Implicit and Explicit Language Learning

Georgetown University Round Table on Languages and Linguistics Series
Selected Titles

IMPLICIT AND EXPLICIT LANGUAGE LEARNING
Conditions, Processes, and Knowledge in SLA and Bilingualism

Cristina Sanz and Ronald P. Leow, Editors

GEORGETOWN UNIVERSITY PRESS
Washington, DC

Library of Congress Cataloging-in-Publication Data

Implicit and explicit language learning: conditions, processes, and knowledge in sla and bilingualism / Cristina Sanz & Ronald P. Leow, editors.
     p. cm. — (Georgetown University round table on languages and linguistics series)
  Includes bibliographical references and index.
  ISBN 978-1-58901-729-0 (pbk. : alk. paper)
1. Second language acquisition—Study and teaching. 2. Bilingualism. 3. Language and languages—Study and teaching. I. Sanz, Cristina. II. Leow, Ronald P. (Ronald Philip), 1954-
  P118.2.I48 2010
  418.0071—dc22   2010036730

⊗ This book is printed on acid-free paper meeting the requirements of the American National Standard for Permanence in Paper for Printed Library Materials.

15 14 13 12 11   9 8 7 6 5 4 3 2
First printing

Printed in the United States of America

Contents

P
18.2
I48
2011

Illustrations

Tables

Acknowledgments

The articles selected for *Implicit and Explicit Language Learning: Conditions, Processes, and Knowledge in SLA and Bilingualism* were first presented at the 2009 Georgetown University Round Table on Languages and Linguistics on March 13–15, hosted by the Department of Spanish and Portuguese and the Linguistics Department at Georgetown University. The present volume is the result of the collaboration and support of many administrative units and individuals. For financial support to host the conference, we would like to thank our sponsors: the Department of Spanish and Portuguese, the Linguistics Department, and the Faculty of Languages and Linguistics.

Thanks also go out to our faculty, staff, and students in the Department of Spanish and Portuguese and Linguistics Department for their excellent support in hosting the 2009 conference. Very special thanks go to Yunkyoung Kang, the research assistant of whom we all dream. Yun's intelligence, diligence, and time-consuming dedication to the many minute details of preparation culminated in the smooth running of a three-day conference that hosted 5 keynote speakers, over 100 presenters and a total attendance of more than 250 national and international researchers, graduate students, and language practitioners. Very special thanks also go to Germán Zárate-Sández and Sarah Grey, from the Department of Spanish and Portuguese, who made sure everyone was fed and happy; they also did a fine job of making sure the conference was successful not only intellectually but also financially. Tech-savvy Jae Goo, from the Linguistics Department, put together a program that was in constant change to the very last minute; this was a major achievement. We would also like to thank the following Georgetown graduate students in applied linguistics—both in the Linguistics and the Spanish and Portuguese departments—who volunteered their services: Yen-Tzu, Sun Hee Hwang, Rebecca Sachs, Natalia Jacobsen, Missy Baralt, Mika Hama, Miguel Angel Novella, Maymona K. Al-Khalil, Marta Tartar, Marissa Fond, Lyn Fogle, Laura Weiss, Laura Kramp, Kerstin Sondermann, Katie Jeong-eun Kim, Kathryn N. Jergovivh', Kateryna Christian, Kaitlyn Tagarelli, Julio Torres, Julie McArthur, Julie Lake, Julie B. Murray, Joo Chung, Jinsok Lee, Jessie Cox, Jessie Grieser, Inge Stockburger, Ibrahim Saleh, Hui-Ju Lin, Hillah Culman, Helen Carpenter, Gregory A. Bennett, Erica L. Lima de Paulo, Elsa Ubeda, Elisabeth Kissling, Elizabeth Karuza, Corinne A. Seals, Claudia Guidi, Carlos Eduardo Balhana, Bo-Ram Suh, Aysun Balkan, Antonio Rico Sulayes, and Anne Micheau Calderon.

To ensure the quality of the articles included in the volume, we would also like to thank our colleagues for their detailed comments and suggestions during the refereeing process of submitted manuscripts: Alfonso Morales-Front, Aurora Bel, Beatriz Lado, Catherine A. Stafford, David Birdsong, Germán Zárate-Sandez, Harriet W. Bowden, Hui-Ju Lin, Iñigo Yanguas, Jae Goo, James F. Lee, Kara

Morgan-Short, Kimberly L. Teague, Laura Weiss, Lisa Zsiga, Melissa Baralt, Nuria Sagarra, Patrick Rebuschat, Sarah Grey, Sheri Anderson, and Silvina Montrul. Special thanks also go out to Sergio Adrada for his careful formatting of this volume.

Finally, we would like to thank Gail Grella of Georgetown University Press for her continuous support. Working with Gail is always a pleasure.

1

Introduction

CRISTINA SANZ AND RONALD P. LEOW
Georgetown University

THE GEORGETOWN UNIVERSITY Round Table on Languages and Linguistics (GURT) is an annual conference with a longstanding tradition. Indeed, GURT 2009 was a special year given that this conference celebrated GURT's fiftieth anniversary. GURT 2009 was cohosted by the Department of Spanish and Portuguese and the Department of Linguistics and was held from March 13 to March 15.

Over the last several decades, neuroscientists, cognitive psychologists, and psycholinguists have investigated the implicit/explicit dichotomy in language development and use from theoretical, empirical as well as methodological perspectives. GURT 2009 provided a forum to address these perspectives in an effort to build connections among them and to draw pedagogical implications when possible. We invited proposals for presentations from research fields related to any aspect pertinent to the conference topic. To this end, this volume, titled *Implicit and Explicit Language Learning: Conditions, Processes, and Knowledge in SLA and Bilingualism,* is a collection of refereed studies that were presented at GURT 2009.

The plenary speakers, representing varied perspectives on the broad scope of this conference theme, were Ellen Bialystok (Psychology, York University, Canada), Nick Ellis (English Language Institute, Psychology and Linguistics, University of Michigan at Ann Arbor), Arthur Reber (Psychology, Brooklyn College), Bill VanPatten (Applied Linguistics and Second Language Studies, Texas Tech University), and Michael Ullman (Neuroscience, Psychology, and Linguistics, Georgetown University). The conference drew over 250 attendees from local, national, and international institutions that included Asia, Europe, and Canada. There were seventy-eight paper presentations, twenty-four poster presentations, three invited panels chaired by ZhaoHong Han (Teachers College), Carmen Pérez-Vidal (Universitat Pompeu Fabra, Spain), and John N. Williams and Patrick Rebuschat (University of Cambridge, UK), and two colloquia.

To provide a relatively balanced representation from the different areas of research disseminated during the conference and to address the broad scope of the conference's focus on *Implicit and Explicit Language Learning: Conditions, Processes, and Knowledge in SLA and Bilingualism,* we faced the challenging task of accepting from the many high-quality submissions we received only a small number of manuscripts for each separate research area. To this end, we have divided the book into these four parts: theory, methodological issues and empirical research, L2 phonology, and bilingualism.

Part I: Theory

In chapter 2 VanPatten discusses how syntax—conceived as a formal component of what is called "language"—resists external efforts to induce its learning. He argues that syntax cannot be learned explicitly; it can only be derived implicitly from the interaction of external data (i.e., input) with internal mechanisms designed solely for the purpose of language (i.e., language processors, Universal Grammar). He also argues, however, that other aspects of language may be amenable to explicit learning, but it is unclear how such learning has any indirect effects on the acquisition/derivation of syntax.

Reber, in chapter 3, reviews Chomsky's model of language, which has dominated linguistics and the psychology of language for the past half century, and finds it wanting in all of its core assumptions. In its place Reber offers an approach that views language as part of a complex mosaic of communicative processes that have pragmatic and functional elements. He also critiques the Chomskyan nativist approach to language acquisition and finds this approach to be inadequate. He proposes a model based on the general mechanism of implicit learning as an alternative approach with promise.

In chapter 4 Ellis reviews various psychological and neurological processes by which explicit knowledge of form-meaning associations impacts upon implicit language learning. He discusses the ways in which language acquisition involves implicit learning from naturalistic usage. Implicit learning provides a distributional analysis, tallying the occurrence of constructions, generalizing schemata from conspiracies of memorized utterances, and forging composites by chunking. These processes provide optimal solutions to the problem spaces of form-function mappings and their contextualized use. At the same time, many aspects of second language are unlearnable from implicit processes alone, although SLA research suggests positive effects of explicit instruction and explicit learning on high levels of adult attainment. Ellis also points out that while explicit and implicit knowledge are distinct and dissociated (they involve different types of representation and are substantiated in separate parts of the brain), they do interact.

Bialystok reports in chapter 5 that the experience of lifelong bilingualism has been shown to lead to both advantages in nonverbal cognitive control and disadvantages in lexical access. These apparently contradictory consequences have typically been explained through separate models that use different explanatory mechanisms for each outcome. Bialystok argues that the two outcomes are in fact consequences of a single system. The need to control attention to two language systems both enhances the domain-general systems for selection and conflict resolution, part of executive functioning, and challenges lexical access through the need to incorporate these high resource systems for ordinary language production. She illustrates the argument by means of a study examining a time-course analysis of word production in a verbal fluency task. Monolinguals and bilinguals who differ in levels of formal language proficiency demonstrate an effect of language knowledge by means of the number of words they produce in an initial burst and an effect of language experience by means of the rate of production of words over time. Bialystok uses these results to support a model based on two central processes that can roughly be called representation (analysis) and control (executive processing).

Part II: Methodological Issues and Empirical Research on Awareness, Pedagogical Contexts, and Individual Differences in SLA

In chapter 6, Leow, Johnson, and Zárate-Sández focus on the methodological issues surrounding the investigation of the relationship between the role of awareness, or lack thereof, and learning. More specifically, the chapter presents a much finer-grained methodological perspective of awareness than what is reported in the current awareness literature in both SLA and non-SLA fields that includes the *what* (is being learned), the *where* (awareness is being investigated, concurrently or nonconcurrently), and the *how* (experimental task, type and location of measurement are employed to investigate awareness). Given this finer-grained perspective of the role of awareness or lack thereof in learning, the chapter concludes that, methodologically, awareness should be investigated along the stages of the acquisitional process (construction vs. reconstruction) and that several variables (e.g., levels of awareness, potential levels of processing at each level of awareness, and potential raising of awareness outside the treatment or experimental phase of the study) need to be considered in any investigation of or report on the construct. To this end, it is strongly proposed that the *what,* the *where,* and the *how* this construct is investigated should be seriously considered when making postulations on the role of awareness in learning.

In chapter 7, Lenet, Sanz, Lado, Howard, and Howard question whether any pedagogical variable affects all subjects to the same extent. Specifically, their experimental study, part of The Latin Project, looks at the interaction between aging and type of feedback. They posit that learning a second language is difficult but not impossible for older adults and cite evidence showing that intentional instructions to learn material such as word pairs or paragraphs often result in larger age-related memory deficits than do more incidental instructions, in part because the strategies that older adults adopt for memorizing are less effective than those adopted by younger adults. They interpret this evidence as suggesting that older adults might benefit from language instruction that encourages more incidental, implicit learning. In their study twenty adults ages sixty-six through eighty-one and twenty college-aged participants were exposed to a lesson on semantic function assignment in Latin under two conditions that differed in degree of explicitness: the presence or absence of grammar rules provided as part of feedback. Their results revealed no significant age deficits in learning, and showed that feedback without grammar rules was more effective than more explicit feedback for the older, but not for the younger, adults. The study also demonstrated retention of limited exposure lasting over five decades, consistent with Bahrick's (1984) *permastore.* Their evidence bodes well for older adults who are motivated to learn a second language, especially when conditions are similar to those in naturalistic rather than academic contexts.

Henshaw, in chapter 8, investigates the role of feedback timing on second language (L2) learners' acquisition of the Spanish subjunctive in adverbial clauses. One hundred two students in a fourth-semester Spanish course took a recognition and interpretation pretest, followed by computerized instruction and practice, based on the tenets of Processing Instruction (VanPatten 2005). Treatment groups differed only with respect to when feedback was provided: (a) immediately after each item, (b) following all items in a task, or (c) twenty-four hours later. A [− feedback] control group was also included. All learners took a recognition and interpretation posttest seven days after the treatment. ANOVAs showed that even though all three [+ feedback] treatment groups outperformed the [− feedback] control group, there were no significant differences between feedback timing groups. This suggests that immediate feedback may not be categorically superior for SLA, thus questioning the widespread assumption in previous CALL studies.

Linck and Weiss report, in chapter 9, that, in studies of L2 aptitude, evidence on the role of executive functions is mixed and there is a noteworthy lack of longitudinal studies. Their current study aimed to fill this gap by examining whether executive functioning predicts acquisition of explicit L2 knowledge in a classroom context. Students enrolled in a university language course were administered two L2 proficiency measures at the beginning and end of a semester. Participants also self-reported their SAT scores and university GPA and completed measures of working memory (WM), inhibitory control, and motivation to learn the L2. After controlling for differences in GPA and L2 motivation, WM accounted for significant additional variance in L2 proficiency at both time points. Critically, WM also uniquely predicted the degree of L2 learning over the semester (with greater WM resources predicting larger improvements). These results provide much needed evidence of WM's role as a component of L2 aptitude, particularly for predicting explicit L2 acquisition during the early stages of learning.

Pérez-Vidal, Juan-Garau, and Mora discuss, in chapter 10, the results of their study undertaken within the Barcelona Study Abroad and Language Acquisition (SALA) project, with data from advanced level Catalan/Spanish bilingual undergraduates (N = 50) acquiring English as a foreign language at an advanced level. A multiyear longitudinal study, data collection from two cohorts of students were collected four times over two and a half years. The data allow for the contrast between formal instruction (FI), taking place at home (AH) prior to a compulsory three-month study abroad period (SA) spent in an English-speaking country, and the SA itself, and its delayed effect. The study reports not only on objective data measuring skill development and writing but also on discrete elements such as accuracy in oral production, phonetic perception, and production. In addition, subjective data measuring individual variables, contact opportunities, and intercultural factors are scrutinized. Pérez-Vidal et al.'s results show that the SA period results in clear benefits in both oral accuracy and written competence, although these gains were already supported by the AH context of learning, which bore fruit later on. Hence, both contexts seem to bring about gains, albeit differentially. In contrast, the three-month-long SA period does not seem to provide enough input or sufficient focused practice with L2 sounds for the learners' phonological competence to develop noticeably.

Rast, in chapter 11, looks into the input processing that takes place in the earliest stages of acquisition, and investigates what French learners of Polish do when faced with a language they know little to nothing about. The Polish input provided to the learners from the moment of first exposure was fully recorded and documented. Learners were tested on initial exposure and at various intervals up to eight hours in order to compare their performance in Polish with the total input they had received up to and including the task. Results are discussed in light of two of VanPatten's (2004) principles of Input Processing: the Primacy of Content Words and the Sentence Location Principle.

In chapter 12 Hilton examines a carefully annotated corpus of oral productions by learners of English or French as an L2, and native speakers of each language, to see what light various hesitation phenomena (silent and filled pauses, retracing, and stutters) shed on questions of implicit and explicit processes in L2 speech. Taking hesitation as an indicator of explicit processing, she interprets the greater incidence of clause-internal hesitation and a higher rate of retracing (characterized by more frequent repetition and reformulation) as evidence that the implicit encoding processes characterizing spoken language frequently fail, in L2 production, to activate language chunks, thereby necessitating an explicit, serial search of the declarative L2 base, which can generate considerable disfluency. This declarative base appears to be qualitatively different from the first language (L1) base—notably lacking in formulaic sequences, which are hypothesized to account for much spoken language fluency.

Part III: Empirical Research on L2 Phonology

Eckman, Iverson, Fox, Jacewicz, and Lee, in chapter 13, report preliminary findings from an ongoing investigation into constraints on the acquisition of both the production and perception of second-language (L2) phonemic contrasts. The results presented in this chapter address two of the three logically-possible ways in which a native language (NL) and target language (TL) can differ with respect to a two-way phonemic contrast. The data support the conclusion that the acquisition patterns for the production of a contrast are not identical to those for the perception of a contrast.

Gordon's study, in chapter 14, explores the effects of L1 vowel inventory size and level of instruction upon English speakers' perception of L2 Spanish front vowels /e/ and /i/. Participants were drawn from three levels of formalized university language instruction. Results revealed that the larger L1 inventory does affect L2 vowel perception as participants at all levels exhibited a high frequency of Multiple Category Assimilation (MCA), or the mapping of one L2 vowel category to more than one L1 vowel category. No significant effects for level of instruction were found, suggesting that even learners with multiple years of L2 learning have no perceptual advantage over beginners or intermediate learners.

Part IV: Empirical Studies on Key Issues in Bilingualism:
Aging, Third Language Acquisition, and Language Separation

In chapter 15, Ingram, Dubasik, Liceras, and Fernández Fuertes' study is the first attempt to examine the early phonological development of English–Spanish two-year-old bilingual twins. They were interested in comparing the phonological system of each twin to the other twin, as well as comparing their emerging Spanish phonological systems with their emerging English phonologies. To do this Ingram et al. developed a scale of phonological similarity to quantify both within-language and within-child comparisons. The results indicated that the phonologies of the twins were 92 percent similar in each language, showing highly similar, but not identical systems. The phonologies of the languages were 71 percent similar, indicating that being twin did not impede early language separation. The highly similar patterns of phonological acquisition between the twins did not impede early language separation.

Lin, in chapter 16, reports on another experimental study conducted within The Latin Project. This chapter examines the relationship between strategies and third language (L3) development and investigated how certain variables, particularly L2 proficiency levels and gender, influence strategies used in L3 development. Participants were ninety male and female L1 Mandarin speakers of three different L2 English levels (low, mid, and high) learning to assign semantic functions to noun phrases in L3 Latin. Correlation analyses revealed positive relationships between compensation strategies reported by all the L2 learners and the grammaticality judgment pretest as well as the sentence written production posttest. Positive correlations were identified between the grammaticality judgment posttest and compensation and metacognitive strategies reported by male learners while a negative correlation was found between the grammaticality judgment delayed test and social strategies reported by female learners. Statistically significant correlations show that the more frequently strategies were used by low L2 learners, the higher L3 scores they attained. Surprisingly, negative correlations were found for the higher L2 learners. Nevertheless, results overall support previous studies showing that female and higher L2 learners use strategies more frequently and that strategies play a role in L3 learning. The results also indicate that factors, such as L2 proficiency, gender, and type of language tests may influence the relationship between learning strategies and L3 development.

Finger, Billig, and Scholl investigate, in chapter 17, whether previously reported bilingual advantages in terms of inhibitory control would also be found in a group of fluent Brazilian bilinguals—speakers of Hunsrückisch and Portuguese—with only four to eight years of formal education. A group of older bilinguals and monolinguals was asked to complete two versions of the Simon task (squares and arrows task) and a Stroop task. Results showed that bilinguals were significantly more accurate in the conflict condition and were slightly faster than monolinguals. These results seem to support previous studies and the hypothesis that bilingualism helps to offset age-related losses in inhibitory control.

With this collection we have aimed to provide a deep and broad view of the topics of interest to those working on the conditions, processes and knowledge that take explicit/implicit as modifiers in SLA and bilingualism. We have been careful to present explicitness as a continuum rather than a contrast to classify types of feedback, to distinguish between processes under attention, those that require awareness and those that take place in the absence of both, as well as to describe the nature of L2 knowledge. We hope our readers—researchers and language practitioners alike—find the theoretical discussions and the operationalization of key constructs presented in this volume informative.

I

Theory

2

Stubborn Syntax: How It Resists Explicit Teaching and Learning

BILL VANPATTEN
Texas Tech University

THE PURPOSE of the present chapter is to remind the reader of a significant fact regarding syntax in adult SLA. Unlike lexical form and meaning, as well as surface elements of morphology such as verbal and nominal inflections, syntax resists explicit efforts at inducing its acquisition. In short, syntax is stubborn. What is more, the claim here is that syntax is not even learned in the traditional sense; instead, it is derived from the interaction of processed input data with certain language-specific internal mechanisms: namely Universal Grammar. This idea is not new (see, for example, Schwartz 1993), but it is often overlooked by those who discuss the roles of explicit and implicit learning in SLA. My belief is that this idea is worth repeating here and that we need to be clearer about our definitions of language when we discuss explicit and implicit learning, especially the effects of explicit teaching and learning, often called *instruction*.

I would like to state up front that the present chapter is not an argument against instruction per se, something that would not make sense given my previous work on instructed SLA and processing instruction (e.g., VanPatten 1996, 2004, 2008; VanPatten and Leeser 2006). Indeed, I would argue that instruction is useful in a variety of domains and that there may be interfaces between syntax and other aspects of language (e.g., morphology, discourse) where instruction might be useful. My argument is centered on syntax alone. I begin with key definitions.

Two Definitions

Two definitions are required for the present discussion: one for syntax and one for explicit learning and teaching. Syntax can mean many things to different people, so I narrow the definition for the present discussion. Syntax involves those properties of language related to and derived from formal and abstract features of a grammar, specifically those that are governed and constrained by Universal Grammar (UG). As an incomplete list of examples, I include the following (divided into two main categories based on the Principles and Parameters framework and its more recent incarnation in the Minimalist Program) (Chomsky 1981, 1995):

1. Universal principles that govern well formedness in all languages (e.g., the Overt Pronoun Constraint, The Extended Projection Principle);
2. Parametric variation across languages—
   a. Features (e.g., interpretable and uninterpretable) and their loci of checking (e.g., VP, DP, CP).
   b. Overt and covert movement arising from feature checking (e.g., Wh-movement, verb movement).
   c. Phrase structure (such as the elements required under X-bar Theory, i.e., Specifiers, Heads, their complements) or the hierarchical projection of functional categories (so that feature checking can occur).

What should be clear from the above examples is that I am not including textbook or laypersons' notions of syntax such as "Object pronouns must precede finite verbs in Spanish" or "In German, the verb is always in second position." Even though these ideas may superficially be related to the abstract features of syntax under discussion here, they are only notations for what people observe on the surface. In addition, some people might confuse morphological inflections with syntax. Teachers of language, for example, often lump verb endings, noun endings, word order, and other things under the term "grammar." Although there is a relationship between morphological inflection and syntax, they are not the same thing. The grammar of language textbooks is by and large not what I mean by syntax.

As for explicit learning and teaching, I lump these together and define them as *any attempts by either learners or teachers to manipulate learning from the outside.* To be sure, I am not referring to processes internal to the learner, such as those that might show up on ERP measures (e.g., Osterhout et al. 2006). The point of my argument is restricted to external manipulation alone, be it from teachers or from learners.

Next, Some Observed Facts

I begin with three well-known facts regarding the acquisition of syntax: (a) it is not instantaneous; (b) it is generally marked by stages of development (e.g., X precedes Y during development); and (c) stages of development are impervious to explicit teaching and learning. All are related so let us begin with a classic example from English. In English, negation has been shown to be acquired over time in overlapping yet ordered stages that look like the following:

Stage 1: Negation external with *no.*
> *No drink beer. No want dinner.*

Stage 2: Negation moved internally.
> *I no drink beer. He no want dinner.*

Stage 3: Appearance of unanalyzed *don't* that alternates with and/or replaces *no.*
> *I don't drink beer. He don't drink beer.*

Stage 4: Appearance of negation with modals and auxiliary *have.*
> *I can't drink beer. He won't eat dinner.*

Stage 5: Appearance of analyzed do with negation (native-like stage)
> *I don't drink beer. He doesn't want dinner.*

Of interest to the present discussion is that such stages cannot be taught away. That is, you cannot grab someone who is in stage 1 and through intensive instruction and practice make that person magically move to the final stage with analyzed *do* (e.g., Schumann's attempt with Alberto; see Schumann 1978). This has been corroborated with other structures and staged development (e.g., Ellis 1989; Pienemann 1987; Towell and Hawkins 1994). Thus, the development of negation and other syntactically governed aspects of language seem to have their own agenda and defy explicit external manipulation (see also Schwartz 1998, and the reviews in Ellis 1994; Gass and Selinker 2008; Lightbown and Spada 2006, and the treatment of these stages in VanPatten and Williams 2007).

Again, to be clear, I am not suggesting that instruction has absolutely no effect on acquisition of language *overall.* What I am saying is that when it comes to syntax, the effect is negligible and is, at best, indirect. Note that although we can describe developmental sequences in terms that do not necessarily reflect theoretical syntax, for example, "negation moved internally," "appearance of negation with modals and auxiliaries," the underlying reasons for these stages can be accounted for in more theoretical terms (e.g., Hawkins 2001).

Another observation about syntactic development concerns L1 influence. It is widely accepted that the L1 somehow plays a role in acquisition (e.g., Herschensohn 2007; Schwartz and Sprouse 1996; Sorace 2003; White 2003). The most widely accepted position is that the L1 provides the initial state, that is, the starting point for all abstract features of syntax. The job of second language acquisition is to overwrite this system, generally referred to as parameter resetting. Many take the position that the L1 has lingering effects such that it may keep learners from becoming native-like, even though L2 learners have access to the same internal mechanisms and knowledge sources that L1 learners do (which I take to be UG). The point I want to make here is that in terms of how syntax develops over time, whatever the effects of the L1 are, they happen outside of learner awareness. They are part of the language system that operates independently of conscious control and thought. To bring this point to the central thesis of this chapter, L1 influence is neither taught nor explicitly learned; it just happens.

Finally, it is worth recalling what we know about research on near-nativeness: is it possible for L2 learners to become native-like with language? This is highly debated in the field of L2 research (see, for example, the overviews in Sorace 2003, as well as Long 2003 and Herschensohn 2007). Over the years we have seen increasingly finer grained analyses of language, and what has emerged is that in its narrowest sense, syntax itself is fully acquirable (e.g., Lardiere 2007; Slabakova 2008). It appears that the interfaces of syntax with other modules of language (e.g., pragmatics, discourse, semantics) are vulnerable to nonnativeness. I will return to this later when I examine the issue of null subjects in a language like Spanish. However, what is often missed is that the research on near-nativeness has examined scores of individuals who have often had extensive classroom experience (presumably involving explicit teaching and learning) and yet some perform in native-like ways and others do not. That is, external manipulation does not guarantee the acquisition of syntax. Likewise, the absence of external manipulation does not mean that syntax cannot be acquired.

Sitting back and reflecting on these observations, there is something about syntax that keeps it from being easily manipulated, if at all. It does not respond to explicit teaching and learning. Simply put, syntax has its own agenda without much regard for instructional efforts. It is stubborn.

What Makes Syntax Stubborn?

The position I take here is that syntax is stubborn because it is not an aspect of language that is learned in the way that learning is traditionally understood. Learning in the traditional sense involves the interaction of learner-directed attention to particular features of an environment with general learning mechanisms (see, e.g., Anderson 2000; Reber 1993; Underwood 1996). As such, learning results in a cognitive change; whatever exists in the mind/brain as a cognitive structure is altered as a result of learning. For example, let us suppose that I do not know how SuperLab works. (SuperLab is a software program used to run psychological experiments.) I sit down with the program, a computer, consult the help index and the tutorial, and after a number of hours I begin to build certain kinds of experiments. My cognitive structures now have something about SuperLab in them that they did not have before. As I work more with SuperLab, I get better at it. This is a classic case of learning. Learning in such cases involves both explicit and implicit learning mechanisms.

But syntax is not learned this way. In fact, syntax is not learned at all. Syntax is derived from the interaction of environmental data (input) and UG (plus the mechanisms that interface UG with the environment) (e.g., Carroll 2001; Schwartz 1993, 1998; White 1989, 2003). This is a standard view within generative circles about how language "grows" in the mind of the learner, be it an L1 acquirer or an adult learner of another language (e.g., Guasti 2004; Montrul 2004; Rothman 2010). Irrespective of the fact that L1 and L2 outcomes may be different (i.e., L1 learners are universally "successful" but L2 learners are not), syntax evolves over time as the mechanisms that create and recreate language in the mind/brain do their work. As Schwartz (1993) aptly describes it, these internal mechanisms cannot make use of explicit information or negative feedback because they are not designed for this. They are designed to operate on data; that is, samples of language. They are not designed to operate on information *about* language. Neither are they designed to operate during production. They are designed to operate on samples of languages that learners get in the input (see also Truscott and Sharwood Smith 2004).

What is more, the acquisition/derivation of syntax involves only implicit processes; that is, how learners come to know that Spanish is a strong agreement language with all of its syntactic reflexes and ramifications (e.g., verb movement, verbal ellipsis, null subjects) and semantic and discourse reflexes (e.g., anaphoric resolution, interpretation of empty categories) happens outside of awareness. It is a by-product of other things the learner is doing during acquisition. In this sense, *syntax happens to learners.* This does not mean that learners do not consciously pay attention when listening to someone else speak or somehow use explicit processes to learn vocabulary, morphology, and other aspects of language. The point here is that what learners do explicitly has little to do with how syntax grows.

Others might argue with this position, especially those in skill theory (e.g., DeKeyser 2007), connectionism (Ellis, this volume), and perhaps sociocultural theory (e.g., Lantolf and Thorne 2007). Skill theorists in particular would argue that language acquisition is like learning anything else, with development proceeding from the accrual of declarative knowledge, to its proceduralization, to (one hopes) its automatization. However, I suggest that scholars take this position because their definition of syntax (and probably language more generally) is different from that used here (for some discussion, see VanPatten 2009). To be sure, there are others who might suggest that UG is unavailable to learners or somehow it is impaired for adults learning an L2 (e.g., Hawkins and Chan 1997; Smith and Tsimpli 1995). But I think the tide has turned since the 1990s; earlier fierce arguments against its role in adult SLA have now softened considerably (see, for example, the special issue of *Studies in Second Language Acquisition,* 2009, on the Fundamental Difference Hypothesis). Scholars are beginning to look at things other than UG to account for differences between successful child L1 acquisition and less-than-successful adult SLA (see also Rothman 2008).

Before making the central thesis of this chapter concrete with an example from the null subject parameter in Spanish, I would like to address a potential objection to the idea that syntax is stubborn and that it is special. The reader familiar with the research on instructed SLA will no doubt know that a tenet of the research is that instruction somehow speeds up acquisition or helps learners obtain higher levels of proficiency (or both) compared with those who do not receive instruction (e.g., Ellis 1994). Assuming this finding is correct and generalizable, there is a real problem with causality when it comes to attributing superior performance by classroom learners over nonclassroom learners: can the superior performance be traced either directly or even indirectly to explicit teaching and learning of syntax? First, no one I know explicitly teaches the kind of syntax we are talking about here; that is, no one teaches learners about movement, the Overt Pronoun Constraint, perfectivity, binding, and other abstract properties of syntax.

But given that there might be a connection between what is taught and the kind of syntax under discussion here, can we claim some kind of causality for explicit teaching? The problem in saying "yes" is that too many intervening factors come to play for us to be sure. For example, there is the confounding variable of exposure. Many of the superior learners used in this line of research have had extended interaction with the language over time, thus creating the possibility that continued exposure to input has pushed the grammar along. There is also the confounding variable of quality of input. Nonclassroom learners used in this line of research often receive restricted varieties of input while classroom learners receive much more elaborated and complex input (see the discussion in Pavesi 1986, for example). My point here is that I think the field of instructed SLA has made a bit too much of the idea that formal instruction in and of itself affects rate and ultimate attainment in L2 learners. Given the number of uncontrolled variables in this kind of research, we have come to a conclusion about the effects of instruction that is more hopeful than it is scientific—even though I personally think that in the end it is probably true that somehow instruction affects rate of learning.

Along the same lines, there are the rather disappointing results of the durability of instruction. In our review of the long-term effects of instruction (VanPatten and Fernández 2004), there simply is no research that reports that, after significant lapsed time, instruction on any kind of syntactic features (clearly not the kind in mind here) holds. For us to say that instruction has some kind of long-term effect on learners that results in higher levels of attainment when it comes to syntax is, again, hopeful at best. And we would do well to remember a fundamental fact about instructed SLA mentioned earlier: instruction does not result in learners skipping stages of development in the acquisition of syntax. These stages appear to be immutable. Syntax is too stubborn to be affected this way.

A Case Scenario: Null and Overt Subjects

In this section I briefly describe aspects of the acquisition of the null subject parameter in Spanish by speakers of English as L1. Through this description I hope to illustrate at several points how syntactic development happens independently of explicit teaching and learning. I begin with a brief description of the null subject parameter.

The Null Subject Parameter

Languages such as Spanish and Italian are characterized as null subject languages, while languages like English and French are not. Null subject languages include a syntactic property by which simple declarative sentences or clauses without subject pronouns are grammatical, as in (1) below. (The word *pro* indicates a null subject.)

(1) Él habla/ *pro* Habla

   He speaks/ *Speaks.

This does not mean that languages like English and French do not allow some kind of null subject, as they clearly do in co-joined sentences, for example: *John speaks a lot and never really says anything.* However, the co-joined sentence cannot exist by itself in English, as shown in (2), but it can in Spanish.

(2) Steve: John speaks a lot.

   (Juan habla mucho.)

   Barry: I know. *And never really says anything.

   (Ya lo sé. Y nunca *pro* dice nada, para decirte la verdad.)

The point is that the null subject is not about whether a grammar allows null subjects. It's about *when* the grammar allows them. In null subject languages, subjectless sentences are simply not ungrammatical under any conditions. (Such sentences may violate discourse conventions, but they do not violate the grammar itself.) What is more, with null subject languages like Spanish and Italian, not only are null subjects allowed in simple declarative sentences, they are required in certain kinds of expressions (examples 3 through 6 represent expletive subjects):

(3) Weather: *Está lloviendo/*Ello está lloviendo.* "It's raining."

(4) Time: *Es la una/*Ello es la una.* "It's one o'clock."

(5) Existential statements: *Hay café./*Allí hay café* "There's coffee."
    (Note that *allí* is unacceptable for "there" if it is meant as a subject.)

(6) Impersonal statements: *Es imposible que así pienses./*Ello es imposible que así pienses.* "It's impossible that you think that way."

(7) Unidentified subjects: Me robaron./*Ellos me robaron. "They robbed me."
    (Here the idea is that the perpetrators are not known.)

The null subject parameter is a bit more complex than the idea that Spanish simply allows null subjects and English does not. What is interesting is that learners are not taught the constraints and options for null subjects, but they do get them. To be sure, they are taught early on with something like "It is not necessary to use subject pronouns in Spanish. The subject is understood from the verb form." But learners are not taught when null subjects are required; yet, they get this early on. In some recent research in our labs at Texas Tech, we have shown that these basic properties of null subjects are acquired by the fourth if not third semester of college-level Spanish. At the same time, the morphological properties of verbs (i.e., person–number endings) are not in place. Thus, learners do not have the very thing that, according to textbooks and teachers, allows them to interpret null subjects. In short, the syntax is in place well before the verbal morphology, suggesting that syntax has its own agenda and is proceeding along without the help of any instruction (see also Rothman and Iverson 2007).

As one more example about what happens with null subjects behind the scenes, let us examine the Overt Pronoun Constraint. The OPC is a principle that governs the interpretation of null and overt pronouns in null subject languages. It states that null subjects can receive a variable interpretation but overt pronouns cannot. In other words, null subject pronouns can refer to a variety of antecedents, but overt subject pronouns are barred from taking quantified DPs (e.g., "no one," "each person"), Wh-phrases (e.g., "who"), and other types of phrases as antecedents. Thus, in (8), both the null and the overt pronoun can refer to *Juan/el hombre* but in (9) and (10) only the null subject can take *nadie* and *quien* as antecedent.

(8) Juan/El hombre admite que *pro*/él es culpable. "John admits he's guilty."

(9) Nadie admite que *pro*/él es culpable. "Nobody admits he's guilty."

(10) ¿Quién admite que *pro*/él es culpable? "Who admits he is guilty?"

In (9) and (10) the overt pronoun can only take an antecedent outside the sentence (i.e., someone else mentioned elsewhere in the discourse). Pérez-Leroux and Glass (1998), for example, demonstrated that learners of Spanish adhere to the OPC early on, and by the time they are at the intermediate levels, are already performing like native speakers when it comes to what they allow to be antecedents for null and overt pronouns. (see also Kanno 1998; Rothman and Iverson 2007). As in the case of required null subjects with certain expressions exemplified above, the OPC is never taught—yet learners clearly get it and it does not take long.

What the above serves to show is that in terms of the purely syntactic properties of the null subject parameter, learners get those properties early in their acquisition of Spanish. In addition, there are properties of the syntax of null subjects (e.g., the OPC) that are not taught, explicitly learned, or could be derived from the input data alone. Both learners and teachers are unaware that the properties of the null subject parameter are being (re)set by learners.

This discussion, of course, gives rise to the question of how learners get null subjects to begin with. Is it through instruction? The answer is no, because even without instruction evidence for null subjects is abundant in the input. Learners readily see and hear sentences such as *Hablo mucho* ("I talk a lot"), *Está lloviendo* ("It's raining"), and *¿Cómo estás?* ("How are you?"). As they encounter these sentences in the input, their parsers/processors must deal with the fact that there are no subjects in them. That is, for the parser to create a successful parse, a subject must be posited. This idea comes from Pritchett (1992), who argued that a major feature of the parser is to make sure that the theta grid of a verb is appropriately represented in the sentence. (The theta grid refers to all the underlying arguments of the verb, such as theme, agent, experiencer, goal, and so on.) If a sentence such as *Hablo mucho* is presented to the parser, the parser is going to ensure that the minimal underlying arguments of "talk" are present. In this case, it would be an agent (i.e., the *talker*). Because there is nothing in the sentence that can be linked to the talker, the parser has two choices: determine the sentence is ungrammatical (parsing fails) or posit something that is not readily evident in the input. Given that UG allows for null subjects, the parser can posit a *pro* in the appropriate place so that a failed parse is avoided. Clearly, all of this happens outside of awareness and without external manipulation. To be sure, teachers and textbooks may tell learners that subject pronouns are not required in Spanish, but this information cannot be used by the internal mechanisms to reset the parameter to [+null subject]. Only processed data can do that.

The reader may have noticed that I used the phrase "the purely syntactic properties of the null subject parameter" earlier, but there is more to null subject languages than the syntax alone. Anyone who has perused the literature on the acquisition of null subjects by L2 learners of Spanish with English L1 knows that in terms of use, learners have difficulty demonstrating native-likeness in a variety of domains at a variety of levels, even advanced. Work by Juana Liceras and her colleagues, for example, has demonstrated that in speaking and writing, learners tend to use far more overt subject pronouns than native speakers (e.g., Liceras 1989; Liceras and Díaz 1998; Liceras, Díaz, and Maxwell 1998). In our work on the resolution of ambiguity with pronouns, advanced learners do not show the preference for antecedent distribution that native speakers do. Native speakers have a relatively strong preference for linking null subject pronouns to the subject of a previous clause or sentence (topic continuity) while not having much of a preference for overt subject antecedents (topic discontinuity) (e.g., Alonso-Ovalle et al. 2002; Jegerski, VanPatten, and Keating, unpublished ms). Learners tend to link both null and overt subject pronouns with subjects of previous clauses. Thus, when presented with *Juan vio a Roberto después que* pro/*él regresó de España,* natives tend to link *pro* with Juan but are 50/50 when it comes to *él* (i.e., it can be either Juan or Roberto). Learners link both *pro* and *él* to Juan. Thus, while the learners clearly have null subject syntax (their judgments of null and overt sentences and their preferences with the OPC are all native-like), they do not use and interpret null and overt subject pronouns like natives. Some characterize this as a problem with the syntax-discourse interface or the syntax-pragmatics interface. It is not a problem with the syntax alone.

The point here is that even though syntax in and of itself has its own agenda and is resistant to outside forces, language is not just syntax. There may be parts of language that are amenable to outside manipulation. For example, can learners be taught and can they learn explicitly to use subject pronouns in a more native-like fashion? This is an empirical question and is quite different from whether or not the null subject parameter can be explicitly taught and learned.

The discussion above leads me to the following: Very often in the explicit/implicit discussion/debate regarding SLA we lose sight of the complexity of language and its multifaceted nature. We tend to overgeneralize, reduce, and simplify language. So when I say that syntax is stubborn, I refer only to syntax. I am not referring to other aspects of language. Indeed, the central question about explicit and implicit learning should not be about the roles of each in SLA but instead about *what aspects of language can be affected by explicit learning and which cannot* (see Schwartz 1993 and Slabakova 2009 for additional discussion).

A Brief Note about the Critical Period

One obvious objection to the ideas presented in this chapter concerns the critical period. Those who believe in the critical period hypothesis would say that the mechanisms available to L1 learners are not available to adults and, thus, syntax cannot be stubborn because it has its own (UG-governed) agenda (e.g., see some of the discussion in Birdsong 1998). Or, while remaining somewhat neutral on whether or not there is a problem with UG availability in adults, there is clearly the difference of children relying largely or entirely on implicit learning while adults rely on explicit learning (e.g., DeKeyser and Larson-Hall 2005). In short, adults are different and thus the central thesis of this chapter is wrong: syntax can and perhaps must be taught and learned explicitly.

Interestingly, the existence of the critical period is irrelevant to the present argument. As almost all the research on the acquisition of syntax has shown (and I briefly touched on this in an earlier section), syntax seems to do what it does with and without explicit learning and teaching. In the case of the acquisition of negation described earlier, these stages are well documented for both classroom and non-classroom learners—yet we know that learners get explicit instruction and practice on negation in English, we know they get explicit instruction and practice on auxiliary *do,* and still the stages emerge. In short, whether adult learners engage implicit or explicit mental processes or engage or do not engage in explicit learning (the real focus of this chapter) makes no difference. Syntax is stubborn.

Conclusion, Including (Once Again) the Issue of Instruction

I would like to begin this conclusion with a partial list of my main points:

- The acquisition of syntax follows developmental sequences.
- Developmental sequences are impervious to external manipulation.
- L1 influence happens outside of awareness.
- Parsing and processing (i.e., the mechanisms that mediate between input and UG) happen outside of awareness.
- Formal syntax and formal syntactic properties are stubborn and resist explicit teaching and learning.

The idea, then, is that as a particular aspect of language, syntax is "gonna do its own thing" in acquisition. However, what syntax decides to do has no bearing on other aspects of language, and how these things respond to instruction (and how they might indirectly influence syntactic development) is open.

During my presentation of these ideas at the 2009 Georgetown University Round Table, an audience member made the following comment: that because syntax is stubborn is precisely why we should teach it. There are two issues underlying this comment that merit attention. The first issue is this: I do not think the audience member, even after my exposition, understood what I mean by syntax—or perhaps that person forgot what I mean by syntax. To be clear, I do not mean syntax as it is used by teachers, laypeople, and a good deal of researchers on explicit/implicit learning. I mean syntax as it is used by syntacticians. Thus, although teachers and textbooks may go about teaching rules of the subjunctive in Spanish, they do not go about teaching the rules of binding (an aspect of syntax that governs the subjunctive). Even though teachers and textbooks may tell learners that a language like Spanish has null subjects, they do not teach the Overt Pronoun Constraint or restrictions on the use of overt pronouns. Although teachers of English may tell learners how to form negation with *do,* they do not teach the properties of (non)verb raising, which govern the placement and appearance of *do* in English.

The second issue is that nowhere have I said syntax as understood by teachers, laypeople, and others should not be taught. To remind people that syntax is stubborn is not the same thing as saying "don't teach formal properties of language." Even though syntax may have its own agenda that cannot be manipulated from the outside, what teachers and curriculum developers think is appropriate for language instruction is up to them. It is to be hoped that their decisions are informed by theory and research. Those familiar with processing instruction (e.g., Farley 2005; VanPatten 2004, 2008) will know that I advocate a type of intervention (not a method) that may help learners create better intake for grammatical development. The reason I advocate this particular kind of intervention is because it is the only one that attempts to operate at the level of processing and parsing. By correcting or altering bad processing, acquisition ought to be aided. While others may disagree, this is the only intervention for grammatical development that makes sense to me from a theoretical—and now, empirical—viewpoint. This idea is shared by others (e.g., Benati and Lee 2008;

Carroll 2001) and is garnering wider appeal in the profession irrespective of any particular model of input processing.

However, I have never suggested that processing instruction guarantees acquisition, nor have I ever advocated that it does anything other than work on processing and parsing—which, in turn, probably has an effect on the underlying grammar of the learner. At no point during processing instruction are we teaching (and hoping learners learn) syntax as it is defined in this chapter. Processing instruction works on the interface between surface properties of language and processing/parsing. The idea is that processing does one thing, and how the syntax organizes itself in the mind/brain of the learner is another. As examples, in VanPatten and Cadierno (1993) we "taught clitic object pronouns" in Spanish via processing instruction, and in Henry, Culman, and VanPatten (2009), we "taught case marking on articles" in German via processing instruction. In both studies, the goal of instruction is to override the First Noun Principle that leads learners to assume the first noun or pronoun is the subject of a sentence. But nowhere do we claim we are teaching syntax, and nowhere do we claim that we are teaching clitic movement, verb movement, or any other syntactic phenomena associated with these particular surface properties of language. And as we have always maintained, it is not the explicit teaching and learning that make the difference; it is the learners' processing of structured input that makes the difference.

Even with these statements, I'm sure at some point someone might claim that I advocate abandoning instruction or that I believe all acquisition involves implicit processes. To be sure, I end with a statement that I hope summarizes the central thesis of this chapter: Syntax is stubborn. It resists direct external manipulation in the form of explicit teaching and learning. Whether or not it can be *indirectly* affected via explicit learning of other aspects of language (e.g., morphology, discourse) is an open question; and whether other aspects of language are affected by instruction is also an open question.

ACKNOWLEDGMENT

I am deeply grateful to Jason Rothman, Ron Leow, and Cristina Sanz for their comments and suggestions on drafts of this chapter.

REFERENCES

Alonso-Ovalle, Luis, S. Fernández-Solera, Lyn Frazier, and Charles Clifton. 2002. Null vs. overt pronouns and the topic-focus articulation in Spanish. *Journal of Italian Linguistics* 14:151–69.

Anderson, John. 2000. *Learning and memory.* 3rd ed. New York: John Wiley & Sons.

Benati, Alessandro, and James F. Lee. 2008. *Grammatical acquisition and processing instruction.* Bristol, UK: Multilingual Matters.

Birdsong, David, ed. 1998. *Second language acquisition and the critical period hypothesis.* Mahwah, NJ: Lawrence Erlbaum Associates.

Carroll, Susanne E. 2001. *Input and evidence: The raw material of second language acquisition.* Amsterdam: John Benjamins.

Chomsky, Noam. 1981. *Lectures on government and binding.* Dordrecht, the Netherlands: Foris.

———. 1995. *The Minimalist Program.* Cambridge, MA: MIT Press.

DeKeyser, Robert. 2007. Skill acquisition theory. In *Theories on second language acquisition,* ed. Bill VanPatten and Jessica Williams, 97–113. Mahwah, NJ: Lawrence Erlbaum Associates.

DeKeyser, Robert, and Jennifer Larson-Hall. 2005. What does the critical period really mean? In *Handbook of bilingualism*, ed. Judith F. Kroll and Anne M. B. De Groot, 88–108. Oxford: Oxford University Press.

Ellis, Rod. 1989. Are classroom and naturalistic acquisition the same? A study of the classroom acquisition of German word order rules. *Studies in Second Language Acquisition* 11:305–28.

———. 1994. *The Study of second language acquisition.* Oxford: Oxford University Press.

Farley, Andrew P. 2005. *Structured input.* New York: McGraw-Hill.

Gass, Susan M., and Larry Selinker. 2008. *Second language acquisition: An introductory course.* 3rd ed. New York: Routledge.

Guasti, Maria T. 2004. *Language acquisition: The growth of grammar.* Cambridge, MA: MIT Press.

Hawkins, Roger. 2001. *Second language syntax.* Oxford: Blackwell.

Hawkins, Roger, and Y. C. Chan. 1997. The partial availability of Universal Grammar in second language acquisition: The "failed features" hypothesis. *Second Language Research* 13:187–226.

Henry, Nicholas, Hillah Culman, and Bill VanPatten. 2009. More on the effects of explicit information in instructed SLA: A partial replication of and a response to Fernández (2008). *Studies in Second Language Acquisition* 31:1–17.

Herschensohn, Julia. 2007. *Language development and age.* Cambridge: Cambridge University Press.

Jegerski, Jill, Bill VanPatten, and Gregory D. Keating. Unpublished ms. *L2 Processing of Anaphoric Pronouns: L1 Transfer at the Syntax-Discourse Interface.*

Kanno, Kazue. 1998. The stability of UG principles in second language acquisition: Evidence from Japanese. *Linguistics* 36:1125–46.

Lantolf, James, and Steven Thorne. 2007. Sociocultural theory and SLA. In *Theories on second language acquisition,* ed. Bill VanPatten and Jessica Williams, 201–24. Mahwah, NJ: Lawrence Erlbaum Associates.

Lardiere, Donna. 2007. *Ultimate attainment in second language acquisition.* Mahwah, NJ: Lawrence Erlbaum and Associates.

Liceras, Juana. 1989. On some properties of the pro-drop parameter. In *Lingusitic perspectives on second language acquisition,* ed. Susan M. Gass and Jacquelyn Schachter, 109–33. Cambridge: Cambridge University Press.

Liceras, Juana, and Lourdes Díaz. 1998. On the nature of the relationship between morphology and syntax: Inflectional typology, f-features, and null/overt pronouns in Spanish interlanguage. In *Morphology and its interfaces in second language knowledge,* ed. Maria-Luise Beck, 307–38. Amsterdam: John Benjamins.

Liceras, Juana, Lourdes Díaz, and Denyse Maxwell. 1998. Null subjects in non-native grammars: The Spanish L2 of Chinese, English, French, German, Japanese, and Korean speakers. In *The development of second language grammars,* ed. Elaine Klein and Gita Martohardjono, 109–47. Amsterdam: John Benjamins.

Lightbown, Patsy, and Nina Spada. 2006. *How languages are learned.* 3rd ed. Oxford: Oxford University Press.

Long, Michael H. 2003. Stabilization and fossilization in interlanguage development. In *The handbook of second language acquisition,* ed. Catherine J. Doughty and Micahel H. Long, 487–535. Oxford: Blackwell.

Montrul, Silvina. 2004. *The acquisition of Spanish: Morphosyntactic development in monolingual and bilingual L1 acquisition and adult L2 acquisition.* Amsterdam: John Benjamins.

Osterhout, Lee, Judith McLaughlin, Ilona Pitkänen, Cheryl Frenck-Mestre, and Nicola Molinaro. 2006. Novice learners, longitudinal designs, and event-related potentials: A means for exploring the neurocognition of second language processing. In *The cognitive neuroscience of second language acquisition,* ed. Marianne Gullberg and Peter Indefrey, 199–230. Oxford: Blackwell.

Pavesi, Maria. 1986. Markedness, discoursal modes, and relative clause formation in a formal and informal context. *Studies in Second Language Acquisition* 8:38–55.

Pérez-Leroux, Ana Teresa, and William R. Glass. 1998. OPC effects on the L2 acquisition of Spanish. In *Contemporary perspectives on the acquisition of Spanish. Vol. 1: Developing grammars,* ed. Ana Teresa Pérez-Leroux and William R. Glass, 149–65. Sommerville, MA: Cascadilla Press.

Pienemann, Manfred. 1987. Psychological constraints on the teachability of languages. In *First and second language acquisition processes,* ed. Carol Pfaff, 143–68. Rowley, MA: Newbury House.

Pritchett, Bradley L. 1992. *Grammatical competence and parsing performance.* Chicago: University of Chicago Press.

Reber, Arthur. 1993. *Implicit learning and tacit knowledge.* Oxford: Oxford University Press.

Rothman, Jason. 2008. Why not all counter-evidence to the critical period hypothesis is equal or problematic: Implications for SLA. *Language and Linguistics Compass* 6:1063–88.

———. 2010. Theoretical linguistics meets pedagogical practice: Pronominal subject use in Spanish as a second language (L2) as an example. *Hispania* 93:52–65.

Rothman, Jason, and Michael Iverson. 2007. On L2 clustering and resetting the null subject parameter in L2 Spanish: Implications and observations. *Hispania* 90:329–42.

Schumann, John H. 1978. *The pidginization process.* Rowley, MA: Newbury House.

Schwartz, Bonnie. 1993. On explicit and negative data effecting and affecting competence and linguistic behavior. *Studies in Second Language Acquisition* 15:147–63.

———. 1998. The second language instinct. *Lingua* 156:133–60.

Schwartz, Bonnie, and Rex Sprouse. 1996. L2 cognitive states and the Full Transfer/Full Access model. *Second Language Research* 12:40–72.

Slabakova, Roumyana. 2008. L2 fundamentals. *Studies in Second Language Acquisition* 31:155–73.

———. 2009. What is easy and what is hard to acquire in a second language? In *Proceedings of the 10th Generative Approaches to Second Language Acquisition Conference (GASLA 2009),* ed. Melissa Bowles, Tania Ionin, Silvina Montrul, and Annie Tremblay, 280–94. Somerville, MA: Cascadilla Press.

Smith, Neil, and Ianthi-Maria Tsimpli. 1995. *The mind of a savant.* Oxford: Blackwell.

Sorace, Antonella. 2003. Near-nativeness. In *The Handbook of second language acquisition,* ed. Catherine J. Doughty and Michael H. Long, 130–51. Oxford: Blackwell.

Towell, Richard, and Roger Hawkins. 1994. *Approaches to second language acquisition.* Clevedon, UK: Multilingual Matters.

Truscott, John, and Michael Sharwood Smith. 2004. Acquisition by processing: A modular perspective on language development. *Bilingualism: Language and Cognition* 7:1–20.

Underwood, Gary, ed. 1996. *Implicit cognition.* Oxford: Oxford University Press.

VanPatten, Bill. 1996. *Input processing and grammar instruction: Theory and research.* Norwood, NJ: Ablex.

———, ed. 2004. *Processing instruction: Theory, research, and commentary* Mahwah, NJ: Lawrence Erlbaum & Associates.

———. 2008. Processing matters. In *Input matters,* ed. Thorten Piske and Martha Young-Scholten, 47–61. Clevedon, UK: Multilingual Matters.

———. 2009. Abstraction in SLA. *Journal of Hispanic and Lusophone Linguistics* 2:199–205.

VanPatten, Bill, and Teresa Cadierno. 1993. Explicit instruction and input processing. *Studies in Second Language Acquisition* 12:225–43.

VanPatten, Bill, and Claudia Fernández. 2004. The long-term effects of processing instruction. In *Processing instruction: Theory, research, and commentary,* ed. Bill VanPatten, 273–89. Mahwah, NJ: Lawrence Erlbaum Associates.

VanPatten, Bill, and Michael J. Leeser. 2006. Theoretical and research considerations underlying classroom practice: The fundamental role of input. In *The art of teaching Spanish: Second language acquisition from research to praxis,* ed. M. Rafael Salaberry and Barbara Lafford, 55–77. Washington, DC: Georgetown University Press.

VanPatten, Bill, and Jessica Williams, eds. 2007. *Theories in second language acquisition.* Mahwah, NJ: Lawrence Erlbaum Associates.

White, Lydia. 1989. *Universal Grammar and second language acquisition.* Amsterdam: John Benjamins.

———. 2003. *Second language acquisition and Universal Grammar.* Cambridge: Cambridge University Press.

3

An Epitaph for Grammar: An Abridged History

ARTHUR S. REBER

University of British Columbia

THE PSYCHOLOGICAL STUDY of language has deep roots, traceable to early speculations about the origins of speech, the "ur" or proto-language, which were later joined by medieval musings about the possibility of linguistic universals and discussed with some sophistication by pioneers like Wilhelm Wundt (1904).

During the early decades of the twentieth century the topic was dominated by descriptivists and behaviorists, and neither group was particularly taken by language's special place in the panoply of things that people do. Descriptivists focused on cataloging things said and written—honest if uninspiring work. Behaviorists approached language as behavior—acknowledging that it was a tad more complex than most of the other varieties they were exploring—but still nothing special. Behaviorism was not quite as indefensible a position as many of its critics believed, but it erred seriously by refusing to climb inside the head of the language user.

Things changed dramatically in the late 1950s. Behaviorism's weaknesses, at least the operant conditioning version championed by B. F. Skinner, were rather painfully exposed when a young linguist, Avram Noam Chomsky, published his review (1959) of Skinner's *Verbal Behavior* (1957). Chomsky's perspective connected in a host of ways with broad movements already under way in psychology, philosophy, linguistics, anthropology, computer sciences, communications, and information theory. It likely would not have enjoyed the success it has without these other links (see Diebold 1965; Osgood and Sebeok [1954] 1965).

Chomsky's critique was accompanied by a radically different view of language, one that reached back to earlier nativist speculations about language origins and universal elements. While topics have changed and models have replaced each other, this Chomsky-inspired approach has dominated theory and thought for nearly a half century, showing how wrong some were in predicting its demise (Reber 1987). The model was grounded in several presumed linguistic and psychological features, the most prominent being:

- Natural languages are formal derivations of a common underlying structure or set of features, known as Universal Grammar, or UG.

- Individual spoken languages select a subset of these principles and emerge with their own idiosyncratic, but bounded, grammars.
- These grammars are *generative;* their functional architectures allow for production of all and only the morpheme sequences that are intuitively acceptable to speakers of that language.
- There exists a biological construct encoded in the human genome known, among other names, as a *Language Acquisition Device* (or LAD) that is programmed with the computational representations of UG. Language acquisition is, therefore, not a learning process in the normal sense, but the maturation, sequencing, or unfolding of a biological system, *a language organ.*
- This unfolding process is based on keying in on those features of the linguistic environment that trigger the relevant computations of UG.
- The language organ or module is encapsulated and cognitively impenetrable, and it shares few if any of its computational properties with other cognitive or behavioral processes.

This model is almost certainly wrong in virtually every possible way. More problematical is the growing suspicion that the dominance of this perspective has been an impediment to progress in the psychological understanding of language acquisition and language use. Whether it has been a long-term benefit to formal linguistics is also doubtful, but I'm not one to pass judgment here. My interest is in the impact of this framework on psychology, about which I want to make four claims:

- There is no such thing as a universal grammar, not in the original sense or in the several, modified, less radical characterizations put forward in recent years.
- There is, in fact, no such thing as grammar, in the sense that is commonly accepted in linguistics and psycholinguistics, as a formal, generative system.
- There is no LAD or any other biological mechanism that guides language acquisition in virtue of being preequipped with the specific content of any language, universal or otherwise.
- There is no encapsulated language organ whose unfolding guides the development of linguistic competence.

In place of the Chomskyan, nativist approach, I propose one based on an empiricist framework that emphasizes communication, pragmatics, and a domain-general acquisition system, such as that put forward in the theory of implicit learning.

Communication

The focus on language as a reified entity has been unwise. Language is best viewed, not as a "thing" to be examined and captured by a formal computational framework, but as a tool for the exchange of information. Language is merely one, albeit a most effective one, of the various ways in which humans exchange knowledge, belief, affect, and intention. It also functions as an adjunct to internal cognitive mechanisms and is intimately related to a host of mental processes. This, of course, is not a new move. Several others (Hauser 1996; Jackendoff 2002) have taken this approach but not, I believe, far enough —although Tomasello's recent book (2008) gets close.

Pragmatic Considerations

This communicative system operates in particular contexts with specific aims and is governed by inter- and intrapersonal social constraints, the boundaries of motoric function, and the desires and intentions of speakers. The pragmatic approach, once a mainstay of the field (Austin 1962; Grice 1969, 1989; Searle 1969) has been marginalized with the emphasis on syntactic models and formalism. It would be useful to bring it back to center stage.

An Implicit Learning System

Discarding nativism carries an obligation to develop an empirical theory of language acquisition. Implicit learning theory was introduced (Reber 1967) for just this purpose. Implicit learning is a process of detecting and representing patterns of covariation among elements in the environment. It is domain-general and capable of capturing the kinds of complex structural relationships found in language. It functions largely independent of conscious modulation and operates effectively during infancy. All are necessary properties. The roles and functions of each of these will become clear as we examine the current state of affairs through the lens of a critique of the Chomskyan, nativist model.

The Illusory Nature of Universal Grammar

The key datum here is that five decades of effort have yielded no progress in identifying the computational properties of UG. There isn't even any consensus on what features are universal. These years are notable for rejecting earlier formal systems for newer candidates. Transformational grammars were set aside in favor of government and binding theory, which, when found wanting, was replaced by principles and parameters, which were succeeded by the current minimalist program with its core operator, *merge*. Chomsky (2005) maintains that these newer approaches are all coherent developments of earlier models. Perhaps, but this claim is not particularly convincing. Even if they are, the deep problem remains: we are no closer to a formalization of UG than we were fifty years ago.

This lack of progress has been acknowledged by many, including Chomsky. With Fitch and Hauser (Chomsky 2005; Fitch, Hauser, and Chomsky 2005: Hauser, Chomsky, and Fitch 2002), he has offered a possible solution. Their approach assumes a faculty of language (FL) that can be parsed into a narrow perspective (FLN) and a broad one (FLB). The former is thought to contain mechanisms and content specific to human language, the latter to be composed of a rich, varied mosaic of forms and functions, mechanisms and structures, processes and operations that have their roots in other species and in perceptual, cognitive, and behavioral systems that evolved for nonlinguistic reasons.

Universal grammar, it is argued, will be found in FLN, not FLB. Fitch, Hauser, and Chomsky (2005) and Hauser, Chomsky, and Fitch (2002) review several principles and operations that could conceivably be part of FLN and conclude that only *recursion* (structures can be nested within other structures, repeatedly) appears essential and that the only operation is *merge*. However, in Fitch, Hauser, and Chomsky (2005) there is a remarkable sentence: "The contents of FLN are to be empirically determined, and could possibly be empty, if empirical findings showed that none of the mechanisms involved are uniquely human or unique to language" (181). It would appear that even Chomsky is willing to consider that the contents of UG are the null set.

Recursion, moreover, isn't a particularly compelling feature of human languages. Johansson (2006) found that removing recursive elements has little or no impact on communication. Christiansen and Devlin (1997) found that recursion is actually relatively uncommon in language and that recursively embedded material is particularly difficult to process, and and Farkaš and Crocker (2008) noted that self-organizing neural networks can capture recursive functions. In short, recursion appears not to be an essential feature of human language.

Is UG Even Needed?

Goldberg (2006), Tomasello (2003, 2008), and Elman and colleagues (Elman 1999; Elman et al. 1996) have all put forward models of language use without assuming a UG. Others, such as Hurford (2006) and Christiansen and Chater (2008), have argued that communicative competence is best viewed as having emerged slowly over time by exploiting biological functions and forms that evolved because they were adaptive in other domains and not specifically for their linguistic role.

Goldberg (2004), who recently engaged in a spirited exchange with Lidz and colleagues (Lidz, Gleitman, and Gleitman 2003; Lidz and Gleitman 2004), maintains that the features of child language that have been taken as evidence of universal grammar can, in fact, be viewed through a broader, pragmatic lens without invoking a universal system. Christiansen and Chater (2008) note that the biological underpinnings of UG are themselves suspect. A highly complex system, populated with abstract principles that pertain only to language and are radically different from other biological systems, defies the basic canons of adaptationism.

Moreover, some approach the problem from a formalist's point of view assuming that empirically determined universals will be directly tied to the properties of UG (Hornstein and Boeckx 2009). Others take a "pragmatic" perspective and anticipate that these observed universals will be found to be linked with more general processing mechanisms. Tomasello (2004) notes that reviews of these various theoretical approaches reveal essentially no overlap in the universals that each argues for. Evans and Levinson (2009) reach an even more troublesome conclusion: that there is no evidence at all for the existence of universal components. Among the thousands of languages spoken today they find not commonality in form and structure but diversity at every turn. This is an uncomfortable place for a field to find itself after nearly a half century of concerted effort.

How We Got Here

These difficulties can be traced to (at least) two factors. First, the Chomskyan approach focused too narrowly on an idealized notion of language. Languages are, as many have noted, "moving targets" that have been shaped by perceptual, learning, and processing biases. Reification was not an effective move. Worse, it invited isolationistic thinking in which language and linguistic functions were seen as encapsulated and impenetrable, distinct from the full range of human cognitive, affective, and social functions.

Second, linguists, their vision clouded by staring too long at syntax, paid insufficient attention to the evolution of language, an intensely active interdisciplinary field of research that was concerned not with formal properties but with the pragmatic *functions* of language. Borrowing methods from perception and the cognitive sciences, from sociobiology and evolutionary psychology, from genetics and developmental biology, researchers have been exploring ways in which language and communicative functions might have evolved by piggybacking on and gradually co-opting older forms and functions.

Two general perspectives have been emerging. One examining basic mechanisms or processes that could support or be exapted for language such as the distinct dorsal and ventral streams of the visual system (Hurford 2003), the mirror neuron system (Arbib 2002), a descended larynx (Fitch and Reby 2001), sensorimotor systems of manual dexterity (Aronoff et al. 2005), the capacity for imaging and schematic representation (see Hampe 2005), and the capacity for sequence learning (Christiansen, Conway, and Onnis 2007; Reber 1993).

The other, somewhat more speculative, approach has looked at social factors that likely played a role in reinforcing the adaptive value of communicative competence. Candidates currently entertained include group size, time pressure, gossip and grooming (Dunbar 1993), group selection for rules of law (Knight 2008), moral codes and cooperation (Locke 2008), the need to talk to oneself (Mirroli and Parisi 2006), social intelligence with accompanying feedback (Bickerton 2009), theory of mind (Dunbar 1993) and mimesis and imitation (Donald 1998). Some (Lightfoot 2000) see language as having emerged as a classic Gould and Lewontin *spandrel.*

Goldberg recently (2008) wondered if the very notion of Universal Grammar hadn't gone missing. Hurford (2008) called it a "notoriously moving target" that has so lost its identity that its critics may, in fact, be "flogging a dead horse" (526). Pinker and Jackendoff (2005) noted, ironically, that it is likely that not all language universals will be manifested in every naturally occurring language. These are the hallmarks of a field in crisis.

So, why do many still cling to the notion that there is some Platonic entity called *language* and that its properties are uniform and part of some larger abstraction called a *universal grammar*? Even among the writings of critics it is rare to find anyone willing to state the obvious. Universal grammar is an illusion, a will-o'-the-wisp, and the very notion has functioned as a classic red herring—in the original sense of that term—an object dragged across the scent path that distracts the searcher. Languages are simply not fixed entities governed by groups of specific rules, things we like to call *grammars.* There are, of course, rich and complex patterns and computational elements in them, but such a richly structured core is characteristic of almost every interesting thing people do. It has been a mistake to isolate language from the rest of the human psyche.

Languages are not merely phonemes and morphemes arranged in particular orders. These sequences are layered, shingled and interwoven, and they cannot be isolated from the rest of the rich and varied communicative system, a supportive structure made up of intonations, prosodic features of pitch, stress, and pausing, of gestures and emphasis, of facial expressions and body movements, of temporal patterns, embodied cognitive structures, references to context, boundary conditions on expression, affect markers, social mores, cultural codes, historical facts, speech acts, Gricean maxims and truth markers, all of which play essential roles combining to yield an efficient channel for transmitting knowledge and meaning.

If UG Is an Illusion Then, a fortiori, There Is No
Generative Grammar of Any Natural Language

There are, of course, patterns of linguistic usage, and these can be thought of as "grammatical" in some sense. However, these do not have generative functions in the classical sense. They are descriptive systems that capture the structure and characterize the ways in which linguistic forms are ordered in specific languages, conventions that have emerged in specific contexts and shared by languages with common ancestry. They can be called grammatical rules, but it would be more accurate to refer to them as patterns of linguistic use. They capture common features of placement and movement of linguistic forms.

However, with the deletion of UG from the explanatory framework, these shared features will need a different schema, one where the "rules" or "patterns" are viewed as entailments of general mechanisms involving agents and actors, actions and the consequences of such, needs and desires and their mental representations. These functions evolved for other reasons and were co-opted early in sapient development by a growing facility with verbal forms of communication. The underlying forms and operative mechanisms are almost certainly not specific to languages or linguistic forms.

If There Is No UG and No Generative Grammar, Then
LAD Is a Theoretically Empty Construct

Despite the widespread acceptance of LAD, there is actually little evidence for it. There are many existence claims and much argument over the specific elements in the linguistic environment necessary to trigger its operations, but most studies produce ambiguous data; the Goldberg–Lidz exchange noted earlier being a classic example. Complicating the situation is the manner in which the issue has played out. When the nativists shanghaied psycholinguistics, LAD became the default position. We should have known better. We should have also been better Humeans, better Popperians. Those who were uneasy with the proposal found themselves on the defensive, trying to show why LAD didn't exist when the burden of proof properly belonged with the claimants.

Proponents, however, ducked this responsibility and adopted a philosophically slippery stance; they put forward reasons why something like a LAD *had to exist.* Among these were:

- language developed too rapidly to have been learned.
- language has an unerring course of development.

▓ linguistic input to the child is too impoverished to permit the induction of the grammar of a natural language.

We now know that the first two are false: language does not develop that quickly and there is no unerring maturational course (Winter and Reber 1994). But the poverty of the stimulus argument lives on, despite a gaping lacuna in the argument for it: the only data entered into the analyses are verbal data, sentences uttered to children viewed as sequences of morphemes, and the domain that appears to be impoverished is syntax. This input may or may not be impoverished (Behme and Deacon 2008), but pragmatically, it doesn't capture the way language is used as a component of a complex, socially focused communication system. The communication network between infants and caregivers, between children and family and friends, teachers, other children and, yes, with artifacts like talking toys, interactive games, computers, telephones, radio, and television uses an immense range of supportive structures, pragmatic scaffoldings, social frameworks, gestural systems, affect markers, paralinguistic elements, metalinguistic features, and all provide a constant stream of input to the infant. The only thing impoverished is the database that's been in use. In fact, language acquisition is more complex than conventional wisdom tells us. Children not only learn to communicate using linguistic channels, but they also acquire the structural features of these paralinguistic, social domains, an impressive array of interlocking skills.

The way to handle this problem is to harken back to the issue of evolution. We, like all species, are biologically tuned to pick up particular kinds of information, especially from displays relevant to the processes of communication. Hauser, Chomsky, and Fitch (2002), as noted above, suggest parsing the language problem into two broad classes, those encompassed by an FLN and those belonging properly to an FLB. The argument constructed to this point has effectively removed the FLN from the picture. But FLB, despite the semantically unfortunate reference of the "FL" part, is a workable construct for it shifts the evolutionary–biology burden to a more tractable problem: identifying the cognitive, affective, motoric and social functions distributed throughout a host of species that can be seen as potential beginnings for human language. This enterprise is very much under way in a wide variety of research domains including evolutionary theory, anthropology, genetics, linguistics, physiology, developmental biology, philosophy, computational and information sciences, and, of course, psychology.

However, whatever is accomplished, we will still be left needing an acquisition system. We may be biologically predisposed to acquire linguistic communicative functions, but we have yet to unpack the properties of the learning mechanism responsible for the process of acquisition. It is going to have to be a process that is eclectic in its capacity to handle the mosaic of inputs it will act on. The theory of implicit learning is a viable candidate here.

Implicit Learning

The concept of implicit learning was introduced over forty years ago (Reber 1967) as an in-principle mechanism for language learning and an alternative to Chomsky's notions that were attracting attention (Reber 1993). However, any acquisition system capable of handling language and communicative functions, whatever its underlying structure ends up looking like, is going to have to display at least six key properties.

- **Implicitness:** It must operate largely without support of consciousness. Conscious control and top-down modulation are virtually nonexistent in infants when they begin this process.
- **Independence of intelligence:** It has to function largely independent of intelligence, for the infant is, if anything, a low-IQ creature. Language is acquired by children with a wide array of cognitive deficits. They may not turn out to be poets or charismatic speakers, but they do learn to communicate, often quite effectively.
- **Social and interpersonal tuning:** The system must be tuned to social and interpersonal functions; communication is for social discourse and subsumes social functions.
- **Robustness:** The mechanism that underlies acquisition needs to be robust as communicative functions are acquired in the face of a host of sensory, motoric, neurological, and psychological disorders and dysfunctions.
- **Evolutionary plausibility:** The system must make evolutionary sense. It should have adaptive elements that are independent of language but capable of functioning with communicative inputs. We should also be able to observe its propaedeutic mechanisms operating in other species and find common functional ground.
- **Neurological features:** The system will have to be linked with identifiable neurological structures and be grounded upon perceptual, cognitive, and affective systems whose neural substrates antedate their current linguistic functions.

Implicit learning is little more, but not less, than the process whereby information is picked up largely independently of awareness of either the process or the products of learning (Reber 1993), and it satisfies all these features. It is, in essence, a covariation detector and shares elements with primitive mechanisms such as those that modulate classical conditioning and more sophisticated ones that can capture sequentially structured inputs with higher-order conditionalized properties and remote dependencies. It is also a process that is fast, effortless, unconscious, procedural, domain independent, bottom up, intuitive, automatic, and associative. It is neurologically robust, is evolutionarily old, and functions independently of age, developmental level, and intelligence (see Reber 1993).

There is also evidence for more sophisticated properties although there is, admittedly, less agreement here. Among these are: sensitivity to attentional focus while using relatively few resources (Hsaio and Reber 1998), capacity for operating in parallel with other processes (Rah, Reber, and Hsiao 2000), establishment of abstract representations (Gómez and Gerken 1999; Gertner, Fisher, and Eisengart 2006; Manza and Reber 1997), and modulation by neural structures implicated in natural language functions (Christiansen, Conway, and Onnis 2007).

The implicit acquisition mechanism is also known to be fully operational during the period of early language acquisition. Equipped with little else, infants as young as three months extract the sequential structure of arbitrary inputs (Gómez 2002; Gómez and Gerken 1999) and accurately capture the features of speech segmentation (Curtin, Mintz, and Christiansen 2005; Saffran 2001; Saffran, Aslin, and Newport 1996). They pick up the morphological properties that mark gender (Brooks et al. 1993), detect phrase markers (Saffran 2001), integrate associative relationships across several syntactic elements (Gómez 2002), and form abstract representations (Gómez and Gerken 1999; Gertner, Fisher, and Eisengart 2006).

The system is, moreover, capable of extracting a key element of natural languages, the statistical links between nonadjacent features (Onnis et al. 2005). In an important series of studies, Gómez, Lany, and colleagues (Gómez and Maye 2005; Lany and Gómez 2008; Lany, Gómez, and Gerken 2007) show how experience with inputs containing complex, nonadjacent features provides infants with the necessary input to form the appropriate representations. Infants' sensitivity to the frequency of these regularities allows them, in Lany and Gómez's words, "to bootstrap . . . learning of a difficult language structure" (2008, 1247).

While these findings emphasize statistical induction routines, other evidence reveals the importance of para- and metalinguistic factors. In a recent report Gliga and Csibra (2009) show that thirteen-month-old infants appreciate the referential nature of words and gestures from parents and caregivers. Rowe and Goldin-Meadow (2009) note that infants are not only sensitive to such gestures but that individual differences in the richness of gestural support during infancy predict later language development.

Summary

The take-home messages? As a starter, we do not need Chomsky. He has been a seminal figure in linguistics and the cognitive sciences, and his legacy is assured. However, the basic architecture of his approach, from its reliance on grammatical formalisms, emphasis on syntax, encapsulation of language separate from the social and pragmatic features of communication and LAD, to its eccentric views on the biology and organicity of language, has diminished its ability to provide the foundation for a mature psychology of language.

In its place I recommend a broader science that focuses on communicative functions, incorporates pragmatic and social elements, one that takes more seriously what the roles and functions of language are and what its evolutionary precursors were. Such a shift in emphasis will be smoothed by a reliance on a general learning mechanism, one that satisfies the various features we know it must have: nonconscious detection of covariation, neurological and psychological robustness, domain generality, age independence, adaptive function, and evolutionary plausibility.

REFERENCES

Arbib, Michael A. 2002. The mirror system: Imitation and the evolution of language. In *Imitation in animals and artifacts,* ed. Chrystopher L. Nehaniv and Kerstin Dautenhahn, 229–80. Cambridge, MA: MIT Press.

Aronoff, Mark, Irit Meir, Carol Padden, and Wendy Sandler. 2005. The roots of linguistic organization in a new language. *Interaction Studies* 9:133–53.

Austin, John L. 1962. *How to do things with words.* Cambridge, MA: Harvard University Press.

Behme, Christina, and S. Hélène Deacon. 2008. Language learning in infancy: Does the empirical evidence support a domain specific language acquisition device? *Philosophical Psychology* 21:641–72.

Bickerton, Derek. 2009. *Adam's tongue.* New York: Hill and Wang.

Brooks, Patricia J., Martin D. S. Braine, Lisa Catalano, Ruth E. Brody, and Vicki Sudhalter. 1993. Acquisition of gender-like noun subclasses in an artificial language: The contribution of phonological markers to learning. *Journal of Memory and Language* 32:76–95.

Chomsky, Noam. 1959. Review of *Verbal Behavior. Language* 35:26–58.

———. 2005. Three factors in language design. *Linguistic Inquiry* 36:1–22.

Christiansen, Morton H., and Nick Chater. 2008. Language as shaped by the brain. *Behavioral and Brain Sciences* 31:489–508.

Christiansen, Morton H., Christopher M. Conway, and Luca Onnis. 2007. Overlapping neural responses to structural incongruities in language and statistical learning point to similar underlying mechanisms. In *Proceedings of the 29th Annual Conference of Cognitive Science Society* 29:173–78.

Christiansen, Morton H., and J. T. Devlin. 1997. Recursive inconsistencies are hard to learn: A connectionist perspective on universal word-order correlations. In *Proceedings of the 19th Annual Cognitive Science Society Conference,* ed. Michael G. Shafto and P. Langley, 113–18. Hillsdale, NJ: Lawrence Erlbaum Associates.

Curtin, Suzanne, Toben H. Mintz, and Morton H. Christiansen. 2005. Stress changes the representational landscape: Evidence from word segmentation. *Cognition* 96:233–62.

Diebold, A. Richard. 1965. A survey of psycholinguistic research, 1954–1964. In *Psycholinguistics: A survey of theory and research problems,* ed. Charles E. Osgood and Thomas A. Sebeok, 205–91. Bloomington: Indiana University Press.

Donald, Merlin. 1998. Mimesis and the executive suite: Missing links in language evolution. In *Approaches to the evolution of language: Social and cognitive bases,* ed. James R. Hurford, Michael Studdert-Kennedy, and Chris Knight, 44–67. New York: Cambridge University Press.

Dunbar, Robin. 1993. Theory of mind and the evolution of language. In *Approaches to the evolution of language: Social and cognitive bases,* ed. James R. Hurford, Michael Studdert-Kennedy, and Chris Knight, 92–110. New York: Cambridge University Press.

Elman, Jeffrey L. 1999. Origins of language: A conspiracy theory. In *The emergence of language,* ed. Brian MacWhinney, 1–27. Hillsdale, NJ: Lawrence Erlbaum Associates.

Elman, Jeffrey L., Elizabeth A. Bates, Mark H. Johnson, Annette Karmiloff-Smith, Domenico Parisi, and Kim Plunkett. 1996. *Rethinking innateness: A connectionist perspective on development.* Cambridge, MA: MIT Press.

Evans, Nicholas, and Stephen C. Levinson, S. 2009. The myth of language universals: Language diversity and its importance for cognitive science. *Behavioral and Brain Sciences* 32:429–48.

Farkaš, Igor, and Mathew W. Crocker. 2008. Syntactic systematicity in sentence processing with a recurrent self-organizing network. *Neurocomputing* 71:1172–79.

Fitch, W. Tecumseh, Marc D. Hauser, and Noam Chomsky. 2005. The evolution of the language faculty: Clarifications and implications. *Cognition* 97:179–210.

Fitch, W. Tecumseh, and David Reby. 2001. The descended larynx is not uniquely human. *Proceedings of the Royal Society, Biological Sciences* 268:2669–75.

Gertner, Yael, Cynthia Fisher, and Julie Eisengart. 2006. Learning words and rules: Abstract knowledge of word order in early sentence comprehension. *Psychological Science* 17:684–91.

Gliga, Teodora, and Gergely Csibra. 2009. 13-month-old infants appreciate the referential nature of deictic words and gestures. *Psychological Science* 20:347–53.

Goldberg, Adele E. 2004. But do we need universal grammar? Comment on Lidz et al. (2003). *Cognition* 94:77–84.

————. 2006. *Constructions at work: The nature of generalization in language.* New York: Oxford University Press.

————. 2008. Universal grammar? Or prerequisites for natural language? Comment on Christiansen and Chater. *Behavioral and Brain Sciences* 31:522–23.

Gómez, Rebecca. L. 2002. Variability and detection of invariant structure. *Psychological Science* 13:431–36.

Gómez, Rebecca L., and LuAnn Gerken. 1999. Artificial grammar learning by one-year olds leads to specific and abstract knowledge. *Cognition* 70:109–35.

Gómez, Rebecca L., and Jessica Maye. 2005. The developmental trajectory of nonadjacent dependency learning. *Infancy* 7:183–206.

Grice, Herbert Paul. 1969. Utterer's meaning and intentions. *The Philosophical Review* 68:147–77.

————. 1989. *Studies in the way of words.* Cambridge, MA: Harvard University Press.

Hampe, Beate, ed. 2005. *From perception to meaning: Image schemas in cognitive linguistics.* Berlin: Mouton de Gruyter.

Hauser, Marc D. 1996. *The evolution of communication.* Cambridge, MA: MIT Press.

Hauser, Marc D., Noam Chomsky, and W. Tecumseh Fitch. 2002. The language faculty: What is it, who has it, and how did evolve? *Science* 298:1569–79.

Hornstein, Norbert, and Cedric Boeckx. 2009. Approaching universals from below: I-Universals in light of a minimalist program for linguistic theory. In *Language universals,* ed. Morton H. Christiansen, Christopher Collins, and Shimon Edelman, 79–99. New York: Oxford University Press.

Hsiao, Andrew T., and Arthur S. Reber. 1998. The role of attention in implicit sequence learning. In *Handbook of implicit learning,* ed. Michael A. Stadler and Peter A. Frensch, 471–94. Thousand Oaks, CA: Sage Publications.

Hurford, James R. 2003. The neural basis of predicate-argument structure. *Behavioral and Brain Sciences* 26:261–83.

————. 2006. Recent developments in the evolution of language. *Cognitive Systems* 7:23–32.

————. 2008. Niche-construction, co-evolution, and domain-specificity. Comment on Christiansen and Chater. *Behavioral and Brain Sciences* 31:526.

Jackendoff, Ray. 2002. *Foundations of language.* New York: Oxford University Press.

Johansson, Sverker. 2006. Working backward from modern language to proto-grammar. In *The evolution of language,* ed. Angelo Cangelosi, Andrew D. M. Smith, and Kenny Smith, 160–67. Hackensack, NJ: World Scientific.

Knight, Chris. 2008. Language co-evolved with the rule of law. *Mind and Society* 7:109–28.

Lany, Jill, and Rebecca L. Gómez. 2008. Twelve-month-old infants benefit from prior experience in statistical learning. *Psychological Science* 19:1247–52.

Lany, Jill, Rebecca Gómez, and LuAnn Gerken. 2007. The role of prior experience in language acquisition. *Cognitive Science* 31:481–507.

Lidz, Jeffrey, Henry Gleitman, and Lila Gleitman. 2003. Understanding how input matters: Verb learning and the footprint of universal grammar. *Cognition* 87:151–78.

Lidz, Jeffrey, and Lila Gleitman. 2004. Yes, we still need universal grammar. *Cognition* 94:85–93.

Lightfoot, David. 2000. The spandrels of the linguistic genotype. In *The evolutionary emergence of language: Social functions and the origins of linguistic form,* ed. Chris Knight, Michael Studdert-Kennedy, and James R. Hurford, 231–47. New York: Cambridge University Press.

Locke, John L. 2008. Cost and complexity: Selection for speech and language. *Journal of Theoretical Biology* 251:640–52.

Manza, Louis, and Arthur S. Reber. 1997. Representing artificial grammars: Transfer across stimulus forms and modalities. In *How implicit is implicit learning?* ed. Dianne C. Berry, 73–106. London: Oxford University Press.

Mirolli, Marco, and Domenico Parisi. 2006. Talking to oneself as a selective pressure for the emergence of language. In *The evolution of language,* ed. Angelo Cangelosi, Andrew D. M. Smith, and Kenny Smith, 214–21. Hackensack. NJ: World Scientific.

Onnis, Luca, Padraic Monaghan, Nick Chater, and Korin Richmond. 2005. Phonology impacts segmentation in speech processing. *Journal of Memory and Language* 53:225–37.

Osgood, Charles E., and Thomas A. Sebeok. (1954) 1965. *Psycholinguistics: A survey of theory and research problems.* Bloomington: Indiana University Press.

Pinker, Steven A., and Ray Jackendoff. 2005. The language faculty: What's special about it? *Cognition* 95:201–36.

Rah, Simon K-Y., Arthur S. Reber, and Andrew T. Hsiao. 2000. Another wrinkle on the dual-task SRT experiment: It's probably not dual-task. *Psychonomic Bulletin & Review* 7:309–13.

Reber, Arthur S. 1967. Implicit learning of artificial grammars. *Journal of Verbal Learning and Verbal Behavior* 6:855–63.

———. 1987. The rise and (surprisingly rapid) fall of psycholinguistics. *Synthese* 72:432–39.

———. 1993. *Implicit learning and tacit knowledge: An essay on the cognitive unconscious.* New York: Oxford University Press.

Rowe, Meredith L., and Susan Goldin-Meadow. 2009. Differences in early gesture explain SES disparities in child vocabulary size at school entry. *Science* 323:951–53.

Saffran, Jenny R. 2001. The use of predictive tendencies in language learning. *Journal of Memory and Language* 44:493–515.

Saffran, Jenny R., Richard N. Aslin, and Elissa L. Newport. 1996. Statistical learning by 8-month-old infants. *Science* 274:1926–28.

Searle, John R. 1969. *Speech acts.* New York: Cambridge University Press.

Skinner, Burrhus Fredric. 1957. *Verbal behavior.* New York: Appleton-Century-Crofts.

Tomasello, Michael. 2003. *Constructing a language: A usage-based theory of language acquisition.* Cambridge, MA: Harvard University Press.

———. 2004. What kind of evidence could refute the UG hypothesis? A commentary on Wunderlich. *Studies in Language* 28:642–44.

———. 2008. *Origins of human communication.* Cambridge, MA: MIT Press.

Winter, Bill, and Arthur S. Reber. 1994. Implicit learning and natural language acquisition. In *Implicit and explicit learning of languages,* ed. Nick C. Ellis, 115–46. London: Academic Press.

Wundt, Wilhelm M. 1904. *Die Sprache.* Vols. 1, 2 of *Völkerpsychologie.* Leipzig: Engelmann.

4

Implicit and Explicit SLA and Their Interface

NICK C. ELLIS
University of Michigan

THIS CHAPTER PROVIDES a historical and cross-disciplinary review of the *Interface Question in SLA* concerning the differences between implicit and explicit language knowledge and the ways in which they interact. The answer to this question is fundamental in that it determines how one believes second languages are learned and whether there is any role for instruction.

Implicit and Explicit Language Learning and Knowledge

Children acquire their first language (L1) by engaging with their caretakers in natural meaningful communication. From this "evidence" they automatically acquire complex knowledge of the structure of their language. Yet paradoxically they cannot describe this knowledge, the discovery of which forms the object of the disciplines of theoretical linguistics, psycholinguistics, and child language acquisition. This is a difference between explicit and implicit knowledge—ask a young child how to form a plural and she says she does not know; ask her "here is a wug, here is another wug, what have you got?" and she is able to reply, "two wugs." The acquisition of L1 grammar is implicit and is extracted from experience of usage rather than from explicit rules—simple exposure to normal linguistic input suffices, and no explicit instruction is needed. Adult acquisition of second language (L2) is a different matter in that what can be acquired implicitly from communicative contexts is typically quite limited in comparison to native speaker norms, and adult attainment of L2 accuracy usually requires additional resources of consciousness and explicit learning.

History of the Interface in Language Education and Applied Linguistics

Differing assumptions about the nature of language representation and its promotion motivated different teaching traditions (Kelly 1969). Traditional Grammar Translation foreign language (FL) instruction and the Cognitive Code method popular in the 1960s and 1970s capitalized on the formal operational abilities of older children and adults to think and act in a rule-governed way. This allowed their instruction, through the medium of language, in pedagogical grammar rules, with lessons focusing on language forms such as, for example, particular tenses and inflectional patterns. These explicit methods were motivated by the belief that perception and awareness of L2 rules necessarily precedes their use. In contrast, FL and L2 teaching methods like "Audiolingualism," which held sway during World War II, and more recent "Natural" and "Communicative" approaches, maintained that adult language learning is, like L1 acquisition, implicit. Since language skill is very different from knowledge about language, they consequently renounced explicit grammar-based instruction. The defining distinction between implicit acquisition and explicit learning of L2 was that of Krashen (1982). He argued that adult L2 students of grammar-translation methods, who can tell more about a language than a native speaker, yet whose technical knowledge of grammar leaves them totally in the lurch in conversation, testify that conscious learning about language and subconscious acquisition of language are different things, and that any notion of a "Strong-Interface" between the two must be rejected. Krashen's Input Hypothesis, an extreme "Non-Interface" position, thus countered that (a) subconscious acquisition dominates in second language performance; (b) learning cannot be converted into acquisition; and (c) conscious learning can be used only as a Monitor, that is, an editor to correct output after it has been initiated by the acquired system. In Krashen's theory, SLA, just like first language acquisition, comes naturally as a result of implicit processes occurring while the learner is receiving comprehensible L2 input. The Input Hypothesis was the theoretical motivation behind Natural and Communicative approaches to instruction.

These foundations suggest that language learning can take place implicitly and explicitly, or, because we can communicate using language, it can be influenced by declarative statements of pedagogical rules (explicit instruction). The central issue of the Interface Question is just how much do explicit learning and explicit instruction influence implicit learning, and how can their symbiosis be optimized? Subsequent research took up this theme.

Empirical analyses of learners in "grammar-free" Communicative, Natural, or Immersion L2 and FL programs demonstrated significant shortcomings in the accuracy of their language (Lightbown, Spada, and White 1993). Critical theoretical reactions to Krashen's Input Hypothesis (e.g., McLaughlin 1987), together with demonstrations that it is those language forms which are attended that are subsequently learned, prompted Schmidt (1990) to propose that conscious cognitive effort involving the subjective experience of noticing is a necessary and sufficient condition for the conversion of input to intake in SLA. Schmidt's Noticing Hypothesis was the theoretical motivation for subsequent research efforts, both in laboratory experiments (Hulstijn and DeKeyser 1997) and in the classroom (Doughty and Williams 1998), into the role of consciousness in SLA. Together, the shortcomings in uptake, the consequently limited end state of naturalistic learners, and the demonstrable role of noticing in SLA, obliged in turn the rejection of the extreme No-Interface position.

Applied Linguistics was thus left with something in between, some form of a Weak Interface position (Ellis 1994; Long 1991) whereby explicit knowledge plays various roles (a) in the perception of, and selective attending to, L2 form by facilitating the processes of "noticing" (i.e., paying attention to specific linguistic features of the input); (b) by "noticing the gap" (i.e., comparing the noticed features with those the learner typically produces in output); and (c) in output, with explicit knowledge coaching practice, particularly in initial stages, with this controlled use of declarative knowledge guiding the proceduralization and eventual automatization of language processing, as it does in the acquisition of other cognitive skills.

The Weak Interface position motivated renewed interest in explicit instruction, but the pendulum didn't swing back all the way to the decontextualized and often meaningless grammar drills of traditional Grammar Translation instruction, which Long (1991) termed Focus on Forms. Instead, instruction was to be integrated into the meaningful communication afforded by more naturalistic approaches: learner errors should be picked up by a conversation partner and corrected in the course of meaningful, often task-based, communication by way of negative evidence which offers some type of explicit focus on linguistic form (Doughty and Williams 1998; Ellis 2000). The period from 1980 through 2000 was a time of concerted research to assess the effectiveness of different types of explicit and implicit L2 instruction. Reviews of these investigations (Ellis and Laporte 1997; Hulstijn and DeKeyser 1997; Lightbown, Spada, and White 1993; Spada 1997), particularly the comprehensive meta-analysis of Norris and Ortega (2000) that summarized the findings from forty-nine unique sample studies and experimental and quasi-experimental investigations into the effectiveness of L2 instruction, demonstrate that focused L2 instruction results in large target-oriented gains, that explicit types of instruction are more effective than implicit types, and that the effectiveness of L2 instruction is durable.

Implicit and Explicit Knowledge and Their Interface in
Psychological Research

These developments ran in parallel to research in psychology demonstrating the dissociations of implicit and explicit memory, and of implicit and explicit learning (Ellis 1994). The separation between explicit and implicit memory was evidenced in anterograde amnesic patients who, as a result of brain damage, lost the ability to consolidate new explicit memories (those where recall involves a conscious process of remembering a prior episodic experience) to update their autobiographical record with their daily activities, to learn new concepts, or to learn to recognize new people or places. Nevertheless, amnesiacs maintained implicit memories (those evidenced by the facilitation of the processing of a stimulus as a function of a recent encounter with an identical or related stimulus but where the person at no point has to consciously recall the prior event) and were able to learn new perceptual skills such as mirror reading and new motor skills (Schacter 1987; Squire and Kandel 1999). They also showed normal classical conditioning, thus the famous anecdote of the amnesic patient who, having once been pricked by a pin hidden in the hand of her consultant, refused thereafter to shake him by his hand while at the same time denying ever having met him before.

The dissociation between explicit and implicit learning was made by Reber (1976), who had people learn complex letter strings (e.g., MXRMXT, VMTRRR) generated by an artificial grammar. In the course of studying these for later recognition, they unconsciously abstracted knowledge of the underlying regularities, to be able to later distinguish between novel strings that either accorded or broke the rules of the underlying grammar. However, like young children who can pass "wug tests" in their native language, these adult participants, too, were unable to explain their reasoning. Such research illustrated quite different styles of learning, varying in the degree to which acquisition is driven by conscious beliefs, as well as in the extent to which they give rise to explicit verbalizable knowledge: Implicit learning is acquisition of knowledge about the underlying structure of a complex stimulus environment by a process that takes place naturally, simply, and without conscious operations. Explicit learning is a more conscious operation, where the individual attends to particular aspects of the stimulus array and volunteers and tests hypotheses in a search for structure.

In brain science, neuropsychological investigations of the results of brain damage demonstrated that different areas of the brain are specialized in their function and that there are clear separations between areas involved in explicit learning and memory and those involved in implicit learning and memory (Ellis and Young 1988). Explicit learning is supported by neural systems in the prefrontal cortex involved in attention, the conscious apperception of stimuli, and working memory; the consolidation of explicit memories involves neural systems in the hippocampus and related limbic structures. In contrast, implicit learning and memory are localized, among other places, in various areas of perceptual and motor cortex.

In psychology, subsequent research in implicit and explicit learning of artificial languages, finite-state systems, and complex control systems showed: (a) When the material to be learned is simple, or where it is relatively complex but there is only a limited number of variables and the critical features are salient, then learners gain from being told to adopt an explicit mode of learning where hypotheses are to be explicitly generated and tested and the model of the system updated accordingly. As a result they are also able to verbalize this knowledge and transfer to novel situations. (b) When the material to be learned is more randomly structured with a large number of variables and when the important relationships are not obvious, then explicit instructions only interfere and an implicit mode of learning is more effective. This learning is instance-based but, with sufficient exemplars, an implicit understanding of the structure will be achieved. Although this knowledge may not be explicitly available, the learner may nonetheless be able to transfer to conceptually or perceptually similar tasks and to provide default cases on generalization (wug) tasks. (c) Whatever the domain, learning the patterns, regularities or underlying concepts of a complex problem space or stimulus environment with explicit instruction, direction, and advances clues, heuristics, or organizers is always better than learning without any cues at all (Reber et al. 1980; MacWhinney 1997a). (d) Although Reber had emphasized that the results of implicit leaning were abstract, unconscious, and rule-like representations, subsequent research showed that there was a very large contribution of concrete memorized knowledge of chunks and sequences of perceptual input and motor output that unconscious processes tally and identify to be frequent across the exemplars experienced in the learning set (Stadler and Frensch 1998).

On the broader stage of cognitive science, the period 1980–2000 showed a parallel shift away from an almost exclusively symbolic view of human cognition to one that emphasised the overwhelming importance of implicit inductive processes in the statistical reasoning which sums prior experience and results in our generalizations of this knowledge as schema, prototypes, and conceptual categories. These are the aspects of cognition that are readily simulated in connectionist models (Elman et al. 1996; Rumelhart and McClelland 1986) and which subsequently have had considerable influence upon our understanding of implicit knowledge of language and its acquisition (Christiansen and Chater 2001).

In cognitive neuroscience technological advances in functional brain imaging using electro-encephalographic (EEG) and functional magnetic resonance imaging (fMRI) triangulated the findings of earlier cognitive neuropsychological studies of brain areas involved in implicit and explicit memory. Subsequent improvements in the temporal and spatial resolution of these techniques afforded much more detailed descriptions of the dynamics of brain activity, promoting a shift of emphasis from knowledge as static representation stored in particular locations to knowledge as processing involving the dynamic mutual influence of interrelated types of information as they activate and inhibit each other over time (Eichenbaum 2002; Frackowiak et al. 2004).

Thus, in the latter part of the twentieth century, research in these various disciplines converged on the conclusion that explicit and implicit knowledge of language are distinct and dissociated, they involve different types of representation, they are substantiated in separate parts of the brain, and yet they can come into mutual influence in processing.

Implicit and Explicit Knowledge and Their Interface in SLA

What is the nature of the implicit knowledge that allows fluency in phonology, reading, spelling, lexis, morphosyntax, formulaic language, language comprehension, grammaticality, sentence production, syntax, and pragmatics? How are these representations formed? How are their strengths updated to statistically represent the nature of language, and how do linguistic prototypes and rule-like processing emerge from usage? These difficult and complex issues are certainly not resolved, and they remain the focus of the disciplines of linguistics, psycholinguistics, and child language acquisition. Nevertheless, there has been a growing consensus over the last twenty or thirty years that the vast majority of our linguistic processing is unconscious, its operations tuned by the products of our implicit learning, which has supplied a distributional analysis of the linguistic problem space, that is, a statistical sampling of language over our entire history of prior usage. Frequency of usage determines availability of representation and tallies the likelihoods of occurrence of constructions and the relative probabilities of their mappings between aspects of form and their relevant interpretations. Generalizations arise from conspiracies of memorized utterances collaborating in productive schematic linguistic constructions (Ellis 2002; Bybee and Hopper 2001; Christiansen and Chater 2001; Bod, Hay, and Jannedy 2003). Implicit learning collates the evidence of language, and the results of this tallying provide an optimal solution to the problem space of form-function mappings and their contextualized use, with representational systems modularizing over thousands of hours on task.

But if these implicit learning processes are sufficient for first language acquisition, why not for second? One part of the answer must be transfer. Transfer phenomena pervade SLA (Weinreich 1953; Lado 1957; Odlin 1989; MacWhinney 1997b).

Our neural apparatus is highly plastic in its initial state. It is not entirely an empty slate, since there are broad genetic constraints upon the usual networks of system-level connections and upon the broad timetable of maturation and myelination, but nevertheless the cortex of the brain is broadly equipotent in terms of the types of information it can represent (Elman et al. 1996). In contrast to the newborn infant, the L2 learner's neocortex has already been tuned to the L1, incremental learning has slowly committed it to a particular configuration, and it has reached a point of entrenchment where the L2 is perceived through mechanisms optimized for the L1. Thus the L1 implicit representations conspire in a "learned attention" to language and in the automatized processing of the L2 in nonoptimal, L1-tuned ways. Details of these constituent processes of contingency, cue competition, salience, interference, over-shadowing, blocking, and perceptual learning can be found in Ellis (2006a, 2006b).

Gathering these strands together, we can conclude:

(a) Implicit and explicit learning are distinct processes.

(b) Implicit and explicit memory are distinguished in their content, their form, and their brain localizations.

(c) There are different types of knowledge of and about language, stored in different areas of the brain, and engendered by different types of educational experience.

(d) A large part of acquisition involves the implicit learning of language from usage.

(e) L1 transfer, learned attention, and automatization all contribute to the more limited achievements of exclusive implicit learning in SLA than in L1A.

(f) Pedagogical responses to these shortcomings involve explicit instruction, recruiting consciousness to overcome the implicit routines that are non-optimal for L2.

(g) Evaluation research in language education demonstrates that such Focus on Form instruction can be effective.

What then are the detailed mechanisms of interface? What are the various psychological and neurobiological processes by which explicit knowledge of form-meaning associations has an impact upon implicit language learning? In the remainder of this chapter I will bring to bear current research in cognitive neuroscience as it relates to this question. I believe that this research broadly supports a Weak Interface position and that additionally it provides an important emphasis for our understanding of language learning and instruction, namely that we must concentrate on dynamic processes (Ellis and Larsen Freeman 2006, 2009) rather than on static conceptualizations of language, representation, and physical interface. The interface, like consciousness, is dynamic, situated, and contextualized: It happens transiently during conscious processing, but the influence upon implicit cognition endures thereafter (Ellis 2005).

Consciousness Provides the Weak Interface

Learning is a dynamic process; it takes place during processing, as Hebb (1949), Craik and Lockhart (1972), and O'Grady (2003) have reminded us from their neural, cognitive, and linguistic aspects on learning. In fluency in our native language, both language processing and language tallying are typically unconscious; our implicit systems automatically process the input, allowing our conscious selves to concentrate on the meaning rather than the form. Implicit, habitual processes are highly adaptive in predictable situations. But the more novelty we encounter, the more the involvement of consciousness is needed for successful learning and problem solving (Baars 1997). As with other implicit modules, when automatic capabilities fail, there follows a call recruiting additional collaborative conscious support (Baars and Franklin 2003): We think about walking only when we stumble, about driving only when a child runs into the road, and about language only when communication breaks down. In unpredictable conditions, the capacity of consciousness to organize existing knowledge in new ways is indispensable.

The psychological processes of interface are exactly that—they are dynamic processes, synchronous with consciousness. The last ten years have seen significant advances in our scientific study of consciousness and its roles in learning and memory (Baars, Banks, and Newman 2003). There have been three major strands of development: (a) cognitive neuroscientific investigation of the neural correlates of consciousness (NCC) (see Koch 2004 for review), (b) cognitive analysis of consciousness (particularly Global Workspace Theory: Baars 1988, 1997), and (c) computational modeling of the events underlying the emergence of self-amplifying resonances across a global network of neuronal coalitions, the dynamic competition among the massively parallel constituency of the unconscious mind that elects (Koch 2004, 24, 173) the current oneness of the fleeting stream of conscious experience (Dehaene and Changeux 2004). These developments inform three issues relating to the Weak Interface: the neurobiology of implicit tallying, the NCC, and the role of consciousness in learning.

The Neurobiology of Implicit Tallying
For the first time, it is now possible, using fMRI and ERP techniques, to image the implicit processing of words which, despite being presented below the threshold for conscious noticing, nevertheless result in subsequent implicit memory effects. The implicit statistical tallying that underlies subsequent priming effects can be seen to take place in various local regions of primary and secondary sensory and motor cortex (Dehaene et al. 2001).

The Neural Correlates of Consciousness
The NCC is a huge, difficult, and fascinating question, and it is generating a correspondingly massive collaborative research effort. A lot more will have been discovered in another ten years. But what is already known is potent enough in its implications for the interface: implicit learning occurs largely within modality and involves the priming, or chunking, of representations or routines within a module; it is the means of tuning our *zombie agents,* the menagerie of specialized sensorimotor processors, such as those identified in Dehaene's research, that carry out routine operations in the absence of direct conscious sensation or control (Koch 2004, chapter 12). In contrast, conscious processing is spread wide over the brain and

unifies otherwise disparate areas in a synchronized focus of activity. Conscious activity affords much more scope for focused long-range association and influence than does implicit learning. It brings about a whole new level of potential associations.

Consciousness and Learning: The Collaborative Mind

Compared with the vast number of unconscious neural processes happening in any given moment, conscious capacity evidences a very narrow bottleneck. But the narrow limits of consciousness have a compensating advantage: consciousness seems to act as a gateway, creating access to essentially any part of the nervous system. Baars's (1988, 1997) *Global Workspace Theory* holds that consciousness is the publicity organ of the brain. It is a facility for accessing, disseminating, and exchanging information and for exercising global coordination and control: consciousness is the interface. "Paying attention—becoming conscious of some material—seems to be the sovereign remedy for learning anything, applicable to many very different kinds of information. It is the universal solvent of the mind" (Baars 1997, sec. 5, 304).

Global Workspace Theory and parallel research into NCC illuminate the mechanisms by which the brain interfaces functionally and anatomically independent implicit and explicit memory systems involved variously in motoric, auditory, emotive, or visual processing and in declarative, analogue, perceptual, or procedural memories, despite their different modes of processing, which bear upon representations and entities of very different natures. Biological adaptations tend to be accretive (Gould 1982). The speech system, for example, is overlaid on a set of organs that in earlier mammals supports breathing, eating, and simple vocalization. Language is overlaid upon systems for the visual representation of the world. Yet, however different the symbolic representations of language and the analogue representations of vision are, they interact so that through language, we create mental images in our listeners that might normally be produced only by the memory of events as recorded and integrated by the sensory and perceptual systems of the brain (Jerison 1976). Likewise, the global broadcasting property of consciousness is overlaid on earlier functions that are primarily sensori-motor. In his major review culminating a lifetime's pioneering work in human neuropsychology, Luria (1973), having separately analyzed the workings of the three principal functional units of the brain (the unit for regulating tone or waking, the unit for obtaining, processing, and storing information, and the unit for programming, regulating, and verifying mental activity), emphasized that it would be a mistake to imagine that each of these units carry out their activity independently: "Each form of conscious activity is always a *complex functional system* and takes place through the *combined working of all three brain units,* each of which makes its own contribution . . . *all three principal functional brain units work concertedly,* and it is only by studying their interactions when each unit makes its own specific contribution, that an insight can be obtained into the nature of the cerebral mechanisms of mental activity" (99–101, italics in original).

Some Component Processes of the Weak Interface

This, then, is the broad framework: Language representation in the brain involves specialized localized modules, largely implicit in their operation, collaborating via long-range associations in dynamic coalitions of cell assemblies representing—among others—the phonological forms of words and constructions and their sensory and motor groundings (Pulvermüller 1999, 2003; Barsalou 1999). L1 usage tunes and automatizes them to perform in particular ways, resulting in our highly specialized L1 processing modules. To break out of these routines, to consolidate the new connections, networks, and routines necessary for L2 processing, consciousness is necessary.

The Weak Interface theory of second language instruction proposed that explicit processing plays a role in SLA by means of "noticing," "noticing the gap," and guided output practice. The remainder of this chapter outlines relevant research on each in turn.

Noticing

The primary conscious involvement in SLA is the explicit learning involved in the initial registration of pattern recognizers for constructions that are then tuned and integrated into the system by implicit learning during subsequent input processing. Neural systems in the prefrontal cortex involved in working memory provide attentional selection, perceptual integration, and the unification of consciousness. Neural systems in the hippocampus then bind these disparate cortical representations into unitary episodic representations. ERP and fMRI imaging confirm these neural correlates of consciousness, a surge of widespread activity in a coalition of forebrain and parietal areas interconnected via widespread cortico-cortico and cortico-thalamic feedback loops with sets of neurons in sensory and motor regions that code for particular features, and the subsequent hippocampal activity involved in the consolidation of novel explicit memories. These are the mechanisms by which Schmidt's noticing helps solve Quine's problem of referential indeterminacy (Ellis 2005).

This means is most relevant where the language form is of low salience and where L1 experience has tuned the learner's attention elsewhere: "Since many features of L2 input are likely to be infrequent, non-salient, and communicatively redundant, intentionally focused attention may be a practical (though not theoretical) necessity for successful language learning" (Schmidt 2001, 23). Instruction is thus targeted at increasing the salience of commonly ignored features by first pointing them out and explaining their structure and, second, by providing meaningful input that contains many instances of the same grammatical meaning-form relationship (Terrell 1991). Once consolidated into the construction, it is this new cue to interpretation of the input whose strengths are incremented on each subsequent processing episode. The cue does not have to be repeatedly noticed thereafter; once consolidated, mere use in processing for meaning is enough for implicit tallying.

A meta-analysis of Norris and Ortega (2000) of twenty-five explicit form-focused treatments from a wide variety of studies with interventions including consciousness raising, input processing, compound focus on form, metalinguistic task essentialness, and rule-oriented focus on form demonstrated an average effect size of these various treatments in excess of 1.2. More generally still, the same meta-analysis demonstrated average effect sizes in excess of 1.0 for sixty-nine different explicit instructional treatments, whether they involved focus on form or more traditional focus on forms. It is true that explicit instruction evidences greater effect on outcome measures that are themselves more explicit and metalinguistic in content (Norris and Ortega 2000), but form-focused instruction results in a medium-sized effect on free constructed production measures too (Norris and Ortega 2000). We need more studies to look at the effects of explicit instruction using outcome measures that particularly focus on different aspects of implicit knowledge and processing (Doughty 2004), but the weight of the evidence to date is in favor of significant interface by the means of attention being focused upon relevant form-meaning connections.

Noticing the Gap
A learner's flawed output can prompt negative feedback in the form of a "corrective recast," that is, a reformulation of his or her immediately preceding erroneous utterance, replacing non-target-like (lexical, grammatical, etc.) items by the corresponding target-language forms. Recasts arguably present the learner with psycholinguistic data that are optimized for acquisition because they make the gap apparent—in the contrast between their own erroneous utterance and the recast they highlight the relevant element of form at the same time as the desired meaning-to-be-expressed is still active, and the language learner can engage in focused input analysis. Long (2006) reviews more than forty descriptive, quasi-experimental, and experimental studies of the occurrence, usability, and use of recasts in classrooms, laboratory settings, and noninstructional conversation, showing that these techniques are generally effective in the promotion of uptake.

Output Practice
Explicit memories can guide the conscious building of novel linguistic utterances through processes of analogy. Formulas, drills, and declarative pedagogical grammar rules can all contribute to the conscious creation of utterances whose subsequent usage promotes implicit learning and proceduralization. Thus, by various means, the learner can use explicit knowledge to consciously construct an utterance in working memory. Anderson's (1988) ACT model described the move from declarative to procedural knowledge as three broad stages: a cognitive stage, where a declarative description of the procedure is learned; an associative stage, where the learner works on productions for performing the process; and an autonomous stage, where execution of the skill becomes rapid and automatic. McLaughlin (1987) described processes of L2 automatization, from the novice's slow and halting production by means of attentive control of construction in working memory to fluent automatic processing with the relevant programs and routines being executed swiftly and without reflection. DeKeyser (2001) provides more recent reviews of automatization and SLA as skill acquisition.

The balance of experimental findings supports the effectiveness for SLA of encouraging learners to produce output. Norris and Ortega (2000) summarized the results of six studies that involved explicit focus on forms followed by output practice which demonstrated a substantial average effect size of 1.39. DeKeyser et al. (2002) report five more recent studies, all of which substantiated that output-based treatments promoted learners to significant improvement on uses of the Spanish subjunctive, acquisition of Spanish copulas, interpretation and production of the Italian future tense, and acquisition of the French causative. Keck et al. (2006) reported a meta-analysis of interaction studies showing that tasks involving opportunities for *pushed output* ($d = 1.05$) produced larger effect sizes than tasks without pushed output ($d = 0.61$) on immediate posttests. Taken together, these studies provide good reason to consider an interface of explicit knowledge upon implicit learning during output too.

Conclusion

In sum, although much of first language acquisition involves implicit learning (Ellis 2002), these mechanisms do not suffice for second language acquisition (SLA) because of learned attention and transfer from L1. SLA must therefore overcome the processing habits of the L1 by recruiting additional resources of explicit learning. The interface between explicit and implicit knowledge is dynamic: It happens transiently during conscious processing, but the influence upon implicit cognition endures thereafter. The various roles of consciousness in SLA include learners noticing negative evidence; their attending to language form, their perception focused by social scaffolding or explicit instruction; their voluntary use of pedagogical grammatical descriptions and analogical reasoning; their reflective induction of meta-linguistic insights about language; and their consciously guided practice that results, eventually, in unconscious, automatized skill. Consciousness creates access: its contents are broadcast throughout the brain to the vast array of our unconscious sources of knowledge, and by these means, consciousness is the interface.

REFERENCES

Anderson, John R. 1988. Acquisition of cognitive skill. In *Readings in cognitive science: A perspective from psychology and artificial intelligence,* ed. Allan M. Collins and Edward Smith, 362–80.

Baars, Bernard J. 1988. *A cognitive theory of consciousness.* Cambridge: Cambridge University Press.

———. 1997. In the theatre of consciousness: Global Workspace Theory, a rigorous scientific theory of consciousness. *Journal of Consciousness Studies* 4:292–309.

Baars, Bernard J., William P. Banks, and James B. Newman, eds. 2003. *Essential sources in the scientific study of consciousness.* Cambridge, MA: MIT Press/Bradford Books.

Baars, Bernard J., and Stan Franklin. 2003. How conscious experience and working memory interact. *Trends in Cognitive Science* 7:166–72.

Barsalou, Laurence W. 1999. Perceptual symbol systems. *Behavioral and Brain Sciences* 22:577–660.

Bod, Rens, Jennifer Hay, and Stephanie Jannedy, eds. 2003. *Probabilistic linguistics.* Cambridge, MA: MIT Press.

Bybee, Joan, and Paul Hopper, eds. 2001. *Frequency and the emergence of linguistic structure.* Amsterdam: John Benjamins.

Christiansen, Morten H., and Nick Chater, eds. 2001. *Connectionist psycholinguistics.* Westport, CO: Ablex.

Craik, Fergus I. M., and Robert S. Lockhart. 1972. Levels of processing: A framework for memory research. *Journal of Verbal Learning and Verbal Behavior* 11:671–84.

Dehaene, Stanislas, and Jean-Pierre Changeux. 2004. Neural mechanisms for access to consciousness. In *The cognitive neurosciences,* ed. by M. Gazzaniga. Cambridge, MA: MIT Press.

Dehaene, Stanislas, Lionel Naccache, Laurent Cohen, Denis Le Bihan, Jean-François Mangin, Jean B. Poline, and Denis Riviere. 2001. Cerebral mechanisms of word masking and unconscious repetition priming. *Nature Neuroscience* 4 (7): 678–80.

DeKeyser, Robert 2001. Automaticity and automatization. In *Cognition and second language acquisition,* ed. Peter Robinson. Cambridge: Cambridge University Press.

DeKeyser, Robert, Rafael Salaberry, Peter Robinson, and Michael Harrington. 2002. What gets processed in processing instruction? A commentary on Bill VanPatten's "Processing Instruction: An Update." *Language Learning* 52:805–24.

Doughty, Catherine. 2004. Effects of instruction on learning a second language: A critique of instructed SLA research. In *Form-meaning connections in second language acquisition,* ed. Bill VanPatten, Jessica Williams, Suzanne Rott, and Mark Overstreet. Mahwah, NJ: Lawrence Erlbaum Associates.

Doughty, Catherine, and Jessica Williams, eds. 1998. *Focus on form in classroom second language acquisition.* New York: Cambridge University Press.

Eichenbaum, Howard 2002. *The cognitive neuroscience of memory.* New York: Oxford University Press.

Ellis, Andrew W., and Andrew W. Young. 1988. *Human cognitive neuropsychology.* Hove, Sussex, UK: Erlbaum.

Ellis, Nick C., ed. 1994. *Implicit and explicit learning of languages.* San Diego: Academic Press.

———. 2002. Frequency effects in language processing: A review with implications for theories of implicit and explicit language acquisition. *Studies in Second Language Acquisition* 24 (2): 143–88.

———. 2005. At the interface: Dynamic interactions of explicit and implicit language knowledge. *Studies in Second Language Acquisition* 27:305–52.

———. 2006a. Language acquisition as rational contingency learning. *Applied Linguistics* 27 (1): 1–24.

———. 2006b. Selective attention and transfer phenomena in SLA: Contingency, cue competition, salience, interference, overshadowing, blocking, and perceptual learning. *Applied Linguistics* 27 (2): 1–31.

Ellis, Nick C., and Nadine Laporte. 1997. Contexts of acquisition: Effects of formal instruction and naturalistic exposure on second language acquisition. In *Tutorials in bilingualism: Psycholinguistic perspectives,* ed. Annette M. DeGroot and Judith F. Kroll. Mahwah, NJ: Lawrence Erlbaum Associates.

Ellis, Nick C., and Dianne Larsen Freeman. 2006. Language emergence: Implications for Applied Linguistics. *Applied Linguistics* 27 (4): Whole issue.

———. 2009. Language as a Complex Adaptive System (Special Issue). *Language Learning* 59: Supplement 1.

Ellis, Rod. 1994. A theory of instructed second language acquisition. In *Implicit and explicit learning of languages,* ed. Nick C. Ellis. San Diego: Academic.

———. 2000. *Learning a second language through interaction.* Amsterdam: John Benjamins.

Elman, Jeff L., Elizabeth A. Bates, Mark H. Johnson, Annette Karmiloff-Smith, Dominic Parisi, and Kim Plunkett. 1996. *Rethinking innateness: A connectionist perspective on development.* Cambridge, MA: MIT Press.

Frackowiak, Richard S. J., Karl J. Friston, Chris D. Frith, Raymond J. Dolan, Cathy J. Price, Semir Zeki, John Ashburner, and William Penny, eds. 2004. *Human brain function.* 2nd ed. London: Academic Press.

Gould, Stephen J. 1982. *The Panda's thumb: More reflections on natural history.* New York: W. W. Norton.

Hebb, Donald O. 1949. *The organization of behaviour.* New York: John Wiley & Sons.

Hulstijn, Jan, and Robert DeKeyser, eds. 1997. Testing SLA theory in the research laboratory. *Studies in Second Language Acquisition* 19:2 (Special Issue).

Jerison, Harry J. 1976. Paleoneurology and the evolution of mind. *Scientific American* 234:90–101.

Keck, Casey M., Gina Iberri-Shea, Nicole Tracy, and Safari Wa-Mbaleka. 2006. Investigating the empirical link between interaction and acquisition: A quantitative meta-analysis. In *Synthesizing research on language learning and teaching,* ed. Lourdes Ortega and John Norris. Amsterdam: John Benjamins.

Kelly, Louis G. 1969. *Twenty five centuries of language teaching.* Rowley, MA: Newbury House.

Koch, Christof. 2004. *The quest for consciousness: A neurobiological approach.* Englewood, CO: Roberts and Company.

Krashen, Stephen D. 1982. *Principles and practice in second language acquisition.* Oxford: Pergamon.

Lado, Robert. 1957. *Linguistics across cultures: Applied linguistics for language teachers.* Ann Arbor: University of Michigan Press.

Lightbown, Patsy M., Nina Spada, and Lydia White. 1993. The role of instruction in second language acquisition. *Studies in Second Language Acquisition* 15 (Special issue).

Long, Michael H. 1991. Focus on form: A design feature in language teaching methodology. In *Foreign language research in cross-cultural perspective,* ed. Kees d. Bot, Ralph Ginsberg, and Claire Kramsch. Amsterdam: John Benjamins.

————. 2006. Recasts in SLA: The story so far. In *Problems in SLA*, ed. Michael Long. Mahwah, NJ: Lawrence Erlbaum Associates.

Luria, Alexander R. 1973. *The working brain: An introduction to neuropsychology.* New York: Basic Books.

MacWhinney, Brian. 1997a. Implicit and explicit processes: Commentary. *Studies in Second Language Acquisition* 19:277–82.

————. 1997b. Second language acquisition and the Competition Model. In *Tutorials in bilingualism: Psycholinguistic perspectives,* ed. Annette M. B. De Groot and Judith F. Kroll. Mahwah, NJ: Lawrence Erlbaum Associates.

McLaughlin, Barry. 1987. *Theories of second language learning.* London: Arnold.

Norris, John, and Lourdes Ortega. 2000. Effectiveness of L2 instruction: A research synthesis and quantitative meta-analysis. *Language Learning* 50:417–528.

Odlin, Terence. 1989. *Language transfer.* New York: Cambridge University Press.

O'Grady, William. 2003. The radical middle: Nativism without Universal Grammar. In *Handbook of second language acquisition,* ed. Catherine Doughty and Michael H. Long. Oxford: Blackwell.

Pulvermüller, Friedman. 1999. Words in the brain's language. *Behavioral and Brain Sciences* 22:253–336.

————. 2003. *The neuroscience of language. On brain circuits of words and serial order.* Cambridge: Cambridge University Press.

Reber, Arthur S. 1976. Implicit learning of synthetic languages: The role of instructional set. *Journal of Experimental Psychology: Human Learning and Memory* 2:88–94.

Reber, Arthur S., Saul M. Kassin, Selma Lewis, and Gary W. Cantor. 1980. On the relationship between implicit and explicit modes in the learning of a complex rule structure. *Journal of Experimental Psychology: Human Learning and Memory* 6:492–502.

Rumelhart, David E., and James L. McClelland, eds. 1986. *Parallel distributed processing: Explorations in the microstructure of cognition.* Vol. 2, *Psychological and biological models.* Cambridge, MA: MIT Press.

Schacter, Daniel L. 1987. Implicit memory: History and current status. *Journal of Experimental Psychology: Learning, Memory, and Cognition* 13:501–18.

Schmidt, Richard. 1990. The role of consciousness in second language learning. *Applied Linguistics* 11:129–58.

————. 2001. Attention. In *Cognition and second language instruction,* ed. Peter Robinson. Cambridge: Cambridge University Press.

Spada, Nina. 1997. Form-focused instruction and second language acquisition: A review of classroom and laboratory research. *Language Teaching Research* 30:73–87.

Squire, Larry R., and Eric R. Kandel. 1999. *Memory: From mind to molecules.* New York: Scientific American Library.

Stadler, Michael A., and Peter A. Frensch, eds. 1998. *Implicit learning handbook.* Thousand Oaks, CA: Sage Publications.

Terrell, Tracy 1991. The role of grammar instruction in a communicative approach. *The Modern Language Journal* 75:52–63.

Weinreich, Uriel. 1953. *Languages in contact.* The Hague: Mouton.

5

How Analysis and Control Lead to Advantages and Disadvantages in Bilingual Processing

ELLEN BIALYSTOK
York University

OVER THIRTY YEARS AGO, I was working on trying to understand the cognitive processes involved in adult second language learning. The problem was surprisingly intractable: the evidence showed slow uneven progress, usually without ever fully mastering the language, and enormous variation between individuals. This language learning task seemed to have no relation to the one we all master effortlessly in our first few years of life. But why should that be? Have our brains changed so much? Is a second language so much more difficult than a first? Are there really dedicated processes for language learning that are available to us for a brief part of our lives, only to desert us later?

Approaching the question from the perspective of what we know about language structure was even more puzzling. Young children who can utter perfectly grammatical sequences have surely never heard of a subject and predicate, modifier and verb, yet all the pieces are selected correctly to comply with some unspoken set of regulations. Adults, in contrast, can expound at great length on parts of speech, verb tense and aspect, and the varieties of modification and yet still fail to make verbs agree and adjectives correspond to their referents. Intensive grammar classes seem to make little difference in this regard.

These observations suggested to me that there was some kind of roadblock between the knowledge built up through experience or instruction and the ability to implement that knowledge into fluent performance. This seemed different from the usual learning experience: for motor skills, continual practice in executing articulated rules eventually improves performance. But this was not the case with language. Adult second language learners were often stuck in a stage of paralysis in which no amount of learning could consolidate the rules, and no amount of practice could improve fluency. Learning could not be explained in terms of a simple progression along one dimension of change.

Analysis and Control in Second Language Acquisition
My interpretation of this situation was that there were two components of skilled performance that needed to be coordinated. In child first language acquisition, the

49

coordination was effortless, but in adult second language acquisition, the synchrony was broken. Skilled performance, it seemed, required both a specialized knowledge base and a set of procedures for using that knowledge. When these two components were at different levels of development, they could not be integrated properly into fluent performance. I labeled the two components analysis of representations and control of attentional processes.

The knowledge base is the representation of information needed to perform in a cognitive domain. Development, however, is not adequately explained by simply the accumulation of knowledge; development also requires the increased organization of that knowledge for it to support higher levels of performance. This evolving organization is handled by the process called "analysis." As knowledge becomes organized and structured, it becomes more explicit and can be articulated and manipulated. For example, children learn a rote sequence that turns out to be counting. As that sequence becomes analyzed, children understand that the sequence comprises of individual numerical entities, each of which has its own cardinal value. Finally, as these cardinal values are understood both individually and in relation to each other as a part of the overall sequence of numbers, they can be manipulated and used for arithmetic calculations. Through this process of analysis, knowledge is continually built up by the addition of new information and by the restructuring of that information that makes it more accessible and suitable as an object of thought.

Another way of thinking about the analysis of knowledge is that information moves along a continuum from implicit knowledge to explicit knowledge. Different degrees of explicitness are required to support different activities. Although an implicit rote knowledge of the sequence of numbers is sufficient for counting, greater levels of explicitness of that sequence are required for understanding cardinality, and even greater levels for carrying out arithmetic calculations. In this sense implicit knowledge is a starting point and should not be confused with the automatized knowledge that is a consequence, or endpoint, of a highly practiced activity. Thus, analysis is responsible for reforming the organizational structure of the representational base to support increasingly complex performance.

The second component, control, was intended to refer to the cognitive procedures used to access knowledge and carry out the necessary operations. This component was not well articulated in the original model, primarily because it relied on general cognitive constructs that were not obviously part of the mechanisms recruited for ordinary language production. The need for the concept, however, was apparent in the attempt to explain the relation between explicit knowledge of language, fluent performance, and metalinguistic awareness. The role for a concept like control was especially clear when there was misleading or irrelevant information that needed to be avoided so that selection of the target information could proceed fluently. Unlike the domain-specific basis of the representational structures for analysis, control was domain-general and resided not in a particular knowledge system but in the resource-limited attention mechanisms of the mind.

In both childhood and adult skill development, progress can be explained in terms of the interaction of analysis and control. New relevant knowledge is built up and integrated into an organized knowledge base, and new attentional procedures are established to support the performance.

An example of the distinction between analysis and control and their differential role in performance was provided with a metalinguistic task administered to children (Bialystok 1986). A standard measure of metalinguistic awareness is to assess the ability to judge the grammaticality of sentences, a task that has been shown to be valid even with young children (de Villiers and de Villiers 1972, 1974). Children's ability to determine whether or not a sentence conforms to the rules of grammatical structures is an indication of their representational knowledge of grammar; in other words, their analysis of linguistic structure. Therefore, children who are sensitive to the abstract rules of grammar will recognize that a sentence such as "Apples growed on trees" violates a formation rule and will decide that the sentence contains a mistake, or, put in the language of research with children, is said the "wrong way." Children can be trained to do this with a reasonable degree of accuracy. Once they have learned this principle and are focused on the well-formedness of sentences, a new type of judgment can be added. Children are reminded that the only criterion is to decide whether or not the sentence is said the "right way" but are warned that some of the sentences will be "silly." This is described as acceptable: it's fun to be silly! Therefore, children must judge that sentences like "Apples grow on noses" are acceptable. The semantic anomaly is extremely salient for children and they are drawn into rejecting the sentence, in spite of repeated cautions that only the way in which the sentence is said must be considered. In other words, children must ignore the salient anomaly in meaning and focus attention on the formal structure of the sentence. Put yet another way, children must use their resources for attentional control to examine their representational base for language structure in order to respond correctly. Thus, the task requires both sufficient analysis of grammatical structure to determine whether or not the sentence matches the correct form and adequate control of attention to focus on the structure and ignore the salient anomaly in meaning. In several experiments, both monolingual and bilingual children were equally successful at determining that a meaningful sentence contained a grammatical error (Apples growed on trees), but bilingual children were more able than comparable monolinguals to respond that a grammatical but anomalous sentence (Apples grow on noses) was said the right way (Bialystok 1986, 1988; Bialystok and Majumder 1998; Cromdal 1999).

This example shows that the distinction between analysis and control not only captured a dissociation in adult second language acquisition in which fluency was separable from knowledge of the language but also explained performance differences in monolingual and bilingual children who were progressing through the stages of language mastery. In both cases the influence of two processes was apparent only because the progress in language acquisition for both children and adults when they were dealing with two languages revealed an asynchrony that was not apparent in child first language acquisition or adult native language performance. More importantly, however, the distinction also captured something more general. Each of these constructs, analysis and control, was rooted in a general cognitive process with a well-established course of development and role in performance. This connection could potentially place language learning and language use in a broader context of cognitive ability and offer an explanation for second language learning and bilingualism that was part of the broad cognitive system.

Costs and Benefits of Bilingualism

Like other experiences that occupy a significant role in an individual's life, such as musical expertise, bilingualism has increasingly been shown to have systematic effects on cognition. To this end, two quite different effects have been reported, each one moving performance in the opposite direction. Bilinguals, on average, have been shown to have deficits relative to monolinguals in tasks based on rapid lexical access. Thus, bilingual adults name pictures more slowly than monolinguals (Gollan et al. 2005; Ivanova and Costa 2008), produce fewer words on verbal fluency tasks (Gollan, Montoya, and Werner 2002; Rosselli et al. 2000), and experience more tip-of-the tongue episodes (Gollan and Acenas 2004). In contrast, bilinguals perform more efficiently than monolinguals on nonverbal tasks assessing executive control. These are tasks that require participants to selectively attend to specific information, inhibit or ignore misleading or competing information, and switch between rules or tasks, all of which are components of the executive function. The tasks include the Simon task in which the position of a stimulus needs to be ignored to respond to its color (Bialystok et al. 2004), the Stroop task in which the printed word needs to be ignored in order to name the color of the ink (Bialystok, Craik, and Luk 2008a), the flanker task in which the direction of flanking arrows must be ignored to respond to the direction of a central target (Costa, Hernandez, and Sebastián-Gallés 2008), and task-switching paradigms in which two sets of rules that apply to a single stimulus are signaled by a cue (Bialystok, Craik, and Ryan 2006). In all these tasks bilinguals show significantly better control over attention than do monolinguals. Paradoxically, linguistic experience leads to costs for language processing but benefits for nonverbal cognitive ability.

The difference between the tasks that lead to a deficit for bilinguals and those that lead to an advantage can be considered in another way as well. All the tasks leading to a bilingual deficit involve rapid retrieval of a lexical item from semantic memory. A crucial factor in determining how efficiently this retrieval will be carried out is the nature of the representational base in semantic memory. To the extent that the linguistic and conceptual representations are organized, structured, and explicit, retrieval of specific items is easy. In other words, these tasks depend on the level of analysis of the linguistic–conceptual representation system. While there is no reason to expect bilinguals to have more poorly defined representational systems in general, there is reason to assume that the representational system for each language is less well articulated and less automatically connected to the conceptual system than it is for bilinguals. For one thing, bilinguals use each of their naming options less often than monolinguals (Gollan et al. 2008), making the efficiency with which a particular item can be accessed less fluent. Bilinguals also know fewer words than monolinguals (Portocarrero, Burright, and Donovick 2007), diminishing the representational base from which performance in these tasks proceeds. In contrast, all the examples of tasks leading to a bilingual advantage involve executive control. Just as in the earlier studies of second language learning and metalinguistic development in bilingual children, the pattern in adult studies leads to the same distinctions between analysis, which is domain specific and equivalent for all participants if the knowledge is equivalent, and control, which is domain general and more efficient in bilinguals.

Why would bilingualism lead to costs in lexical retrieval and benefits in nonverbal control? The linguistic and nonlinguistic tasks that produce these results require the involvement of both representation (analysis) and attention (control), but the emphasis in each case is different. The primary component for verbal retrieval is representation, but the primary component for the nonverbal tasks is control. Thus, the general disadvantage for bilinguals in representation and the general advantage in control determines performance in these paradigms, even though both components are involved in each.

The similarity between lexical retrieval tasks and nonverbal control tasks can be understood by the diagram in figure 5.1. In picture naming there is potential conflict from the two verbal forms that correspond to the target item. These compete for attention in selection, so bilinguals experience a delay in choosing the appropriate target label. There is no ambiguity about the stimulus to be named, so the difference between the performance of monolinguals and bilinguals is due to the

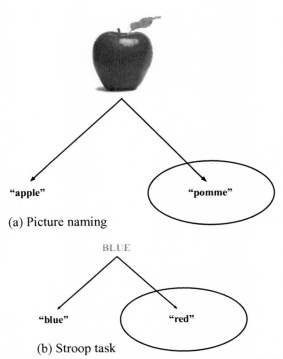

(a) Picture naming

(b) Stroop task

Figure 5.1 Similarity between Lexical Retrieval Tasks and Nonverbal Control Tasks. Illustration of the competition for selection involved in performing (a) a picture-naming task for bilinguals and (b) a Stroop task for all participants.

additional choice required for bilinguals to select from the appropriate language. In the Stroop task it is the stimulus itself that creates the conflict by indicating two different responses, only one of which conforms to the task rules, namely, the ink color. However, the more salient response is the meaning given by the color word, so it is effortful to avoid producing this more automatic response in order to comply with the instructions and simply name the ink color. It is this ability to override a habitual or primed response to produce a less typical response that is enhanced in bilinguals.

Why is this easier for bilinguals? The central premise in the explanation is the claim that both languages for fluent bilinguals are constantly active when one of them is being used, even in strongly monolingual contexts. This claim is supported by large amounts of evidence using behavioral and neuroimaging techniques (Dijkstra, Grainger, and van Heuven 1999; Rodriguez-Fornells et al. 2005). Therefore, the selection problem inherent in the Stroop task is one encountered continually by bilinguals—how to choose between two competing options when both alternatives have some claim to selection. This constant practice has the effect of enhancing those attentional processes for bilinguals, reducing the interference effect of irrelevant distractors. Thus, in a situation where all else is equal, as in the Stroop task or the flanker task, the bilinguals are less bothered by the interference and perform more efficiently than the monolinguals. The situation is not the same for picture naming or word generation. In these cases the bilinguals are both challenged by the need to choose between competing options, a problem that does not apply to the monolinguals, and to carry out this performance from the base of a less analyzed or less richly represented linguistic system. Hence, tasks based on rapid lexical retrieval are performed more poorly by bilinguals than monolinguals, all else being equal.

Interactions between Representation and Control

In simple terms, bilinguals perform more poorly than monolinguals on tasks based on linguistic representation but better than monolinguals on tasks based on executive control. In reality, however, this dichotomy is too simple. All cognitive performance depends on both the representational and control demands of the task and the corresponding levels of the individual. Therefore, actual cognitive performance is not likely to be described in terms of relying on one or the other of these components but rather in terms of the interaction between them. These interactions are especially apparent in linguistic tasks that also carry significant demands for executive control.

These interactions can be seen in the two main conditions of a standard verbal fluency task. In general, these are tasks used as standardized neuropsychological assessment tools in which participants are asked to generate as many words as possible in sixty seconds that conform to a criterion. In one condition, called semantic or category fluency, the criterion is to name as many words as possible that are members of a particular category, such as animals, girls' names, or clothing items. The task demand corresponds with the organizational structure of the semantic representation, so generating appropriate items is a straightforward matter of searching through a system in which candidate items are associated in representational space. Thus, the number of items generated is a reflection of the integrity and size of the semantic network. The primary factor determining performance, therefore, is language proficiency in general and vocabulary size in particular.

The second condition is called letter or phonemic fluency. The instruction in this case is to generate words that begin with a target letter, usually given as F, A, and S in different trials. In addition to the arbitrary grouping criterion, the condition also includes a set of restrictions that require constant monitoring and updating. These exclusions are proper names, numbers, and words that are morphological variants of words already generated. Therefore, the letter-fluency task is more difficult than the category fluency task for two reasons: the responses are not already grouped together in organized representations, and the exclusions increase the demands for monitoring and working memory. For these two reasons, performance in the letter-fluency task provides a reflection not only of language proficiency as was the case for category fluency but also for executive control. Moreover, the difference in performance between the two conditions is roughly the extent to which executive control is involved in the task.

Several studies have used verbal fluency tasks to compare monolingual and bilingual performance, generally finding that monolinguals generate more words than bilinguals. This is sometimes found for both category and letter fluency (e.g., Bialystok, Craik, and Luk 2008a) and sometimes just for category fluency with smaller or nonsignificant differences for letter fluency (e.g., Gollan, Montoya, and Werner 2002). However, the studies rarely provide formal assessments of language proficiency or vocabulary knowledge for the bilinguals, but including such information allows for more precise predictions. Category fluency is primarily an assessment of proficiency, and since on average bilinguals have lower proficiency and smaller vocabularies than comparable monolinguals in each language, bilinguals should generate fewer words in the category-fluency test. Letter fluency is an assessment of both proficiency and control, and since on average bilinguals have greater control than monolinguals, this advantage should help them to overcome the deficit found in category fluency and improve performance, possibly to the level of monolinguals. This is the pattern found in a study of monolingual and bilingual young adults in which the bilinguals had a significantly lower English vocabulary score than monolinguals (Bialystok, Craik, and Luk 2008b).

The claim that bilinguals have a smaller vocabulary is based on a small but significant shift in the mean of normally distributed vocabulary scores for individuals from the two groups. The consequence of this shift in the mean is that on average randomly selected monolinguals will have a higher vocabulary than randomly selected bilinguals, even though a large number of bilinguals actually have a higher vocabulary score than monolinguals in that language. Therefore, it is possible to erase the usual bilingual deficit in linguistic representation by selecting those bilinguals who are matched with monolinguals on vocabulary. This selection procedure changes the predictions for group performance on the two conditions of the verbal fluency test. Category fluency reflects vocabulary and proficiency, so the matched group of monolinguals and bilinguals should generate equivalent numbers of words on this task. Letter fluency reflects vocabulary plus control, so with no deficit to overcome in vocabulary, bilinguals should outperform monolinguals on this task because of their advantage in executive control. In the study by Bialystok, Craik, and Luk (2008b), an additional group of bilinguals who were matched to the monolinguals on vocabulary score was also tested. In this case, the matched bilinguals obtained the same score as monolinguals on category fluency but generated more words than participants in the other two groups on the letter-fluency task. Thus, linguistic representation is not an inevitable deficit for bilinguals, and when it is controlled, bilinguals can outperform monolinguals even on the verbal tasks for which they have traditionally demonstrated deficits.

A more detailed examination of this interaction was undertaken in another study that examined not only the number of words produced by each group on each of the fluency tasks but also the time course performance of each group over the sixty seconds. Following a procedure developed by Rohrer and Wixted (1995), the number of words produced in each five-second interval was plotted against time. Typically, participants produce a burst of words at the beginning of the period that trails off over the minute. The extent of the initial burst is reflected in the intercept, indicating the richness of the immediately available vocabulary. The effortfulness of retrieving each item, or the control required to select new items, is reflected in the slope of the decline. If each selection requires an additional choice between competitors in the two languages, then the slope for bilinguals should be flatter, signaling slightly longer selection process for each item.

We tested three groups of participants—monolinguals, bilinguals whose vocabulary scores were lower than those of monolinguals, and bilinguals selected because their vocabulary scores were equivalent to those of monolinguals (Luo, Luk, and Bialystok 2010). Measures of working memory and nonverbal general intelligence were identical for participants in all three groups. The two relevant comparisons are the intercept point, indicating the representational system for the lexicon with a higher intercept signaling better proficiency, and the slope, indicating the control processes involved in retrieving each item, with a flatter slope signaling more processing, presumably to select among competitors. Overall, the number of words produced provides a general assessment of performance in the task. Beginning with this last statistic, participants in all three groups produced a similar number of responses to category-fluency instructions, but vocabulary-matched bilinguals produced more words than participants in the other two groups for letter fluency, replicating the results of the previous study for letter fluency, although not for category fluency (Bialystok, Craik, and Luk, 2008b). More important, the characteristics of the time–course graphs were consistent with the predictions. Essentially, the unmatched bilinguals had a lower intercept than either the monolinguals or the vocabulary-matched bilinguals, but the two bilingual groups both demonstrated flatter slopes than the monolingual group. This pattern of results reflects the interaction of both factors: the typically lower proficiency and representational analysis of bilinguals and the increased control needed to monitor selection from the two competing language alternatives.

These examples illustrate the costs and benefits of bilingualism on language and cognitive performance and the ability of an account based on differences in representation and control to explain those patterns. Typically, the representation of linguistic structures for bilinguals is weaker for each language than it is for comparable monolinguals, so tasks that depend primarily on the richness of the analysis of the representational base are performed more poorly by bilinguals. But representation and analysis are specific to a domain, and there are no generalized costs to representations in other domains of expertise. However, control of attention and executive procedures for monitoring information, conflict resolution, and task switching are more advanced for bilinguals, and these processes are general across all domains of expertise.

In the terms of representation and control, this description can account for a wide range of cognitive functions, encompassing a variety of domains and levels of skilled performance. Essentially, everything we do depends on adequate representational and control systems to support that performance. But it was not obvious in the tentative utterances of adult second language learners or in the early insights into language structure by bilingual children that these activities were resting on exactly the same mechanisms as all other cognitive performance, two essential foundations that appeared as one because their development was usually coordinated. It turns out, however, that understanding the representation and control elements of skilled performance in general provides a reasonable account of learning and development for language ability. Moreover, it shows us that language is not special and that the power of experience to modify cognition is profound.

ACKNOWLEDGMENTS

This work was partially supported by grant R01HD052523 from the U.S. National Institutes of Health, grant MOP57842 from the Canadian Institutes of Health Research, and by grant A2559 from the Natural Sciences and Engineering Research Council of Canada. This chapter is based on a keynote address given at the Georgetown University Round Table of Languages and Linguistics, March 13–15, 2009, Washington, DC.

REFERENCES

Bialystok, Ellen. 1986. Factors in the growth of linguistic awareness. *Child Development* 57:498–510.

———. 1988. Levels of bilingualism and levels of linguistic awareness. *Developmental Psychology* 24:560–67.

Bialystok, Ellen, Fergus I. M. Craik, Raymond Klein, and Mythili Viswanathan. 2004. Bilingualism, aging, and cognitive control: Evidence from the Simon task. *Psychology and Aging* 19:290–303.

Bialystok, Ellen, Fergus I. M. Craik, and Gigi Luk. 2008a. Cognitive control and lexical access in younger and older bilinguals. *Journal of Experimental Psychology: Learning, Memory, and Cognition* 34:859–73.

———. 2008b. Lexical access in bilinguals: Effects of vocabulary size and executive control. *Journal of Neurolinguistics* 21:522–38.

Bialystok, Ellen, Fergus I. M. Craik, and Jennifer Ryan. 2006. Executive control in a modified anti-saccade task: Effects of aging and bilingualism. *Journal of Experimental Psychology: Learning, Memory, and Cognition* 32:1341–54.

Bialystok, Ellen, and Shilpi Majumder. 1998. The relationship between bilingualism and the development of cognitive processes in problem-solving. *Applied Psycholinguistics* 19:69–85.

Costa, Albert, Mireia Hernandez, and Nuria Sebastián-Gallés. 2008. Bilingualism aids conflict resolution: Evidence from the ANT task. *Cognition* 106:59–86.

Cromdal, Jakob. 1999. Childhood bilingualism and metalinguistic skills: Analysis and control in young Swedish–English bilinguals. *Applied Psycholinguistics* 20:1–20.

de Villiers, Jill G., and Peter. A. de Villiers. 1972. Early judgments of semantic and syntactic acceptability by children. *Journal of Psycholinguistic Research* 1:299–310.

————. 1974. Competence and performance in child language: Are children really competent to judge? *Journal of Child Language* 1:11–22.

Dijkstra, Ton, Jonathan Grainger, and Walter J. B. van Heuven. 1999. Recognition of cognates and interlingual homographs: The neglected role of phonology. *Journal of Memory and Language* 41:496–518.

Gollan, Tamar H., and Lori-Ann R. Acenas. 2004. What is a TOT? Cognate and translation effects on tip-of-the-tongue states in Spanish–English and Tagalog–English bilinguals. *Journal of Experimental Psychology: Learning, Memory, and Cognition* 30:246–69.

Gollan, Tamar H., Rose I. Montoya, Cynthia Cera, and Tiffany C. Sandoval. 2008. More use almost always means a smaller frequency effect: Aging, bilingualism, and the weaker links hypothesis. *Journal of Memory and Language* 58:787–814.

Gollan, Tamar H., Rose I. Montoya, Christine Fennema-Notestine, Shaunna K. Morris. 2005. Bilingualism affects picture naming but not picture classification. *Memory & Cognition* 33:1220–34.

Gollan, Tamar H., Rose I. Montoya, and Grace Werner. 2002. Semantic and letter fluency in Spanish–English bilinguals. *Neuropsychology* 16:562–76.

Ivanova, Iva, and Albert Costa. 2008. Does bilingualism hamper lexical access in highly-proficient bilinguals? *Acta Psychologica* 127:277–88.

Luo, Lin, Gigi Luk, and Ellen Bialystok. 2010. Effect of language proficiency and executive control on verbal fluency performance in bilinguals. *Cognition*.

Portocarrero, Jose S., Richard G. Burright, and Peter J. Donovick. 2007. Vocabulary and verbal fluency of bilingual and monolingual college students. *Archives of Clinical Neuropsychology* 22:415–22.

Rodriguez-Fornells, Antoni, Arie van der Lugt, Michael Rotte, Belinda Britti, Hans-Jochen Heinze, and Thomas F. Munte. 2005. Second language interferes with word production in fluent bilinguals: Brain potential and functional imaging evidence. *Journal of Cognitive Neuroscience* 17:422–33.

Rohrer, Doug, and John T. Wixted. 1995. Retrieval from semantic memory and its implications for Alzheimer's disease. *Journal of Experimental Psychology: Learning, Memory, and Cognition* 21:1127–39.

Rosselli, Monica, Alfredo Ardila, Katia Araujo, Viviana A. Weekes, Virginia Caracciolo, Mabel Padilla et al. 2000. Verbal fluency and verbal repetition skills in healthy older Spanish–English bilinguals. *Applied Neuropsychology* 7:17–24.

II

Methodological Issues and
Empirical Research on Awareness,
Pedagogical Contexts, and
Individual Differences in SLA

6

Getting a Grip on the Slippery Construct of Awareness: Toward a Finer-Grained Methodological Perspective

RONALD P. LEOW, ELLEN JOHNSON, AND GERMÁN ZÁRATE-SÁNDEZ
Georgetown University

"CONSCIOUSNESS AS AN OBJECT of intellectual curiosity is the philosopher's joy and the scientist's nightmare" (Tulving 1993, 283). No one will disagree with this statement given that the multifaceted nature of the construct "awareness" makes it undoubtedly one of the slipperiest to operationalize and measure in both second language acquisition (SLA) and non-SLA fields such as cognitive psychology, cognitive science, and neuroscience. Indeed, the role of awareness, or lack thereof, in *learning* is explicitly or implicitly subsumed in a remarkable number of variables in these fields, including type of learning (e.g., subliminal, incidental, implicit, explicit), type of learning condition (e.g., implicit, explicit), type of awareness (e.g., language, metacognitive, phenomenal, situational, self, conscious, unconscious), and constructs such as noticing, detection, perception, and consciousness. This chapter focuses on the methodological issues surrounding the investigation of the relationship between the role of awareness, or lack thereof, and learning. More specifically, the chapter presents a much finer-grained methodological perspective of awareness than what is reported in the current awareness literature in both SLA and non-SLA fields and includes the *what* (is being learned), the *where* (awareness is being investigated, concurrently or nonconcurrently), and the *how* (experimental task, type, and location of measurement are employed to investigate awareness). Given this finer-grained perspective of the role of awareness or lack thereof in learning, the chapter concludes that, methodologically, awareness should be investigated along the stages of the acquisitional process (*construction* vs. *reconstruction*) and that several variables need to be considered in any investigation of or report on the construct.

Defining What Constitutes Awareness in Learning

Early definitions of and references to awareness in fields outside SLA are clear indications of the vagueness of what constitutes awareness. For example, Garrett (1943) wrote, "Awareness is the searchlight of consciousness. It is the process by means of which the individual consciousness as a whole seeks out and finds its associational affinities everywhere in the universe" (12). In cognitive psychology, Merikle, Smilek, and Eastwood (2001) conflate the terms "awareness" and "consciousness" when they state that "any evidence that perception is not necessarily accompanied by an awareness of perceiving attracts attention because it challenges the idea that perception implies consciousness" (116). Similarly, in cognitive science, Schacter (1989) uses "consciousness" interchangeably with "phenomenal awareness" to refer to what Dimond (1976) called "the running span of subjective experience" (377). In SLA the definition that appears to underlie many of its studies on the role of awareness in learning is Tomlin and Villa's restricted definition derived from SLA (e.g., Schmidt 1990) and cognitive science (e.g., Schacter 1992). According to Tomlin and Villa (1994), awareness is "a particular state of mind in which an individual has undergone a specific subjective experience of some cognitive content or external stimulus" (193).

A careful survey of many studies in SLA and other fields purporting to investigate the role of awareness in learning reveals quite a wide range of methodological approaches employed to investigate this slippery construct. Many studies appear to assume that the role that awareness plays at one stage along the acquisitional process (that is, from input > intake > developing L2 grammar > output) may be reflective of the role played at a different stage along this process. More specifically, awareness may be investigated at the concurrent (online) stage of *construction* where the encoding or accessing of incoming experimental information takes place and at the non-concurrent (offline) stage of *reconstruction* where the retrieval of stored knowledge of the construct (Litman and Reber 2005) occurs. At the stage of *construction,* learners receive and process online the incoming information while at the stage of *reconstruction* they indicate offline—*after* they have processed the incoming information—whether they were aware of the targeted underlying rule, lexical item, color, symbol, and so forth, during the experimental phase or exposure. The stages where awareness plays a role in relation to the acquisitional process in SLA research are visually presented in figure 6.1.

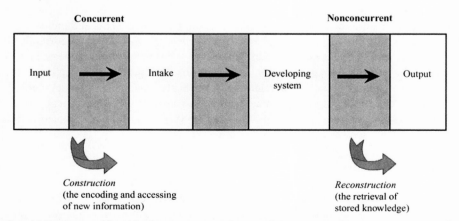

Figure 6.1 The Stages of the Role of Awareness in Relation to the Acquisitional Process in SLA Research

In addition, research designs also appear to be clearly incompatible, in many instances, with each other, given that the targeted information, experimental tasks, and type of measurement tasks are inherently different, leading to a nebulous picture of what role awareness does play in learning.

To address these potential methodological mismatches in the awareness literature in both SLA and other fields, this chapter reports on a *finer-grained perspective* of this construct, namely, the *what* (is being learned), the *where* (awareness is being investigated, *construction* vs. *reconstruction*), and the *how* (experimental task, type and location of measurement employed to investigate awareness). This finer-grained methodological perspective of awareness is visually displayed in figure 6.2.

Fields outside of SLA

Without doubt, awareness as a construct has its roots many decades ago outside the field of SLA, in cognitive science and cognitive psychology, although it is usually referred to or conflated with the construct of "consciousness." Its presence in relation to perception and learning has been investigated since at least the late '60s when Reber's (1967) Artificial Grammar Learning (AGL) experiments seemed to indicate that the rule system that underlies certain letter strings (e.g., VXVS) could be learned unconsciously or implicitly. AGL studies appear to share the common assumption that there is a clear dissociation between our ability to perform on a task and our ability to verbally express the knowledge that is guiding our performance (Shanks 2005). This does not mean that awareness is always verbalizable; one can be aware of something and not be able to verbally report on it (despite a positive correlation between confidence and accuracy).

Table 6.1 is a concise review that addresses the *what,* the *where,* and the *how* of the research designs of several important studies in fields other than SLA that have empirically investigated the role of awareness in learning.

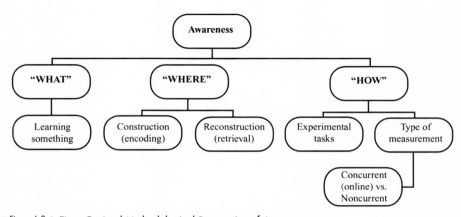

Figure 6.2 A Finer-Grained Methodological Perspective of Awareness

■ Table 6.1.
Selected Review of the *What*, the *Where*, and the *How* of Non-SLA Studies on Awareness

Author(s)	What	Where	Exp Task	How Type of measurement	How Location
Reber (1967)	Artificial grammar learning (AGL)	Reconstruction	Study letter strings	Rule verbalization; GJT	Offline
Eich (1984)	Word pairs	Reconstruction	Dichotic listening task	Recognition & memory tests (post) verbal report	Offline
Nissen and Bullemer (1987)	Sequence of light positions	Reconstruction	SRT, ± tone-counting	Verbal reports; questionnaire	Offline
Schunn and Dunbar (1996)	Knowledge for problem solving	Construction/ Reconstruction	Priming, problem solving	Stroop latencies, recognition	Online, offline
Merikle and Joordens (1997)	Colors of varying stimulus quality	Construction/ Reconstruction	Stroop priming-focused or divided attention	Perceptual ID, stem completion, cued recall, recognition, ID of masked words	Online, offline
Pilotti, Gallo, and Roediger (2000) and Tunney and Shanks (2003)	Imaged written and spoken words vs. nonimaged written AGL	Reconstruction	Hear/image/read NS-S words; ± familiar	GJT/Confidence rating (binary & continuous)	Offline

Brown and Besner (2004)	Embedded & nonembedded words	Reconstruction	GJT/Confidence rating	Embedded word recall/questioning	Offline
Fay, Isingrini, and Pouthas (2005)	Word stems	Reconstruction	Stem completion	Reaction times, questionnaire	Offline
Smith and Squire (2005)	Sequence (hierarchy) of characters	Construction/ Reconstruction	Word completion	Questionnaire	Online, offline
Haider and Frensch (2005)	Numeric series	Reconstruction	Exposure to hierarchy & testing	Interview	Offline
Sung and Tang (2007)	Reverse errors	Reconstruction	Filling in missing #	Eye tracking (gaze time)	Offline
Gross and Greene (2007)	Sequence of pictures (regular and reverse patterns)	Construction	Accuracy judgment	Questionnaire	Online
Dienes and Seth (in press)	Artificial grammar learning (AGL)	Reconstruction	Analogical inference	Experiment 1: Wager (1 or 2 sweets/ 10 sweets) or provide confidence ratings (guessing or sure to some degree)	Offline
		Reconstruction	Memorize letter strings	Experiment 2: Provide one form of confidence rating (no-loss gambling)	Offline

The What

Table 6.1 reveals quite an impressive array of targeted experimental information that has been employed to address the role of awareness in learning targeted information, such as letter strings in fields other than SLA. Such information has included artificial grammars, word pairs, colors, numeric series, lexical items (e.g., word stems, words), sequences of words, numbers, light positions, characters, and pictures. Although all of the information to be learned is verbally presented, it is challenging to compare this diverse range of input.

The Where

As can be seen in table 6.1, it appears that the majority of non-SLA studies (e.g., Brown and Besner 2004; Eich 1984; Fay, Isingrini, and Pouthas 2005; Gross and Greene 2007; Haider and Frensch 2005; Nissen and Bullemer 1987; Pilotti, Gallo, and Roediger 2000; Reber 1967; Smith and Squire 2005) opted to investigate the role of awareness at the *reconstruction* stage of the acquisitional process. That is, the designs focused on participants' knowledge of the experimental information rather than on their concurrent processing of the information as it was being constructed. Nevertheless, some of these studies did address awareness at both stages of *construction* and *reconstruction* (e.g., Merikle and Joordens 1997; Schunn and Dunbar 1996; Tunney and Shanks 2003) while one (Sung and Tang 2007) examined it only during the *construction* stage.

The How

One relatively popular experimental task in the non-SLA fields is that presented in a sequence format, which introduces participants to strings of information (characters, pictures, light positions, numbers, or other symbols). An example of a sequence format is found in Nissen and Bullemer (1987). Experiment 1 was a serial reaction time (SRT) task that assessed the learning of a sequence of light positions on a microcomputer screen under repeating conditions and random conditions. Another well-used experimental task is the completion task, which entails filling in missing information such as stems, words, or numbers (see Fay, Isingrini, and Pouthas 2005 for an example).

The Stroop task is another experimental task that has been employed in several studies to address, for example, the effects of (masked) priming or divided attention (e.g., Merikle and Joordens 1997). The classic Stroop task is a test of a participant's capacity to direct attention to specific information in stimuli with conflicting information, for example, presenting the word RED with a blue outline. Participants are required to classify the stimulus (that may be preceded by a prime that could be the word RED or BLUE) with the correct color. Similarly, problem-solving tasks are also frequently used, as in Schunn and Dunbar (1996).

The methodology of measuring awareness has also been addressed in the *how* of non-SLA awareness studies. For example, Tunney and Shanks (2003) compared two subjective measures of awareness based on reports of confidence (four options, binary and continuous scales) and a grammaticality judgment task (GJT) to explore whether they provide evidence of implicit cognition in artificial grammar learning (AGL).

Table 6.1 also indicates that awareness was measured predominantly via offline measurements that include questionnaires, embedded word recall/questioning, interviews, grammaticality judgment tasks, recognition and memory tests, cued recalls, wagering and so on. Instructions for questionnaires or interviews typically requested that participants state an underlying rule if possible while the grammaticality judgment tasks required participants to judge whether a sentence was grammatically (in)correct. Recall or memory tasks required participants to remember what they had been exposed to during the experimental phase of the study. Wagering typically involves giving participants a specific amount of tokens or money and asking them to wager specific amounts of tokens or money based on their level of confidence whether some data, for example, followed a specific rule or pattern.

Online measurements included eye-tracking and reaction times, verbal reports, and Stroop latencies. Eye-tracking and reaction times are arguably the two most popular online measurements employed in non-SLA fields. An example of eye-tracking is found in Sung and Tang (2007) in which gaze time was measured using EyeLink II; it began one character to the left of the two targeted characters and finished one character to the right (four characters in total). Reaction times were operationalized as the amount of time participants took to respond to some experimental stimulus during the experimental phase and were typically measured in milliseconds.

SLA Field

The role of awareness in *language* learning is arguably subsumed in many instruction or exposure strands of SLA research (cf. Leow 2007 for further discussion). In many of these studies, the construct of awareness was not teased out as an independent variable but explicitly or implicitly was assumed to play a role in input processing via the construct of noticing (Schmidt 1990 and elsewhere). The earliest study to investigate the role of awareness was Leow (1997), who employed concurrent data-elicitation procedures (e.g., think-aloud protocols) to operationalize and measure this construct. To date, there are at least eleven studies that have empirically addressed the role of awareness in learning. The next section reports on the *what,* the *where,* and the *how* of the research designs of these studies. This report is provided in table 6.2.

The **What**

As can be seen in table 6.2, the targeted items in 73 percent of these studies (Alanen 1995; Leow 1997, 2000; Rebuschat 2008; Robinson 1995; Rosa and Leow 2004; Rosa and O'Neill 1999; Sachs and Suh 2007) have included several grammatical features (e.g., imperatives, subjunctive clauses, pseudo clefts, syntax) in two main languages, namely, English and Spanish, while the remaining 27 percent have investigated lexical items such as novel words (Hama and Leow 2010; Williams 2005) and Spanish vocabulary (Martínez-Fernández 2008).

The **Where**

Table 6.2 reveals that almost two-thirds (64 percent) of the studies have investigated the role of awareness at the *construction* stage (Hama and Leow 2010; Leow 1997, 2001; Martínez-Fernández 2008; Rosa and Leow 2004; Rosa and O'Neill 1999;

Table 6.2.
Selected Review of the *What*, the *Where*, and the *How* of SLA Studies on Awareness

Author(s)	What	Where	Exp. Task	How		
				Type of measurement	Location	
Alanen (1995)	Grammatical features (Finnish)	Reconstruction	Written text	GJT	Offline
Robinson (1995)	Grammatical features (English)	Reconstruction	Stimulus sentences	Questionnaire	Offline
Leow (1997)	Grammatical features (Spanish)	Construction	Problem-solving task	Verbal reports	Online
Rosa and O'Neill (1999)	Grammatical features (Spanish)	Construction	Problem-solving task	Verbal reports	Online
Leow (2000)	Grammatical features (Spanish)	Construction	Problem-solving task	Verbal reports/questionnaire	Online/Offline
Rosa and Leow (2004)	Grammatical features (Spanish)	Construction	Problem-solving task	Verbal reports	Online
Williams (2005)	Lexical items (novel)	Reconstruction	Stimulus sentences	Oral interview	Offline
Sachs and Suh (2007)	Grammatical features (English)	Construction	Written text	Verbal reports	Online
Martínez-Fernández (2008)	Lexical items (Spanish)	Construction	Written text	Verbal reports	Online
Rebuschat (2008)	Grammatical features (semiartificial)	Reconstruction	Stimulus sentences	Oral interview, plausibility judgment task, elicited imitation, classification task	Offline
Hama and Leow (2010)	Lexical items (novel)	Construction	Stimulus sentences	Verbal reports, oral interview	Online/offline

Sachs and Suh 2007) whereas the other 36 percent have reported on its role at the *reconstruction* stage (Alanen 1995; Rebuschat 2008; Robinson 1995; Williams 2005).

The How

According to table 6.2, SLA studies have employed at least three types of experimental tasks, including problem-solving tasks (36 percent), stimulus sentences (36 percent), and written texts of varying features (27 percent). An example of a problem-solving task is the crossword puzzle employed by Leow (1997, 2000) to expose his participants to the L2 data. The puzzle was carefully designed to provide mismatches between the stem-changing vowels in an effort to, via concurrent verbal reports, operationalize and measure participants' attention to and awareness of the targeted vowel-changing stems before statistically measuring for their effects on participants' postexposure performances.

An example of stimulus sentences can be found in Williams's (2005) study in which participants were provided with noun phrases with four novel determiners that carried both distance (known to participants) and animacy (unknown to participants) information. The training phase was focused on the distance information. Significantly performing above chance on a two-option postexposure assessment task would indicate that the animacy rule was learned without awareness.

Table 6.2 also shows that, unlike fields outside of SLA, awareness was measured predominantly via online think aloud protocols or verbal reports (64 percent) with the remaining 36 percent employing offline measurements, relatively similar to those in the non-SLA field that include questionnaires, oral interviews or offline verbal reports, confidence ratings, elicited imitation, classification task, and grammaticality or plausibility judgment tasks. The instructions for thinking aloud usually were of the non-metalinguistic type that simply required participants to think aloud or verbalize whatever they were thinking while interacting with the L2 data. The protocols were subsequently coded for levels of awareness and then statistically analyzed in relation to, for example, participants' recognition and production of the targeted items in the input, after exposure to the L2 data. Instructions for questionnaires or oral interviews typically requested that participants state an underlying rule if possible while the grammaticality judgment tasks required participants to judge whether a sentence was grammatically (in)correct and/or underline the incorrect form or structure and/or provide a correction of the incorrect form or structure. Two studies employed both online and offline measurement tasks (Hama and Leow 2010; Leow 2000).

What the Review Reveals

Answers to the questions of the *what*, the *where*, and the *how* of research designs provide several interesting revelations that do need to be considered carefully in any investigation of or report on the role of awareness or lack thereof in learning in both non-SLA and SLA fields. First of all, the *what* in non-SLA and SLA fields is inherently different, with the latter field investigating natural languages that are intrinsically different from the targeted information employed in the non-SLA fields such as colors, sequences, nonsense words, pictures, and symbols. The closest target to natural languages found in non-SLA fields are the artificial languages employed by researchers such as Reber and his associates, though artificial languages cannot be equated with natural languages for obvious reasons.

Where awareness is investigated is determined by whether measurement is performed concurrently (at the stage of *construction*) via online data-elicitation procedures or nonconcurrently (at the stage of *reconstruction*) via offline data elicitation procedures. As reported in tables 6.1 and 6.2, the non-SLA fields has predominantly chosen/targeted the *reconstruction* stage for their measurement while the SLA field has opted, for the most part, to measure awareness at the stage of *construction,* that is, concurrently.

How awareness is measured is also fairly different in the non-SLA and SLA fields. The experimental tasks appear to overlap more in format than in content. Problem-solving tasks and stimulus sentences are relatively popular in both fields. However, the most popular measurement in the non-SLA field appears to be the offline questionnaire whereas online verbal reports are predominantly employed in the SLA field.

In addition to the *what,* the *where,* and the *how,* a careful review of the awareness literature in the SLA field also reveals that investigating this construct needs to take into account the findings that there appear to be *levels* of awareness (see Leow 1997; Martínez-Fernández 2008; Rosa and Leow 2004; Rosa and O'Neill 1999; Sachs and Suh 2007). Regarding grammatical information, Leow reports three levels of awareness (at the level of *noticing,* at the level of *reporting,* and awareness at the level of *understanding*) while both Rosa and Leow, and Rosa and O'Neill report two levels of awareness: awareness at the level of noticing [+N] and awareness at the level of understanding [+U], which are more in line with Schmidt's (1990) postulated levels of awareness. Sachs and Suh (2007) also report two levels: level 1 is CC (cognitive change, considered awareness at the level of noticing) while level 2 combines Leow's reporting and understanding levels to include MA (meta-awareness) and MR (morphological rule formation), both considered awareness at the level of understanding. For lexical items, Martínez-Fernández reports two levels: "noticing of one word aspect" and "noticing of two word aspects." (2008).

In addition to levels of awareness, there also appear to be levels of processing within each level of awareness. For example, in Suh's (2009) study, coding for awareness at the level of noticing includes three distinct types of processing: simple reading, translation of L2 > L1, and pausing after the targeted verb and repeating it. Similarly, for awareness at the level of understanding, both partial and full reports of the underlying grammatical rule being targeted in the study are included at this level.

Finally, care needs to be taken when the potential exists for some level of awareness of the targeted information to be raised outside the treatment or experimental phase of the study. For example, Hama and Leow (2010) found levels of awareness raised during the testing phase, as revealed by verbal reports gathered during this phase but not reported on the offline questionnaire. The failure to control for access to this important information may lead to lower internal validity of the study.

Conclusion
A much finer-grained methodological perspective of the construct of awareness reveals that awareness should be investigated along the stages of the acquisitional

process (construction vs. reconstruction) and that several variables (e.g., levels of awareness, potential levels of processing at each level of awareness, and potential raising of awareness outside the treatment or experimental phase of the study) need to be carefully considered in any investigation of and report on the construct. To this end it is strongly proposed that the *what,* the *where,* and the *how* this construct is investigated should be seriously considered when making postulations on the role of awareness in learning. Even viewed from a finer-grained methodological perspective, awareness still remains the scientist's nightmare, albeit quite a fascinating one.

REFERENCES

Alanen, Riikka. 1995. Input enhancement and rule presentation in second language acquisition. In *Attention and awareness in foreign language learning,* ed. Richard W. Schmidt, 259–302. Honolulu: University of Hawai'i Press.

Brown, Matthew, and Derek Besner. 2004. In sight but out of mind: Do competing views test the limits of perception without awareness? *Consciousness and Cognition* 13 (2): 421–29.

Dienes, Zoltán, and Anil Seth. In press. Gambling on the unconscious: A comparison of wagering and confidence ratings as measures of awareness in an artificial grammar task. *Consciousness and Cognition.*

Dimond, Stuart J. 1976. Brain circuits for consciousness. *Brain, Behavior, and Evolution* 13:376–95.

Eich, Eric. 1984. Memory for unattended events: Remembering with and without awareness. *Memory & Cognition* 12:105–11.

Fay, Séverine, Michel Isingrini, and Viviane Pouthas. 2005. Does priming with awareness reflect explicit contamination? An approach with a response-time measure in word-stem completion. *Consciousness and Cognition* 14:459–73.

Garrett, Eileen J. L. 1943. *Awareness.* New York: Creative Age Press.

Gross, William L., and Anthony J. Greene. 2007. Analogical inference: The role of awareness in abstract learning. *Memory* 15:838–44.

Haider, Hilde, and Peter A. Frensch. 2005. The generation of conscious awareness in an incidental learning situation. *Psychological Research* 69:399–411.

Hama, Mika, and Ronald P. Leow. 2010. Learning without awareness revisited: Extending Williams (2005). *Studies in Second Language Acquisition* 32 (3): 465–91.

Leow, Ronald P. 1997. Attention, awareness, and foreign language behavior. *Language Learning* 47 (3): 467–505.

———. 2000. A study of the role of awareness in foreign language behavior: Aware versus unaware learners. *Studies in Second Language Acquisition* 22 (4): 557–84.

———. 2007. Input in the L2 classroom: An attentional perspective on receptive practice. In *Practice in second language learning: Perspectives from applied linguistics and cognitive psychology,* ed. Robert DeKeyser, 21–50. New York: Cambridge University Press.

Litman, Leib, and Arthur S. Reber. 2005. Implicit cognition and thought. In *The Cambridge handbook of thinking and reasoning,* ed. Keith J. Holyoak and Robert G. Morrison, 431–53. New York: Cambridge University Press.

Martínez-Fernández, Ana. 2008. Revisiting the Involvement Load Hypothesis: Awareness, type of task and type of item. In *Selected proceedings of the 2007 Second Language Research Forum,* ed. Melissa Bowles, Rebecca Foote, Silvia Perpiñán, and Rakesh Bhatt, 210–28. Somerville, MA: Cascadilla Proceedings Project.

Merikle, Philip M., and Steve Joordens. 1997. Parallels between perception without attention and perception without awareness. *Consciousness & Cognition* 6:219–36.

Merikle, Philip M., Daniel Smilek, and John D. Eastwood. 2001. Perception without awareness: Perspectives from cognitive psychology. In *The cognitive neuroscience of consciousness,* ed. S. Dehaene. Cambridge, MA: MIT Press.

Nissen, Mary J., and Peter Bullemer. 1987. Attentional requirements of learning: Evidence from performance measures. *Cognitive Psychology* 19 (1): 1–32.

Pilotti, Maura, David A. Gallo, and Henry L. Roediger. 2000. Effects of hearing words, imaging hearing words, and reading on auditory implicit and explicit memory tests. *Memory & Cognition* 28:1406–18.

Reber, Arthur S. 1967. Implicit learning of artificial grammars. *Journal of Verbal Learning and Verbal Behavior* 6 (6): 855–63.

Rebuschat, Patrick. 2008. Implicit learning of natural language syntax. PhD diss. University of Cambridge.

Robinson, Peter. 1995. Aptitude, awareness, and the fundamental similarity of implicit and explicit second language learning. In *Attention and awareness in foreign language learning,* ed. Richard W. Schmidt, 303–57. Honolulu: University of Hawai'i Press.

Rosa, Elena M., and Ronald P. Leow. 2004. Awareness, different learning conditions, and L2 development. *Applied Psycholinguistics* 25:269–92.

Rosa, Elena M., and Michael D. O'Neill. 1999. Explicitness, intake, and the issue of awareness. *Studies in Second Language Acquisition* 21 (4): 511–56.

Sachs, Rebecca, and BoRam Suh. 2007. Textually enhanced recasts, learner awareness, and L2 outcomes in synchronous computer-mediated interaction. In *Conversational interaction in second- language acquisition: A series of empirical studies,* ed. Alison Mackey, 197–227. Oxford: Oxford University Press.

Schacter, Daniel L. 1989. On the relation between memory and consciousness: Dissociable interactions and conscious experience. In *Varieties of memory and consciousness: Essays in honour of Endel Tulving,* ed. Henry L. Roediger and Fergus I. M. Craik. Mahwah, NJ: Lawrence Erlbaum Associates.

———. 1992. Priming and multiple memory systems—Perceptual mechanisms of implicit memory. *Journal of Cognitive Neuroscience* 4 (3): 244–56.

Schmidt, Richard W. 1990. The role of consciousness in second language learning. *Applied Linguistics* 11 (2): 129–58.

Schunn, Christian D., and Kevin N. Dunbar. 1996. Priming, analogy, and awareness in complex reasoning. *Memory & Cognition* 24 (3): 271–84.

Shanks, David R., 2005. Implicit learning. In *Handbook of Cognition,* Koen L. Lamberts and Rob L. Goldstone, 202–20. London: Sage.

Smith, Christine, and Larry R. Squire. 2005. Declarative memory, awareness, and transitive inference. *Journal of Neuroscience* 25:10138–46.

Suh, BoRam. 2009. Type of written feedback, awareness, and L2 learning. Paper presented at the 2009 Georgetown University Round Table, March, Washington, DC.

Sung, Yung-Chi C., and Da-Lun Tang. 2007. Unconscious processing embedded in conscious processing: Evidence from gaze time on Chinese sentence reading. *Consciousness and Cognition* 16:339–48.

Tomlin, Russell S., and Victor Villa. 1994. Attention in cognitive science and second language acquisition. *Studies in Second Language Acquisition* 16 (2): 183–203.

Tulving, Endel. 1993. Varieties of consciousness and levels of awareness in memory. In *Attention: selection, awareness, and control: A tribute to Donald Broadbent,* ed. Alan Baddeley and Lawrence Weiskrantz, 283–99. Oxford: Clarendon Press.

Tunney, Richard J., and David R. Shanks. 2003. Does opposition logic provide evidence for conscious and unconscious processes in artificial grammar learning? *Consciousness & Cognition* 12 (2): 201–18.

Williams, John N. 2005. Learning without awareness. *Studies in second language acquisition* 27:269–304.

7

Aging, Pedagogical Conditions, and Differential Success in SLA: An Empirical Study

ALISON E. LENET AND CRISTINA SANZ
Georgetown University

BEATRIZ LADO
University of San Diego

JAMES H. HOWARD JR.
The Catholic University of America and Georgetown University Medical Center

DARLENE V. HOWARD
Georgetown University

LEARNING A SECOND LANGUAGE is difficult but not impossible for older adults. There is evidence that intentional instructions to learn material such as word pairs or paragraphs often result in larger age-related memory deficits than do more incidental instructions, in part because the strategies that older adults adopt for memorizing are less effective than those adopted by younger adults. This suggests that older adults might benefit from language instruction that encourages more incidental, implicit learning. In our study twenty adults aged sixty-six through eighty-one and twenty college-aged participants were exposed to a lesson on semantic function assignment in Latin under two conditions that differed in degree of explicitness: the presence or absence of grammar rules provided as part of feedback. Our results revealed no significant age deficits in learning and showed that feedback without grammar rules was more effective than more explicit feedback for the older, but not for the younger, adults. The study also demonstrated retention of limited exposure to high school Latin lasting over five decades, consistent with Bahrick's (1984) *permastore*. Contrary to common belief, our evidence bodes well for older adults who are motivated to learn a second language, especially when conditions are similar to those in naturalistic rather than academic contexts.

Introduction

Why second language acquisition becomes more difficult with aging is unclear. The *critical period hypothesis* (e.g., Penfield and Roberts 1959) was later replaced by the idea of a *sensitive period* (Hyltenstam and Abrahamsson 2000). However, these notions have now been nearly dismissed in favor of the *linear decline hypothesis* that says the ability to learn a second language decreases steadily with age. For example, Hakuta, Bialystok, and Wiley (2003) used 1990 census data to show a negative linear relationship between age of arrival (AOA) in a new country and end-state L2 acquisition. Flege, Yeni-Komshian and Liu (1999) found that L1 Korean/L2 English bilingual speakers' foreign accent positively correlated with their AOA in the US, while accuracy in morphosyntax was negatively correlated. Similarly, Birdsong (2006) highlighted a negative correlation between AOA and ultimate attainment, and that a later AOA often led to more errors in grammatical judgment and a higher degree of nonnative accent.

Sources of Age Effects: Biological

Brain changes that occur with aging likely contribute to these linear age-related declines in grammar learning. For example, there is some evidence (e.g., reviewed by Ullman 2001) that syntax is processed mainly in the frontal cortex and basal ganglia, areas that show structural and functional declines beginning in young adulthood (e.g., Hedden and Gabrieli 2005; Raz et al. 2005). Birdsong (2006) noted the importance of dopamine in SLA, and several studies show a decrease in dopamine receptors beginning around age twenty (Li, Lindenberger, and Sikström 2001; Volkow et al. 1998). Further, while some forms of implicit learning are relatively spared with aging, others are not, particularly the learning of subtle, complex sequential structure that calls on frontostriatal systems (e.g., Bennett, Howard, and Howard 2007; Gagnon, Bedard, and Turcotte 2005; Howard et al. 2008).

Sources of Age Effects: Cognitive and
Social–Affective Factors

Park (2000) suggested the main deficits that occur with cognitive aging are decreases in simultaneous processing and storage capacity (working memory capacity, WMC), processing speed, and inhibitory control. Inhibitory control may explain bilinguals' advantage in cognitive tasks (Bialystok, this volume) and L3 learning, as it helps suppress irrelevant input (Sanz 2000). WMC is important in SLA because it enables the short-term rehearsal of sequences and their consolidation into language (Ellis and Sinclair 1996). SLA studies examining the interaction between WMC and pedagogical treatments (e.g., Erlam 2005; Sanz et al., unpublished ms.)—including explicit feedback (Lado 2008; Lin 2009) and recasts (Mackey et al., in press; Sagarra 2007)—have also identified WMC as a predictor of success in language development.

Decreased speed and attention also contribute to uneven success in adult SLA (Kemper 1992). Whether attention (with awareness) is required for SLA is debated (Hama and Leow, in press; Williams 2005), but it is important for learning complex sequences hidden in grammar (Cohen, Ivry, and Keele 1990).

Social–affective factors that covary with age may also contribute to age effects. For example, younger learners are exposed to literacy, which increases their exposure to the input (Bialystok and Hakuta 1999). Motivation, self-esteem, attitude, and desire to assimilate (Long 1999; Singleton 2001) are factors internal to the learner that can further affect L2 success.

Adults Can Attain Native-Like Proficiency in a Foreign Language

Despite the factors working against older learners, recent views (e.g., Birdsong 1992; Birdsong and Molis 2001) suggest SLA is possible across the lifespan, and is influenced by individual differences (IDs) and external conditions. Marinova-Todd (2003) showed that some adults who arrived in an English-speaking country after the age of sixteen were indistinguishable from native speakers on certain language measures. Birdsong (1992) examined English speakers (mean age of forty) who were first exposed to French after puberty and found that many with significant exposure to the language reached native-like abilities in grammaticality judgment tests. Bongaerts, Mennen, and van der Silk (2000) studied late learners of Dutch and found that adults (mean age of forty) could demonstrate native-like accent with enough practice. Finally, Birdsong and Molis's (2001) replication of Johnson and Newport (1989) demonstrated, unlike the original study, that a number of late learners showed native-like attainment.

Age-Appropriate Pedagogical Conditions

For decades SLA research has been examining the effects of pedagogical conditions and IDs in language development. Only recently, however, have studies explored how IDs mediate the effects of such pedagogical variables as type of practice and exposure to grammar lessons or feedback (e.g., work by Erlam 2005; Mackey et al., in press; Sagarra 2007; and Sanz et al. 2009).

There is evidence in cognitive psychology that intentional instructions to learn material, such as word pairs or paragraphs, often result in larger age-related memory deficits than do more incidental instructions (e.g., Old and Naveh-Benjamin 2008), in part because the strategies that older adults adopt for memorizing are not as effective as those adopted by younger adults. In contrast, automatic processing without the active use of strategies may be unaffected by age (Hasher and Zacks 1979). Further, there is evidence that trying to learn can even hurt implicit forms of learning under some conditions (e.g., Howard and Howard 2001; Song et al. 2009).

Midford and Kirsner (2005) offered evidence that the optimal method of L2 teaching might differ between younger and older adults. They used Reber's (1967) artificial grammar paradigm to examine the effects of explicit and implicit methods of L2 teaching in older (mean age 65.9) and young adults (mean age 20.6). They varied type of instruction (explicit or none), and grammar complexity. Explicit instruction told participants to look for the underlying pattern of the artificial grammar, which they were later asked to describe. Results indicated that the older group was least disadvantaged in the most implicit condition and most disadvantaged in the simple grammar, particularly with explicit instruction. The older group showed deficits in all conditions but were least disadvantaged in the most implicit condition.

The present experiment attempts to extend Midford and Kirsner's results, using a real language and operationalizing the degree of explicitness. The Explicit treatment combines feedback on accuracy with a grammar explanation, while the Less Explicit treatment provides only accuracy feedback. L2 development is measured by accuracy in assignment of semantic functions to noun phrases in L2 Latin. Interpretation, production, and grammaticality judgment tests are given in pretests, and in posttests immediately following treatment, and one week after treatment to observe retention. Based on Midford and Kirsner's findings, we predicted that older adults would learn better in the Less Explicit than the Explicit condition.

Methods

Participants

Participants were twenty older adults (eleven female, nine male) who had previously participated in an experiment in the Georgetown University Cognitive Aging Lab and who expressed interest in returning. They ranged in age from sixty-six to eighty-one ($m = 72.3$). These older adults were compared to twenty Georgetown students (thirteen female, seven male, age range eighteen to twenty-one, $m = 18.7$) who were part of a dissertation study (Lado 2008). All participants were monolingual (English) and had no significant exposure to any case-marking language (e.g., German, Turkish). Participants were assigned to one of two treatment groups: Less Explicit or Explicit feedback. The treatment groups were matched for gender and background in Latin and other foreign languages. The older treatment groups did not differ significantly from each other on Mini-Mental State Examination Score ($m = 29$, $sd = 1$), WAIS-III Vocabulary ($m = 66$, $sd = 9.7$), WMS-III Digits Span Forward ($m = 9$, $sd = 2.3$), or WMS-III Digit Span Backwards ($m = 6$, $sd = 1.9$).

Procedure

Procedures and materials followed the Latin Project's design. The experiment was administered in three sessions in the iMac language Lab or the Cognitive Aging Lab. Tests and treatments were delivered by a computer application that combines Flash and ColdFusion programming tools. Except for treatment assignment, all participants were treated identically, following the procedure detailed below. Further details on testing and treatment materials may be found in Lado's (2008) dissertation.

Vocabulary training. After a questionnaire that assessed language experience, each subject received a Latin vocabulary lesson consisting of thirty-five nouns and eleven verbs. Each lexical item was presented with a picture, an English translation, and a sound file. The nouns were presented with gender- and case-appropriate endings (singular and plural nominative and accusative forms). Verbs were presented in third person singular and plural forms. Items were presented once for twelve to fifteen seconds each, and the lesson advanced automatically.

▨ Table 7.1
Experiment Procedures

Day 1	Day 2 (1–2 Days after Day 1)	Day 3 (1 week after Day 2)
• Vocabulary training	• Grammar training 2 rounds Explicit or Less Explicit	• No training
• Pretest	• Posttest	• Delayed test

Presentation was followed by a quiz. If participants did not reach a 60 percent accuracy level, they were automatically prompted to go through the vocabulary lesson again. If they reached the 60 percent threshold, they were quizzed again on those items they had failed. The procedure was repeated until 100 percent accuracy was reached, at which point participants completed a pretest.

Grammar pretest. This test, like the post- and delayed tests, was divided into four sections: aural interpretation, written interpretation, written grammaticality judgment, and written production. All items, as well as test ordering, were randomized, except for the production test, which was always administered last. All treatment and critical sentences consisted of two human nouns performing transitive actions. The Written Interpretation test required matching the correct sentence with the picture appearing on the screen with two people in costume, one of whom was performing an action on the other. The Aural Interpretation test was similar except that the input was oral. In the Grammaticality Judgment test, a sentence appeared on the screen and participants used the keyboard to indicate whether or not the sentence was grammatical. In all three tests participants could choose an "I don't know" option. In the Sentence Production test, participants created Latin sentences to depict a picture. The roots and Latin endings were provided in boxes, and participants were instructed to drag and drop so as to avoid typing errors.

Treatments. On their second test day, participants were assigned to either the Explicit or the Less Explicit group. Both treatments consisted of six untimed versions of a task that provided input-based practice and asked participants to read or listen to a Latin sentence and to pick a picture or English translation that represented what they saw or heard. After they entered their response, both feedback groups were told if they were correct or incorrect, as in *Oops! That's incorrect!* The Explicit group also received a grammatical explanation, as in *Oops! -us is a subject ending,* and *-um is an object ending.* Feedback in both groups was visible for six seconds. All subjects completed two lessons, each lasting approximately thirty minutes.

Posttest. Following the treatments on Day 2, the participants completed a posttest.

One-week-delayed grammar test. Identical to the others, this assessed retention.

Results
Performance in the Older Group
Figure 7.1a–d shows the mean number correct on each of the four grammar tests for the older adults broken down by Time (pre-, post-, delayed) and Treatment (Less Explicit and Explicit). Visual examination suggests the Less Explicit group is in the direction of performing better than the Explicit group for all four tests. However, when separate mixed design Treatment × Time ANOVAs were conducted for each measure, only Grammaticality Judgment yielded a significant Treatment × Time interaction, $F(2,32) = 3.323$, $p = .0488$. For Grammaticality Judgment, the Less Explicit treatment yielded significantly higher scores during the posttest than the Explicit treatment,

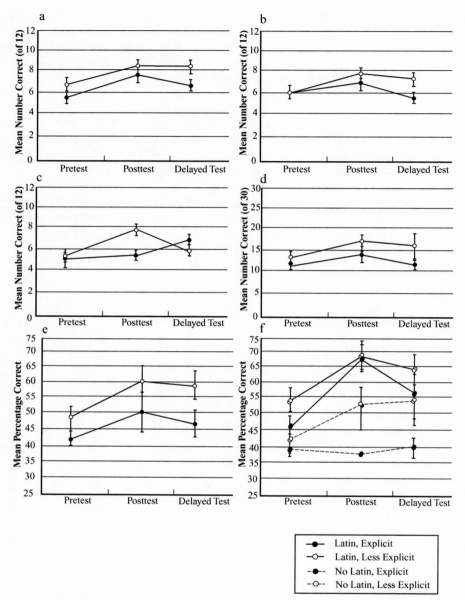

Figure 7.1 Mean Number of Correct Performances of the Older Adults on the Four Grammar Tests. (a) Mean number correct on the Written Interpretation test. (b) Mean number correct on the Aural Interpretation test. (c) Mean number correct on the Grammaticality Judgment test. (d) Mean number correct on the Sentence Production test. (e) Mean percent correct combined across the four tests. (f) The effect of Latin experience on combined test performance of the older participants.

$t(18) = 2.304, p = .0334$. Grammaticality Judgment also yielded a main effect of Time $F(2, 32) = 4.644, p = .0170$, indicating there was learning over the three testing days. For Written Interpretation, there was a main effect of Time $F(2, 32) = 4.045, p = .0271$. For Aural Interpretation there were no significant effects. For Sentence Production there was a main effect of Time, $F(2, 28) = 3.660, p = .0387$; this effect was carried by the Less Explicit group, which showed a significant effect of Time, $F(2,12) = 4.105$, $p < .0438$, while the Explicit group did not, $F(2,16) = .945$, *ns*.

Combining the Measures
To improve statistical power, scores from the four tests were combined into one composite measure by averaging percentage scores from all four tests for each participant (fig. 7.1e). Only the Less Explicit feedback group showed a main effect of Time $F(2,16) = 6.969, p = .0067$, and was therefore the only older group to show significant learning.

Previous Latin Experience in the Older Group
Because some older participants ($n = 5$ in the Less Explicit group, $n = 4$ in the Explicit group) reported previous coursework in Latin, the effect of their Latin experience on their overall performance was assessed via the composite measure, as shown in figure 7.1f. There was a main effect of Latin experience, $F(1,14) = 12.337, p = .0034$, suggesting previous Latin experience enhanced performance.

Learning in the Young Group
Figure 7.2a–d show the performances of the younger group on the four tests. Neither treatment was significantly better on any of the four tests, that is, there were no main effects nor interactions for Treatment. Participants in the Explicit group showed a main effect of Time on the Written Interpretation test ($F[2, 18] = 5.004, p = .0187$), and on the Grammaticality Judgment test ($F[2,16] = 6.695, p = .0077$) and this effect was marginally significant for the Sentence Production test ($F[2,18] = 3.143, p = .0675$). Participants in the Less Explicit group showed a significant Time effect only on the Grammaticality Judgment test, $F[2,18] = 5.812, p = .0113$. The composite measure of the younger groups (fig. 7.2e) suggests that for the young adults, in contrast to the older, Explicit feedback was superior to Less Explicit. Separate ANOVAs revealed significant learning in the Explicit group $F(2,18) = 11.583, p = .0006$, but only marginally significant learning in the Less Explicit group $F(2,18) = 3.268, p = .0616$.

Age and Learning
Because prior Latin exposure influenced performance, and younger participants did not have previous exposure, older adults with this exposure were excluded from the age comparison. Figure 7.3 shows the composite measure of participants without previous Latin experience for both age and treatment groups. There was no main effect of Age, showing that there were no significant age deficits in this experiment. There was a main effect of Time, $F(2,52) = 8.468, p = .0007$, indicating overall learning among participants without previous Latin exposure.

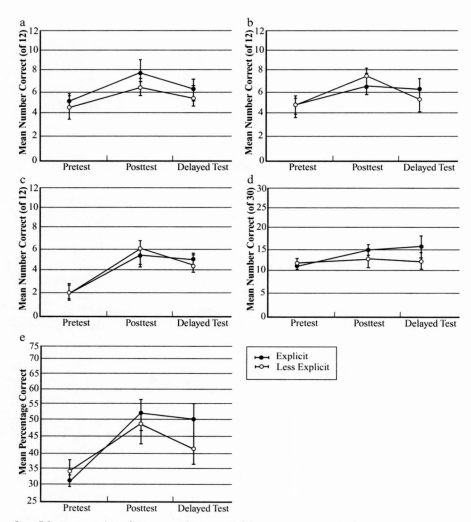

Figure 7.2 Mean Number of Correct Performances of the Younger Group on the Four Grammar Tests. (a) Mean number correct on the Written Interpretation test. (b) Mean number correct on the Aural Interpretation test. (c) Mean number correct on the Grammaticality Judgment test. (d) Mean number correct on the Sentence Production test. (e) Mean percent correct combined across the four tests.

Discussion

Overall, our results are consistent with Midford and Kirsner's (2005) findings that the older group did better in the Less Explicit form of the task, whereas the young did not. However, the age deficits seen by Midford and Kirsner are not as pronounced in the current study.

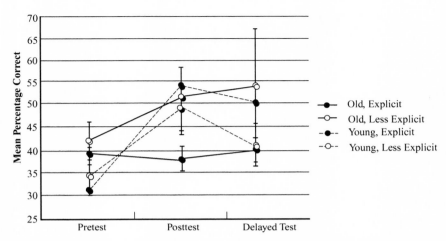

Figure 7.3 Composite Measure of Participants without Previous Latin Experience for Both Age and Treatment Groups.

We have identified evidence of overall learning in the older group that was not significantly less than in the young group, even when those with previous Latin experience were removed (fig. 7.3). This supports the notion that older adults are still capable of learning complex morphosyntax (Birdsong 1992; Marinova-Todd et al. 2003). It is possible the older adults were very motivated, as they were recruited from past experiments in the lab and had expressed interest in coming back, and they asked about their progress frequently. While this experiment did not provide prolonged exposure to a second language, the ability of these older adults to learn a complex structure that required realignment of cue preference (from word order to subject–verb agreement and case morphology) in Latin in a short time is noteworthy.

The hypothesis that Less Explicit feedback would be more effective than Explicit for older participants received support. While only one measure (Grammaticality Judgment) yielded the predicted Treatment × Time interaction, it is evident from the individual and composite graphs that the Less Explicit feedback was more helpful to the older adults than the Explicit. This holds true especially when the adults with previous Latin experience ($n = 9$) are removed (fig. 7.3). In the young group the opposite pattern is occurring, favoring the Explicit feedback. The small sample size may explain the lack of significant Treatment effects in the young group.

A common complaint from older adults in the Explicit training group was that the feedback was not presented for enough time. While our purpose was to match the timing between the groups, this may account for the relative success of the older Less Explicit group. Future studies could be self-paced. Another possibility is that the Explicit feedback was distracting and encouraged older adults to try to memorize the rules contained in the feedback, and their strategies were unsuccessful, actually hurting the learning of the syntax. Further research could ask participants to find patterns in the grammar during the training phase to see if effortful processing would diminish the advantage of the Less Explicit group. This could even take the form of verbalization of thoughts during the grammar tests, which shows the potential to aid younger adult learners of a second language (Sanz et al. 2009).

The analyses also yielded evidence of retention despite a five-decade lag between exposure to Latin in high school and current testing (fig. 7.1f). Bahrick (1984) used regression analysis to examine the recall and recognition of adults who were one to fifty years beyond the end of their high school and/or college Spanish instruction. Reading comprehension, recall, and vocabulary and grammar recognition were related to the level of initial instruction and the grades received in the Spanish course. Bahrick concluded there existed a fifty-year *permastore* for adults who studied Spanish in school, despite having engaged in little to no rehearsal in the interim. In the present experiment older participants who claimed to have limited recollection of Latin exposure had higher baseline performances than participants with no previous Latin (young and old).

Conclusion

Our results suggest that older adults are as capable as college-aged learners of developing new L2 knowledge after limited exposure, especially under the right conditions. This is encouraging for adults motivated to become bilingual and carries implications for the field of aging and SLA. It is sobering that, contrary to general beliefs in the teaching profession, more grammar does not always mean faster rates of acquisition. Clearly, a one-size-fits-all approach to language teaching is not the best solution, and the field needs to continue investigating the interaction between individual differences, including adult age, and pedagogical variables.

NOTE

This study is part of The Latin Project©, developed to investigate the relationship among bilingualism, cognition, and language development. All materials, including the treatment and test components, were developed by Cristina Sanz, Harriet Bowden, and Catherine Stafford, with support from Spencer Foundation and Georgetown's GSAS grants to Sanz and assistance from Bill Garr from Georgetown University Information Systems. The older participants were tested as part of Alison E. Lenet's senior honors thesis and the younger participants were part of Beatriz Lado's dissertation (2008). The study was supported by NIH/NIA Grant R37AG1545.

REFERENCES

Bahrick, Harry P. 1984. Semantic memory content in permastore: Fifty years of memory for Spanish learned in school. *Journal of Experimental Psychology: General* 113:1–29.

Bennett, Ilana J., James H. Howard Jr., and Darlene V. Howard. 2007. Age-related differences in implicit learning of subtle third-order sequential structure. *Journals of Gerontology: Series B, Psychological Sciences and Social Sciences* 62:98–103.

Bialystok, Ellen, and Kenji Hakuta. 1999. Confounded age: Linguistic and cognitive factors in age differences for second language acquisition. In *Second language acquisition and the critical period hypothesis,* ed. David Birdsong, 161–81. Mahwah, NJ: Lawrence Erlbaum Associates.

Birdsong, David. 1992. Ultimate attainment in second language acquisition. *Language* 68:706–55.

———. 2006. Age and second language acquisition and processing: A selective overview. *Language Learning* 56:9–49.

Birdsong, David, and Michelle Molis. 2001. On the evidence for maturational constraints in second-language acquisition. *Journal of Memory and Language* 44:235–49.

Bongaerts, Theo, Susan Mennen, and Frans van der Silk. 2000. Authenticity of pronunciation in naturalistic second language acquisition: The case of very advanced late learners of Dutch as a second language. *Studia Linguistica* 54:298–308.

Cohen, Asher, Richard Ivry, and Steven Keele. 1990. Attention and structure in sequence learning. *Journal of Experimental Psychology: Learning, Memory, and Cognition* 16:17–30.

Ellis, Nick, and Susan Sinclair. 1996. Working memory in the acquisition of vocabulary and syntax: Putting language in good order. *Quarterly Journal of Experimental Psychology: Section A* 49:234–50.

Erlam, Rosemary. 2005. Language aptitude and its relationship to instructional effectiveness in second language acquisition. *Language Teaching Research* 9:147–71.

Flege, James, Grace Yeni-Komshian, and Serena Liu. 1999. Age constraints on second language acquisition. *Journal of Memory & Language* 41:78–104.

Gagnon, Sylvain, Marie-Josee Bedard, and Josee Turcotte. 2005. The effect of old age on supra span learning of visuo-spatial sequences under incidental and intentional encoding instructions. *Brain Cognition* 59:225–35.

Hakuta, Kenji, Ellen Bialystok, and Edward Wiley. 2003. Critical evidence: A test of the Critical-Period Hypothesis for second-language acquisition. *Psychological Science* 14:31–38.

Hama, Mika, and Ronald P. Leow. In press. Learning without awareness revisited: Extending Williams (2005). *Studies in Second Language Acquisition* 32.

Hasher, Lynn, and Rose T. Zacks. 1979. Automatic and effortful processes in memory. *Journal of Experimental Psychology: General* 108:356–88.

Hedden, Trey, and John D. E. Gabrieli. 2005. Healthy and pathological processes in adult development: New evidence from neuroimaging of the aging brain. *Current Opinion in Neurology* 18:740–47.

Howard, Darlene V., and James H. Howard Jr. 2001. When it does hurt to try: Adult age differences in the effects of instructions on implicit pattern learning. *Psychonomic Bulletin & Review* 8:798–805.

Howard James H., Jr., Darlene V. Howard, Nancy A. Dennis, and Andrew J. Kelly. 2008. Implicit learning of predictive relationships in three-element visual sequences by young and old adults. *Journal of Experimental Psychology: Learning, Memory, and Cognition* 34:1139–57.

Hyltenstam, Kenneth, and Niclas Abrahamsson. 2000. Who can become native-like in a second language? All, some, or none? On the maturational constraints controversy in second language acquisition. *Studia Linguistica* 54:150–66.

Johnson, Jacqueline, and Elissa Newport. 1989. Critical period effects in second language learning: The influence of maturational state on the acquisition of ESL. *Cognitive Psychology* 21:60–99.

Kemper, Susan. 1992. Language and aging. In *Handbook of aging and cognition,* ed. Fergus I. M. Craik and Timothy Salthouse, 213–70. Mahwah, NJ: Lawrence Erlbaum Associates.

Lado, Beatriz. 2008. *The role of bilingualism, type of feedback, and cognitive capacity in the acquisition of non-primary languages: A computer-based study.* PhD diss., Georgetown University, Washington, DC.

Li, Shu-Chen, Ulman Lindenberger, and Sverker Sikström. 2001. Aging cognition: From neuromodulation to representation. *Trends in Cognitive Sciences* 5:479–86.

Lin, Hui-Ju. 2009. *Bilingualism, feedback, cognitive capacity, and learning strategies in L3 development.* PhD. diss., Georgetown University, Washington, DC.

Long, Michael. 1999. Maturational constraints on language development. *Studies in Second Language Acquisition* 12:251–85.

Mackey, Alison, Rebecca Adams, Catherine Stafford, and Paula Winke. In press. Exploring the relationship between modified output and working memory capacity. *Language Learning* 60.

Marinova-Todd, Stefka H. 2003. Know your grammar: What the knowledge of syntax and morphology in an L2 reveals about the critical period for second/foreign language acquisition. In *Age and the acquisition of English as a foreign language: Theoretical issues and field work,* ed. Maria del Pilar Garcia-Mayo and Maria Luisa Garcia Lecumberri, 59–73. Clevedon, UK: Multilingual Matters.

Midford, Richard, and Kim Kirsner. 2005. Implicit and explicit learning in aged and young adults. *Neuropsychology & Cognition* 12:359–87.

Old, Susan R., and Moshe Naveh-Benjamin. 2008. Differential effects of age on item and associative measures of memory: A meta-analysis. *Psychology and Aging* 23:104–18.

Park, Denise C. 2000. The basic mechanisms accounting for age-related decline in cognitive function. In *Cognitive aging: A primer,* ed. Denise C. Park and Norbert Schwarz, 3–21. Philadelphia: Psychology Press.

Penfield, Wilder, and Lamar Roberts. 1959. *Speech and brain mechanisms.* Princeton, NJ: Princeton University Press.

Raz, Naftali, Ulman Lindenberger, Karen M. Rodrigue, Kristin M. Kennedy, Denise Head, Adrienne Williamson, et al. 2005. Regional brain changes in aging healthy adults: General trends, individual differences and modifiers. *Cerebral Cortex* 15:1676–89.

Reber, Arthur S. 1967. Implicit learning of artificial grammars. *Journal of Verbal Learning and Verbal Behavior* 6:855–63.

Sagarra, Nuria. 2007. From CALL to face-to-face interaction: The effect of computer-delivered recasts and working memory on L2 development. In *Conversational interaction in second language acquisition: A series of empirical studies,* ed. Alison Mackey, 229–76. Oxford: Oxford University Press.

Sanz, Cristina. 2000. Bilingual education enhances third language acquisition: Evidence from Catalonia. *Applied Psycholinguistics* 21:23–44.

Sanz, Cristina, Hui-Ju Lin, Beatriz Lado, Harriet W. Bowden, and Catherine A. Stafford. 2009. Concurrent verbalizations, pedagogical conditions, and reactivity: Two CALL studies. *Language Learning* 59:3–71.

———. Unpublished ms. Pedagogical conditions and working memory capacity in early language development: Two CALL studies.

Singleton, David. 2001. Age and second language acquisition. *Annual Review of Applied Linguistics* 21:77–89.

Song, Sunbin, Brynn Marks, James H. Howard Jr., and Darlene V. Howard. 2009. Evidence for parallel explicit and implicit sequence learning systems in older adults. *Behavioural Brain Research* 196:328–32.

Ullman, Michael. 2001. A neurocognitive perspective on language: The declarative/procedural model. *Nature Reviews Neuroscience* 2:717–26.

Volkow, Nora, Gene-Jack Wang, Joanna Fowler, Yu-Shin Ding, Ruben Gur, et al. 1998. Parallel loss of pre- and postsynaptic dopamine markers in normal aging. *Annals of Neurology* 44:143–47.

Williams, John N. 2005. Learning without awareness. *Studies in Second Language Acquisition* 27:269–304.

8

Effects of Feedback Timing in SLA: A Computer-Assisted Study on the Spanish Subjunctive

FLORENCIA HENSHAW
University of Illinois at Urbana–Champaign

AMONG SECOND LANGUAGE ACQUISITION RESEARCHERS, there is consensus that feedback can play an important role in helping second language learners "to confirm, disconfirm, and possibly modify the hypothetical, transitional rules of their developing grammars" (Chaudron 1988, 134). More specifically, feedback that is immediate may be best for learners to confirm or refute interlanguage hypotheses, which is key for learning to take place (Loschky and Bley-Vroman 1993; Tomasello and Herron 1989). However, no studies in the field of SLA have offered empirical confirmation to the assumption that immediate feedback is indeed more beneficial to learners than delayed feedback. Furthermore, the many cognitive psychology studies on feedback timing present conflicting findings: some suggest that delayed feedback is superior for verbal retention (Kulhavy and Anderson 1972; Phye and Andre 1989; Surber and Anderson 1975), whereas others indicate an advantage for immediate feedback (Brosvic et al. 2006; Dihoff et al. 2003; Pressey 1950), and still others report no difference in performance based on feedback timing (Buzhardt and Semb 2002; Gaynor 1981; Goda 2004; Gottlieb 1989).

Given the discrepancy in results among cognitive psychology studies and the lack of SLA research on feedback timing, it seems reasonable to question the assumption that immediate feedback is more beneficial to L2 learners than delayed feedback. Thus, the present study evaluates the effects of feedback timing on grammar acquisition in a computer-assisted language learning (CALL) task by comparing the learning outcomes of three treatment groups that differ only with respect to when feedback is provided: (a) immediately, following each item, (b) following all items in a task, or (c) twenty-four hours later. A [− feedback] control group is also included to determine whether the provision of feedback itself was beneficial to the learners.

Research on Feedback in SLA

The vast majority of studies examining the role of feedback in SLA have focused on the effectiveness of implicit and explicit feedback, especially during oral interaction.

In these studies, implicit feedback has typically been operationalized as recasts (Carroll and Swain 1993; Leeman 2003; Lyster 2004), while forms of explicit feedback tend to include a metalinguistic explanation (Carroll and Swain 1993; Ellis, Loewen, and Erlam 2006). Along the explicitness continuum lie other forms of oral corrective feedback, such as prompts, which contain both implicit and explicit elements (Lyster 2004). In CALL most studies have considered metalinguistic explanations as explicit feedback, and the provision of "right"/"wrong" answers as implicit feedback (Rosa and Leow 2004; Sanz 2004; Sanz and Morgan-Short 2004). While there is no doubt that metalinguistic explanations are explicit, the operationalization of implicit feedback has been cause for debate, since indicating whether answers are correct or incorrect could be "more accurately labeled as *semiexplicit*" (Ellis, Loewen, and Erlam 2006, 348). Even though these differences in operationalization make it difficult to compare studies and generalize, results tend to suggest an advantage for explicit over implicit corrective feedback, in that the more explicit the feedback, the greater the improvement in performance (Ellis, Loewen, and Erlam 2006). Researchers have proposed that attentional factors may play an important role in determining the efficacy of feedback.

All of these studies, involving either oral interaction or computerized instruction, examined the effects of feedback provided immediately following learner utterances or responses. In fact, the ability to provide "immediate, individualized feedback" is considered an advantage of CALL (Bowles 2005; Heift and Rimrott 2008; Rosa and Leow 2004; Sanz 2004; Sanz and Morgan-Short 2004). However, one would be hard-pressed to find empirical evidence to support this assumption. While the role of feedback has been well documented in SLA, very few studies in the field have investigated the effects of feedback timing to determine if, in fact, immediate feedback is more beneficial to learners than delayed feedback. Timing of correction has been discussed in the realm of reactive Focus on Form, where it is generally suggested that learners benefit most from corrective feedback if it is provided at the time when the need to fill a gap between their interlanguage and the target language arises (Doughty 2001; Doughty and Williams 1998; Tomasello and Herron 1989). Nonetheless, the goal of those studies was to determine the extent to which instructors should draw learners' attention to form in an interactional context without disrupting meaningful communication, rather than to compare the effectiveness of immediate versus delayed correction.

Research on Feedback Timing

In addition to being labeled as implicit or explicit, feedback can be categorized according to when it is provided to the learners during practice. Specifically, the present study is concerned with three types of feedback: Item-by-Item immediate (IBI-i), End-of-Session immediate (EOS-i), and End-of-Session delayed (EOS-d). IBI-i feedback is defined as "automatically (under machine control) given to the learner immediately upon completion of a question during instruction"; EOS-i consists of "feedback automatically displayed at the end of a large segment of instruction"; and twenty-four-hour EOS-d is "program-controlled feedback provided to a learner within 24 hours of completion of an instructional segment" (Dempsey and Wager 1988, 21). These three types of feedback were specifically selected as the focus of this study in consideration of what is utilized in CALL research and in foreign language (FL) classroom instruction. As mentioned before, SLA studies evaluating feedback in CALL tend to utilize IBI-i feedback under the assumption that this type is the most beneficial to learners (Bowles 2005; Rosa and Leow 2004; Sanz 2004; Sanz and Morgan-Short 2004). On the other hand, in most FL classrooms, learners receive feedback either immediately upon completion of an activity (EOS-i), or at the next class meeting (EOS-d), in the case of homework. In technology-enhanced courses that incorporate the use of online learning programs such as Blackboard and WebCT, students usually receive feedback on their performance after responding to an entire activity (EOS-i).

In the field of cognitive psychology, extensive research has been conducted to evaluate the effects of feedback timing on verbal retention. In one of the first empirical studies on feedback timing, Pressey (1950) addressed the question of whether immediate knowledge of results could improve test scores. In his study, participants took a series of multiple-choice quizzes in class and were given feedback in two different ways. Subjects in the IBI-i group utilized special punchboards that would allow them to answer until they got each response correct, thus providing them with immediate feedback, while those in the twenty-four-hour EOS-d group received their scores the following day in class. Two months later, a comprehensive exam was administered to all students, and the results showed that the IBI-i group had outperformed the EOS-d group. These findings do not seem surprising, considering that participants in the IBI-i group had the option of responding iteratively, while those in the EOS-d group were never given the chance to correct their answers.

Contrary to what Pressey (1950) found, other cognitive psychology researchers have reported an advantage for delayed feedback on verbal retention. In their now classic study, Kulhavy and Anderson (1972) set out to empirically test the Delay-Retention Effect (DRE), according to which "learners who receive immediate knowledge of the correct responses, or feedback, retain less than learners for whom feedback is presented after a period of delay" (Kulhavy and Anderson 1972, 505). To this end, the authors administered a multiple-choice test on introductory psychology to 194 high school students, who received either EOS-i or twenty-four-hour EOS-d feedback. All participants took the same test a week later, and the results revealed that those who had received EOS-d feedback performed significantly better. The authors explained the results by proposing the Interference-Perseveration Hypothesis: "Learners forget their incorrect responses over the delay interval, and thus there is less interference with learning the correct answers from the feedback" (Kulhavy and Anderson 1972, 506). In addition, the authors suggested that the superiority of EOS-d feedback may be due to the fact that students pay more attention to the feedback after the delay.

Although Kulhavy and Anderson's investigation has become a cornerstone among cognitive psychology studies on feedback timing, it certainly presents some limitations. First, the retention interval was not the same for all groups: participants took the posttest seven days after the first day of treatment, rather than seven days after receiving feedback. That is, the interval between provision of feedback and posttest was seven days for the EOS-i group, but only six days for the EOS-d group. Second, the tests used during treatment and the posttest were identical, which raises the question of whether students were actually able to retain verbal material or simply had better photographic memory. These two limitations combined make the results questionable: the EOS-d group may have been able to remember more correct answers because their retention interval was twenty-four hours shorter than the EOS-i group, and not because of the DRE. This problem could have been avoided by including novel items that tested participants on the same concepts but with different wording.

The studies mentioned thus far tested participants on general psychology concepts, which may arguably involve a set of different cognitive skills than those involved in the acquisition of a foreign language. A more relevant study to SLA was conducted by Brosvic et al. (2006) on the acquisition of Esperanto vocabulary. Their investigation comprised five feedback conditions (twenty-four-hour EOS-d, EOS-i, IBI-i with a scoring sheet, IBI-i with a research assistant, and a [-feedback] control group), in addition to two response conditions (respond until correct, versus only one response permitted). Every six hours of instruction, for a period of ten weeks, participants took fifty-item multiple-choice examinations based on the vocabulary items learned in class and were provided feedback according to the treatment group in which they had been placed. Assessment measures included a cumulative 100-item posttest delivered one week after completion of all practice sessions, and two delayed posttests administered after three and six months, respectively. Given that there were no significant differences between the two IBI-i conditions, Brosvic et al. (2006) aggregated the results as one "immediate feedback" group. Similarly, the twenty-four-hour EOS-d and EOS-i groups were also collapsed into a single "delayed feedback" group due to lack of significant differences between groups. Their findings indicated that the group receiving immediate feedback was more successful at correcting initially wrong responses in all the examinations, including the three- and six-month delayed posttests, especially when iterative responding was available.

The advantage for IBI-i feedback found by Brosvic et al. (2006) might be questionable, given some of the limitations of the study. First, as a result of having such a large number of treatment groups, the sample size for each group was very small (n = 10). The authors considered the lack of differences between groups as rationale for aggregating results, but they failed to take into consideration that the lack of differences could have been due to the small sample size. It seems reasonable to question whether grouping the EOS-i and twenty-four-hour EOS-d conditions under one label is appropriate, when all previous studies in cognitive psychology have examined them separately. Lastly, it is unclear why the IBI-i group was the only feedback condition that included the intervention of a research assistant, who sat with two students at a time and provided them with feedback. Although it is hard to say if this served as an advantage in any way, it certainly was a very different procedure than the one for either the EOS-i or EOS-d conditions.

In the field of SLA, to my knowledge, only two studies have examined the effects of feedback timing on L2 grammar acquisition, and neither found any differences between various feedback timing conditions (Dabaghi 2006; Goda 2004). In a study investigating the effectiveness of oral error correction, Dabaghi (2006) manipulated both the timing (immediate versus delayed) as well as the type of feedback (explicit versus implicit). A total of fifty-six Iranian students of English as a Foreign Language participated in the study. It is not clear whether proficiency level was controlled for, since the author omits the characteristics of the participants. Subjects were asked to read a story and then retell it to the researcher in their own words. Implicit feedback was provided in the form of recasts, while explicit feedback consisted of metalinguistic information. Feedback was provided either as the learner was retelling the story (immediate) or after concluding the story (delayed). Learning gains were measured according to performance in individualized posttests on the errors that had been corrected for each participant. The author fails to mention when or how the posttest was administered, although presumably the delay and format were the same for all groups. Results showed that while there was a significant effect for feedback type (i.e., explicit feedback was significantly more effective than implicit feedback), "immediate error correction and delayed error correction were equally effective in drawing the learners' attention to discrepancies between their interlanguage and target language forms" (Dabaghi 2006, 12). Given the scarce amount of information provided by the author, it is unclear whether all participants received the same amount of feedback or whether all errors (morphological, syntactic, lexical) were corrected. Beyond these possible limitations in the experimental design, Dabaghi's (2006) findings might be of limited relevance for the purposes of the present study, since oral feedback could be construed as different from written feedback.

A computer-assisted study by Goda (2004) compared IBI-i and EOS-i feedback on computer-assisted tasks involving twenty questions that were randomly selected from the grammar section of the Test of English as a Foreign Language (TOEFL). One of the tasks consisted of selecting the phrase among four possible choices that best completed a sentence, while in the other task, learners had to identify the erroneous word in a sentence, out of four indicated options. As a consequence of the lack of criteria in selecting the experimental items, the level of difficulty may have varied greatly from item to item. Participants were ninety-two students of English as a Foreign Language in Taiwan, who had an average of ten years of English instruction and were majoring in Applied Foreign Languages. Neither a pretest nor a proficiency test was administered to screen participants. Results showed that both IBI-i and EOS-i groups improved in their ability to select the proper structure and identify errors, but that there were no significant differences between the two groups. A possible explanation for this result is that the delay in the provision of feedback did not differ considerably between the two groups since practice consisted of only twenty multiple-choice items, which likely took participants a very short amount of time to complete. The results may have also been affected by the heterogeneity in structures tested, in combination with the lack of control for proficiency or previous knowledge.

Research Questions

In light of the conflicting results and methodological limitations in cognitive psychology research, as well as the scarce number of studies on feedback timing in SLA, the present study proposes to determine whether timing of feedback during written multiple-choice tasks, as used in previous CALL and cognitive psychology studies, has an effect on L2 learners' grammar acquisition. Unlike previous studies, only one grammatical structure—the Spanish subjunctive—will be tested to ensure a constant level of difficulty from item to item, and both old and novel items will be included to evaluate the learners' ability to generalize their knowledge to contexts different from those seen during practice. Two different types of multiple-choice tasks will be used to measure comprehension abilities: recognition of when subjunctive should be employed and interpretation of the use of subjunctive.

Thus, the following research questions are proposed to guide this investigation:

(a) Does feedback timing (IBI-i vs. EOS-i vs. EOS-d) during written multiple-choice tasks have an effect on L2 learners' *recognition* of new and old exemplars of the Spanish subjunctive with adverbial clauses of time?

(b) Does feedback timing (IBI-i vs. EOS-i vs. EOS-d) during written multiple-choice tasks have an effect on L2 learners' *interpretation* of new and old exemplars of the Spanish subjunctive with adverbial clauses of time?

It is hypothesized that, if the assumption made by CALL researchers is correct, the group receiving feedback immediately after each item should make greater gains in learning outcomes, as measured by posttest scores, than either of the other experimental groups.

Method
Participants
Participants were 102 undergraduate students at the University of Illinois at Urbana–Champaign (UIUC) enrolled in one of two fourth-semester Spanish courses: "Introduction to Spanish Grammar" and "Spanish in the Professions." During the data-collection period, the use of the subjunctive with adverbial clauses was not formally presented in either of the courses. Students at lower levels were not selected because previous research has suggested that prior to the fourth semester, students may not be ready to acquire the subjunctive (Pereira 1996). Furthermore, fourth-semester students had prior exposure to and knowledge of the future tense in Spanish, which they needed to be able to recognize in the main clauses of some of the items in the tasks. To control for any prior knowledge of the target structure, only participants who scored less than chance, 25 percent, on both the recognition and interpretation items on the pretest, were included in the final sample.

All participants were monolingually raised native speakers of English, with normal vision and hearing. They had less than one semester of immersion in a Spanish-speaking country, and less than two semesters of other foreign language study, in order to ensure no knowledge of subjunctive in other languages. This information was gathered through a language background questionnaire administered prior to the treatment session.

Participants were randomly assigned to one of four treatment conditions:

▓ IBI-i (n = 27): Feedback was provided immediately after submission of each response.

▓ EOS-i (n = 27): Feedback was provided immediately after submission of all forty responses.

▓ EOS-d (n = 27): Feedback was provided twenty-four hours after submission of all forty responses.

▓ Control (n = 21): No feedback was provided.

All groups, including the control group, received explicit information on the target form, followed by forty items of practice. Participants in the IBI-i, EOS-i, and EOS-d groups received explicit feedback in the form of a "That's right!" or "Not quite" answer followed by a one-sentence metalinguistic explanation restating the target rule. Feedback was provided after both correct and incorrect responses to ensure that every participant received the same amount and type of feedback. The control group, on the other hand, did not receive any feedback on their responses.

Target Structure

The target structure in this study is the Spanish subjunctive with adverbial clauses of time, which was chosen because of its complexity for L2 learners (Terrell, Baycroft, and Perrone 1987) and because its redundancy and low communicative value make it a perfect candidate for a study employing Processing Instruction (PI). While the use of subjunctive with noun clauses and adjectival clauses has been the target of previous PI research (Collentine 1998; Farley 2001, 2004), its use with adverbial clauses of time has not yet been investigated.

The rule to determine if the verb in the subordinate clause should be in indicative or subjunctive may be summarized as follows: if the action of the subordinate clause is a future-time event, the subjunctive is used, as in (1); otherwise, indicative is used, as in (2).

(1) Carlos va a comer cuando llegue a casa.

"Carlos is going to eat when (he) gets-subj. home"

(2) Carlos come cuando llega a casa.

"Carlos eats when (he) gets-ind. home"

There are several conjunctions of time that can introduce a subordinate clause requiring the indicative or the subjunctive. In the present study, only five conjunctions were utilized: *cuando* ("when"), *después de que* ("after"), *tan pronto como* ("as soon as"), *hasta que* ("until"), and *en cuanto* ("as soon as"). These adverbial conjunctions were selected because they are the most frequently taught and used in Spanish textbooks and were therefore most likely to be familiar to learners.

Instructional Materials

All treatment materials were designed following the tenets of PI, a grammar instruction method based on how learners process input (VanPatten 2005). According to this approach, learners are first given explicit information (EI) followed by Structured Input (SI) activities.

During the EI module all participants received nonparadigmatic information in English about how the subjunctive is formed, where it is located within a sentence (in subordinate clauses), and when it is used with adverbial clauses of time.

The information was nonparadigmatic because only the conjugation of -AR verbs in third person singular was presented, and all information was accompanied by examples in Spanish. The content was adapted from the corresponding explanations found in two textbooks that follow the PI methodology, *¿Sabías Que . . .?* and *Sol y Viento*. Subsequently, following the tenets of PI, all participants were warned about a particular processing strategy that might negatively affect their acquisition of the target form, which in the case of the subjunctive mood is the Preference for Nonredundancy: "Learners are more likely to process nonredundant meaningful grammatical forms before they process redundant meaningful forms" (VanPatten 2005, 268). The subjunctive is redundant to the learners not only because it is not used in English in that particular context, but also because the same meaning can be retrieved elsewhere in the sentence: the notion of futurity is conveyed by the verb in the main clause. In addition, learners were warned not to utilize future tense in place of subjunctive. As in English, the future tense is not used in the subordinate clause in Spanish, despite the fact that the action implies a future intent.

The practice items were SI activities designed according to VanPatten's (2005) guidelines:

- Present one thing at a time.
- Keep meaning in focus.
- Use both written and oral input.
- Have the learner do something with the input.
- Keep the learner's processing strategies in mind.

The processing strategy taken into account was the Sentence Location Principle: "Learners tend to process items in sentence initial position before those in final position and those in medial position" (VanPatten 2005, 269). When creating the activities, the main clause was separated from the subordinate clause, and the verb in the subordinate clause was always placed at the beginning of each item, so that it would be the first word read on the screen or heard in the audio. This ensured that the verbs in subjunctive would be in utterance-initial position, and that the verb in the main clause would "no longer take precedence for processing over the subjunctive verb endings" (Farley 2005, 47).

During the recognition task, participants heard the first half of a sentence on a character from the TV show *The Simpsons* and were asked to select the phrase that best completed it. The audio portion contained the main clause and the conjunction of time. The choices on the screen were two subordinate clauses, one containing a verb in present indicative and the other in present subjunctive. Thus, learners were forced to process the verb in the subordinate clause to complete the task. Likewise, in the interpretation task, participants listened to the second half of a sentence about a character from the TV show *Family Guy* and were asked to select the phrase that best started it. The audio portion included the subordinate clause only, while the choices on the screen were of two main clauses with the same conjunction of time, but one was a habitual event, containing a verb in present tense, and the other was a future event, containing a verb in either the synthetic or the periphrastic future. During both the recognition and the interpretations tasks, meaning was kept on focus by having participants indicate whether each statement could also apply to themselves and, based on their answers, draw a conclusion regarding which character in *The Simpsons* or *Family Guy* was most like themselves.

A total of forty practice items were presented to all the groups in the same order: twenty recognition items, followed by twenty interpretation items. Each set of twenty items consisted of: ten requiring indicative (two per conjunction; five old exemplars and five new exemplars) and ten requiring subjunctive (two per conjunction; five old exemplars and five new exemplars). Furthermore, verbs that needed to be in subjunctive in the recognition task appeared in indicative in the interpretation task, and vice versa. This ensured that all conjunctions and verb forms were presented with the same frequency, thus eliminating the possibility that practice could favor one over another. Vocabulary in the tasks was controlled and included high-frequency words that fourth-semester students are likely to recognize (e.g., *comer* "to eat," *dormir* "to sleep," *tarea* "homework"), as well as cognates.

Assessment Measures

The pretest served as both a baseline and screening tool. It consisted of forty multiple-choice items, which included ten recognition items (five requiring indicative and five requiring subjunctive), ten interpretation items (five habitual actions and five future-event actions), and twenty distracters on aspectual and temporal differences in Spanish. The purpose of the items that required the use of indicative was to control for overextension of the subjunctive as a consequence of the instructional treatment. Each item consisted of a sentence in Spanish with a blank where a word or phrase had been omitted, followed by four possible choices: one in present subjunctive, one in present indicative, one in future, which was the right answer for half of the interpretation items, and one in past tense (imperfect or preterite), which was included to mimic the choices in the distracter items. Only one choice was correct for each item. The posttest had the same multiple-choice format as the pretest, but it comprised sixty items to account for twenty new exemplars (ten recognition items and three interpretation items), divided in the same fashion as the pretest items. A sample recognition item and a sample interpretation item are provided in (3) and (4), respectively.

(3) La abuela va a cocinar tan pronto como _____ la comida.
    "The grandmother is going to cook as soon as (she) _____ the food."

a. va a comprar	b. compra	c. compre	d. compraba
a. "is going to buy"	b. "buys-ind."	c. "buys-subj."	d. "bought."

(4) La secretaria _____ atención cuando escuche las instrucciones.
    "The secretary _____ attention when (she) hears-subj. the instructions."

a. ponga	b. pone	c. puso	d. va a poner
a. "pays-subj."	b. "pays-ind."	c. "paid"	d. "is going to pay"

Procedure

This study followed a classic pretest–posttest design. In week 1, participants completed the language background questionnaire and the pretest online. At least one week later, participants who scored at chance or less on the pretest came in to a computer lab and were granted access to the Blackboard site where materials had been uploaded. All participants were familiar with Blackboard, which is used campuswide. The treatment and posttests were administered individually: EI was presented in a Learning Module, allowing subjects to advance at their own pace; recognition and interpretation SI tasks were delivered as a single forty-item quiz, in which questions appeared one at a time and could not be revisited. Seven days after the practice session, subjects in the IBI-i, EOS-i, and control groups took the posttest, while those in the EOS-d group took it seven days after receiving feedback. The rationale for choosing a delay of seven days is twofold. First, it follows the research design of several cognitive psychology studies on feedback timing (Gottlieb 1989; Kulhavy and Anderson 1972; Surber and Anderson 1975). Second, it authentically reflects what tends to occur in a FL classroom setting: students learn about a structure, practice in class, then take an exam at least one week later.

Results

Both the pretest and the posttest were scored as follows: 1 point for each correct answer, and 0 points for incorrect answers. The total was tallied for each subject, and the scores were then analyzed using SPSS 17 (alpha level was set at .05). Mean scores and standard deviations for all assessments and groups are summarized in table 8.1. The following sections discuss the results of inferential statistics used to answer each of the two research questions.

Research Question 1: Recognition of Old and New Exemplars

To find out whether feedback timing had an effect on the learners' ability to recognize the use of subjunctive on old exemplars, pretest and posttest scores were analyzed using a repeated measures ANOVA, with Time (pretest, posttest) as the within-subjects factor and Group (IBI-i, EOS-i, EOS-d, Control) as the between-subjects factor. The results revealed a significant effect for Time, $F(1,98) = 126.739, p < .0001$, but no

Table 8.1.
Descriptive Statistics for All Groups and Tests: Mean Scores (SD)

Group	Recognition Pretest MIN = 0 MAX = 1	Recognition Posttest MIN = 0 MAX = 5	Interpretation Pretest MIN = 0 MAX = 1	Interpretation Posttest MIN = 0 MAX = 5	Recognition New Items MIN = 0 MAX = 5	Interpretation New Items MIN = 0 MAX = 5
IBI-i	.56 (.51)	2.89 (1.67)	.59 (.50)	1.81 (1.30)	2.67 (1.80)	2.04 (1.58)
EOS-i	.56 (.51)	2.33 (1.92)	.52 (.51)	2.15 (1.52)	2.04 (1.99)	2.04 (1.61)
EOS-d	.44 (.51)	2.93 (1.52)	.59 (.50)	2.22 (1.70)	2.74 (1.95)	1.96 (1.79)
Control	.76 (.44)	1.81 (1.25)	.57 (.51)	1.43 (1.03)	1.38 (1.16)	1.05 (1.02)

significant effect for Group, $F(1,98) = 1.415, p = .243$. There was a significant inter-action between Time and Group, $F(3,98) = 3.387, p = .021$, indicating that although all feedback groups improved significantly on their ability to recognize the use of sub-junctive, the improvement of the [-feedback] control was not as great, as seen in fig-ure 8.1 below.

To investigate whether feedback timing had an effect on the learners' ability to generalize to new contexts, a one-way ANOVA was performed on posttest scores of new recognition items. There was a significant difference between groups, $F(3,98) = 2.95, p = .036$, as seen in figure 8.2. A posthoc Tukey's HSD test revealed that this contrast was due to a significant difference between the EOS-d group and the control group ($p = .05$), as well as a difference that approached statistical significance between the IBI-i group and the control group ($p = .07$). Large effect sizes were observed for these two contrasts ($d = .85$ for both), suggesting that provision of feedback, regard-less of timing, had a much greater impact than not receiving feedback on recognition of subjunctive in novel items. It is important to also note that none of the groups re-ceiving feedback outperformed any other feedback group, as there were no significant differences between the IBI-i, EOS-i, and EOS-d groups.

Research Question 2: Interpretation of Old and New Exemplars

Similar analyses as those conducted on recognition scores were performed on inter-pretation scores. The repeated measures ANOVA on old interpretation items revealed a significant effect for Time, $F(1,98) = 88.947, p < .0001$, but not for Group, $F(1,98) = 1.161, p = .329$, and no significant interaction between Time and Group, $F(3,98) = 1.61, p = .192$, suggesting that all groups, including the [-feedback] control group, made equally significant gains from pretest to posttest in their ability to interpret the use of subjunctive, as seen in figure 8.3.

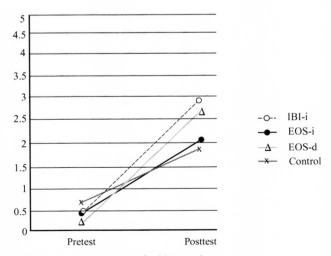

Figure 8.1 Group Mean Scores: Recognition of Old Exemplars

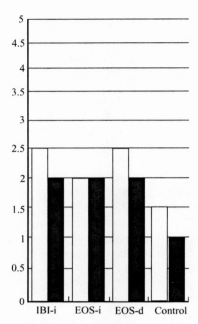

▓ Figure 8.2 Group Mean Scores on Recognition and Interpretation of New Exemplars

A one-way ANOVA performed on scores from interpretation of new items yielded a difference between groups that approached statistical significance, $F(3,98) = 2.163$, $p = .097$. A graph of mean scores shows this trend toward significance with higher posttest scores for the feedback groups in comparison with the [− feedback] control group (see fig. 8.2).

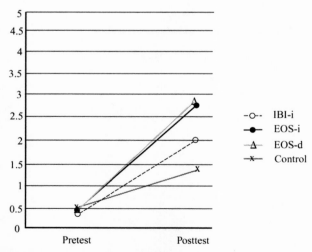

▓ Figure 8.3 Group Mean Scores: Interpretation of Old Exemplars

Overextension of Subjunctive

To ensure that participants were not overusing the subjunctive as a consequence of instruction, a repeated measures ANOVA was performed on old recognition items where indicative was required. There was no significant effect for Time, $F(1,98) = 1.375, p = .244$, no significant effect for Group, $F(1,98) = 1.241, p = .299$, and no significant interaction between Group and Time: $F(3,98) = .08, p = .971$. To evaluate the overextension of the subjunctive on new recognition items where indicative was required, a one-way ANOVA was conducted, and it revealed no significant differences between groups, $F(3,98) = 1.447, p = .234$. These results confirm that learners were not employing a test-taking strategy by selecting the subjunctive choice for all items, neither were they overextending the use of subjunctive to all adverbial clauses on time as a result of instruction.

Summary of Results

Both research questions were answered negatively: no effect was found for feedback timing on L2 learners' recognition or interpretation of new and old exemplars of the Spanish subjunctive with adverbial clauses of time. All groups receiving feedback significantly improved in their ability to recognize and interpret the use of subjunctive in previously seen items, from pretest to posttest, and there were no statistically significant differences between feedback groups in their ability to recognize or interpret the use of subjunctive in new exemplars. However, explicit feedback itself had a differential effect on the learners' ability to recognize the use of subjunctive in both new and old exemplars, given that all three feedback groups significantly outperformed the [-feedback] control group in those tasks.

Discussion and Conclusion

The goal of the present study was to empirically test the assumption made by CALL researchers that immediate feedback is more beneficial to L2 learners than delayed feedback. Specifically, the research questions examined whether feedback timing (IBI-i vs. EOS-i vs. EOS-d) would have an effect on L2 learners' recognition and interpretation of new and old exemplars of the Spanish subjunctive with adverbial clauses of time. The results indicated that feedback timing does not seem to have a differential effect on L2 learners' acquisition of the target structure, confirming what had been previously found by Goda (2004) and Dabaghi (2006). That is, contrary to what the assumption made by CALL researchers would predict, students who received immediate feedback (IBI-i) performed similarly to students who received the other two feedback types (EOS-i and EOS-d).

Nonetheless, the results revealed a poorer performance on the part of the control group, which did not receive any type of feedback. In fact, with respect to recognition, it was noted that the feedback groups significantly outperformed the control group on both old and new items. This finding suggests that the provision of feedback itself may have a beneficial effect on L2 learners' acquisition of the Spanish subjunctive, irrespective of when it is provided. The fact that participants receiving feedback outperformed those who did not is in line with numerous empirical studies that have shown a facilitative role for feedback in SLA (Carroll and Swain 1993; Leeman 2003; Lyster 2004; Muranoi 2000). Furthermore, it could be argued that the explicitness of the feedback was especially helpful for learners to confirm or refute interlanguage hypotheses, given the fact that several studies have shown an advantage for explicit feedback, especially in CALL (Bowles 2005; Nagata 1993; Nagata and Swisher 1995; Rosa and Leow 2004). Future studies should explore whether utilizing a less explicit instructional treatment or type of feedback might yield different effects for feedback presented at different times.

Another possible explanation for the lack of differences between feedback groups may be due to one major limitation of this study: the limited number of experimental items that required the use of the subjunctive in the pretest and posttest. Subtle differences between feedback groups may have been lost as a consequence of having only five target items, which undoubtedly reduced the statistical power of the analyses.

Overall, the findings of this study cast serious doubts on the assumption that immediate feedback in a CALL task is categorically more beneficial to L2 learners than delayed feedback. However, the present study is limited in that it focused on only one particular grammar structure in Spanish, and it did not examine production data. Therefore, the effects of feedback timing on learners' acquisition of other structures or on their production skills are unknown. Further research is needed to address these possibilities and shed more light on the effects of feedback timing in SLA.

REFERENCES

Bowles, Melissa. 2005. *Effects of verbalization condition and type of feedback on L2 development in a CALL task.* PhD diss., Georgetown University.

Brosvic, Gary, Michael Epstein, Roberta Dihoff, and Michael Cook. 2006. Acquisition and retention of Esperanto: The case for error correction and immediate feedback. *Psychological Record* 56:205–18.

Buzhardt, Jay, and George Semb. 2002. Item-by-Item versus End-of-Test feedback in a computer-based PSI course. *Journal of Behavioral Education* 11:89–104.

Carroll, Susanne, and Merrill Swain. 1993. Explicit and implicit negative feedback: An empirical study of the learning of linguistic generalizations. *Studies in Second Language Acquisition* 15:357–66.

Chaudron, Craig. 1988. *Second language classrooms: Research on teaching and learning.* Cambridge: Cambridge University Press.

Collentine, Joseph. 1998. Processing Instruction and the subjunctive. *Hispania* 81:576–87.

Dabaghi, Azizollah. 2006. Error correction: Report on a study. *Language Learning Journal* 34:10–13.

Dempsey, John, and Susan Wager. 1988. A taxonomy for the timing of feedback in computer-based instruction. *Educational Technology* 28:20–25.

Dihoff, Roberta, Gary Brosvic, Michael Epstein, and Michael Cook. 2003. Provision of feedback during preparation for academic testing: Learning is enhanced by immediate but not delayed feedback. *Psychological Record* 53:533–48.

Doughty, Catherine. 2001. Cognitive underpinnings of focus on form. In *Cognition and second language instruction,* ed. Peter Robinson, 206–57. Cambridge: Cambridge University Press.

Doughty, Catherine, and Jessica Williams. 1998. Pedagogical choices in focus on form. In *Focus on form in classroom: Second language acquisition,* ed. Catherine Doughty and Jessica Williams, 197–261. Cambridge: Cambridge University Press.

Ellis, Rod, Shawn Loewen, and Rosemary Erlam. 2006. Implicit and explicit corrective feedback and the acquisition of L2 grammar. *Studies in Second Language Acquisition* 28:339–68.

Farley, Andrew. 2001. Processing instruction and meaning-based output instruction: A comparative study. *Spanish Applied Linguistics* 5:57–94.

———. 2004. Processing instruction and the Spanish subjunctive: Is explicit information needed? In *Processing Instruction: Theory, research and commentary,* ed. Bill VanPatten, 227–40. Mahwah, NJ: Lawrence Erlbaum Associates.

————. 2005. *Structured input: Grammar instruction for the acquisition-oriented classroom*. New York: McGraw Hill.

Gaynor, Patricia. 1981. The effect of feedback delay on retention of computer-based mathematical material. *Journal of Computer Based Instruction* 8:28–34.

Goda, Yoshiko. 2004. *Feedback timing and learners' response confidence on learning English as a foreign language (EFL): Examining the effects of a computer-based feedback and assessment environment on EFL students' language acquisition*. PhD diss., Florida Institute of Technology.

Gottlieb, James. 1989. *The effects of feedback timing and learner response confidence on delayed retention of verbal information*. PhD diss., Florida State University.

Heift, Trude, and Anne Rimrott. 2008. Learner responses to corrective feedback for spelling mistakes in CALL. *System* 36:196–213.

Kulhavy, Raymond, and Richard Anderson. 1972. Delay-retention effect with multiple-choice tests. *Journal of Educational Psychology* 63:505–12.

Leeman, Jennifer. 2003. Recasts and second language development: Beyond negative evidence. *Studies in Second Language Acquisition* 25:37–63.

Loschky, Lester, and Robert Bley-Vroman. 1993. Grammar and task-based methodology. In *Tasks and language learning: Integrating theory and practice,* ed. Graham Crookes and Susan Gass, 123–67. Clevedon, UK: Multilingual Matters.

Lyster, Roy. 2004. Differential effects of prompts and recasts in form-focused instruction. *Studies in Second Language Acquisition* 26:399–432.

Muranoi, Hitoshi. 2000. Focus on form through interaction enhancement: Integrating formal instruction into a communicative task in EFL classrooms. *Language Learning* 50:617–73.

Nagata, Noriko. 1993. Intelligent computer feedback for second language instruction. *Modern Language Journal* 77:330–39.

Nagata, Noriko, and Virginia Swisher. 1995. A study of consciousness-raising by computer: The effect of metalinguistic feedback on second language learning. *Foreign Language Annals* 28:337–47.

Pereira, Isabel. 1996. *Markedness and instructed SLA: An experiment in teaching the Spanish subjunctive*. PhD diss., University of Illinois at Urbana–Champaign.

Phye, Gary, and Thomas Andre. 1989. Delayed retention effect: Attention, perseveration, or both? *Contemporary Educational Psychology* 14:173–85.

Pressey, Sidney. 1950. Development and appraisal of devices providing immediate automatic scoring of objective tests and concomitant self–instruction. *Journal of Psychology* 29:417–47.

Rosa, Elena, and Ronald Leow. 2004. Computerized task-based exposure, explicitness, type of feedback, and Spanish L2 development. *Modern Language Journal* 88:192–216.

Sanz, Cristina. 2004. Computer delivered implicit versus explicit feedback in processing instruction. In *Processing Instruction: Theory, research and commentary,* ed. Bill VanPatten, 241–55. Mahwah, NJ: Lawrence Erlbaum Associates.

Sanz, Cristina, and Kara Morgan-Short. 2004. Positive evidence vs. explicit rule presentation and explicit negative feedback: A computer-assisted study. *Language Learning* 54:35–78.

Surber, John, and Richard Anderson. 1975. Delay-retention effect in natural classroom settings. *Journal of Educational Psychology* 67:170–73.

Terrell, Tracy, Bernard Baycroft, and Charles Perrone. 1987. The subjunctive in Spanish interlanguage: Accuracy and comprehensibility. In *Foreign language learning: A research perspective,* ed. Bill VanPatten, Trisha Dvorak, James Lee, 19–32. Cambridge: Newbury House.

Tomasello, Michael, and Carol Herron. 1989. Feedback for language transfer errors: The garden path technique. *Studies in Second Language Acquisition* 11:385–95.

VanPatten, Bill. 2005. Processing instruction. In *Mind and context in adult second language acquisition,* ed. Cristina Sanz, 267–81. Washington, DC: Georgetown University Press.

9

▦ Working Memory Predicts the Acquisition of Explicit L2 Knowledge

JARED A. LINCK
The Pennsylvania State University

DANIEL J. WEISS
The Pennsylvania State University

▦ THE ROLE OF EXECUTIVE FUNCTIONING in second language (L2) aptitude remains unclear. While some studies report a relationship between working memory (WM) and L2 learning (e.g., Mackey et al. 2002), others have argued against this association (e.g., Juffs 2004). There is also evidence that being bilingual incurs benefits to inhibitory control (e.g., Bialystok et al. 2004), and recent studies have reported that individual differences in inhibitory control are related to online L2 processing (e.g., Linck, Hoshirno, and Kroll 2008). However, few studies have adopted a longitudinal approach to assessing the predictive validity of these executive functions. The current study aimed to fill this gap by examining whether executive functioning predicts acquisition of explicit L2 knowledge in a classroom context. Students enrolled in their first, second, or third semester of university language courses participated in experimental sessions at the beginning and end of a semester. In both sessions, participants completed two L2 proficiency measures that assessed explicit knowledge of L2 vocabulary and grammar. In addition, participants performed individual difference measures of WM, inhibitory control, and motivation to learn the L2 and reported their university grade-point average (GPA) and SAT scores. We found that L2 motivation and GPA both reliably predicted initial L2 proficiency (i.e., first testing session performance). In a series of hierarchical regression analyses controlling for differences in L2 motivation and GPA, WM accounted for significant additional variance in initial L2 proficiency. WM reliably predicted the degree of L2 learning across testing sessions (greater WM resources predicted larger improvements in L2 proficiency), whereas no other predictor accounted for these changes. These results support the notion that the executive function of WM is an important component of L2 aptitude (e.g., Miyake and Friedman 1998; Robinson 2005), particularly for predicting explicit L2 acquisition during the early stages of learning.

Working Memory Predicts the Acquisition of Explicit
L2 Knowledge

For decades, researchers and practitioners alike have been interested in predicting which learners are likely to succeed in acquiring a foreign language. Variables have been proposed and explored empirically (for a review, see Dörnyei 2006), with the goal of identifying separable components of language learning ability—i.e., *language aptitude* (Dörnyei 2005; Skehan 2002). WM and inhibitory control abilities have been identified as being likely contributors to language aptitude (e.g., Abutalebi and Green 2007; Hummel 2009; Kroll and Linck 2007). Although a number of studies have reported relationships between WM and aspects of L2 learning (e.g., Harrington and Sawyer 1992; Miyake and Friedman 1998), no study to date has examined the predictive utility of working memory or inhibitory control within a longitudinal design. Thus, the current study was designed to investigate the predictive validity of two executive functions—WM and inhibitory control—in L2 learning in a classroom context.

Drawing from theoretical developments in the field of cognitive psychology, there has been increased interest in examining how WM contributes to language aptitude (see Dörnyei 2006; Hummel 2009; Miyake and Friedman 1998). Working memory refers to a specific set of cognitive processes that are crucial to the processing, storage, and retrieval of information in memory (e.g., Baddeley and Hitch 1974). WM is thought to include a short-term storage component (i.e., short-term memory) and an attentional control component known as the central executive. Although short-term memory and the central executive component of WM are correlated, they are empirically and conceptually distinguishable (Engle et al. 1999). Indeed, recent WM models emphasize the role of the central executive in exerting cognitive control over the contents of short-term memory as the primary determiner of individual differences in WM (e.g., Engle 2002).

There is a growing body of evidence of the role of WM in L2 learning. Individual differences in WM have been correlated with L2 proficiency as measured by the TOEFL scores (Harrington and Sawyer 1992), reading comprehension tasks (e.g., Miyake and Friedman 1998), as well as with the use of feedback from recasts in conversational interactions (Mackey et al. 2002). Further, evidence from psycholinguistic studies of online language processing suggests that using an L2 imposes cognitive processing demands that necessitate the control of attention by WM (e.g., Hernandez and Meschyan 2006; see Kroll and Linck 2007). Indeed, there is a growing body of research demonstrating the impact of WM on L2 online processing (for a review, see Michael and Gollan 2005). Therefore, it is plausible that individuals with greater WM resources are better equipped to handle the cognitive processing demands of mastering an L2. It is important to note that the capacity and efficiency of the short-term memory component of WM (independent of the central executive) are also known to be related to certain L2 learning outcomes, including vocabulary learning in the lab (Atkins and Baddeley 1998), vocabulary use and production skill (O'Brien et al. 2006), and oral fluency development (O'Brien et al. 2007).

However, not all researchers are convinced of the role that WM plays in L2 learning. Juffs (2004) reported finding no evidence of a relationship between performance on a reading span task and online L2 sentence comprehension and subsequently suggested that researchers have overstated the usefulness of WM measures in accounting for differences in L2 learning. It is important to note, though, that Juffs included native English speakers in his sample but also failed to find WM effects on English "garden path" sentences (a finding that has been well documented in the monolingual literature; see, for example, Novick, Trueswell, and Thompson-Schill 2005). The available (albeit mixed) correlational data provide some evidence of the relationship between WM and L2 learning (e.g., Harrington and Sawyer 1992; Hummel 2009; Mackey et al. 2002; Mikaye and Friedman 1998) but do not establish the predictive validity of WM. For evidence that WM is a predictor of L2 learning, WM must be linked to differences in L2 learning outcomes over multiple points in time.

There is growing evidence from research on executive functions that WM and inhibitory control both contribute to the cognitive control of memory and attention but, importantly, that they support different aspects of cognitive control (e.g., Miyake et al. 2000). Inhibitory control refers to one's ability to ignore distracting but irrelevant information or to suppress more habitual responses in order to perform a less dominant response (e.g., Green 1998). These skills may be particularly relevant to L2 learning given the observation that both languages are active in the mind of an L2 learner and can interfere with one another (e.g., Dijkstra and Van Heuven 2002; Kroll, Sumutka, and Schwartz 2005). Inhibitory control has also been implicated in L2 use (e.g., Abutalebi and Green 2007) independent of WM. There is preliminary correlational evidence that individual differences in inhibitory control are related to L2 picture naming (Linck, Hoshino, and Kroll 2008). Moreover, recent work by Bialystok and colleagues comparing monolinguals to balanced bilinguals suggests that a bilingual's lifetime of experience juggling two languages in the mind incurs advantages in inhibitory control abilities (e.g., Bialystok et al. 2004; Bialystok, Craik, and Luk 2008). Taken together, these results raise the question of whether individual differences in inhibitory control might predict one's ability to master an L2. To the best of our knowledge, this hypothesis has not yet been systematically tested.

The Current Study

We designed this experiment to examine the predictive validity of executive functioning in L2 learning in a classroom context. Using a longitudinal (test–retest) design, we tested the hypothesis that individual differences in WM and inhibitory control predict L2 proficiency at the beginning and end of a semester-long language course for university students enrolled in an introductory language class. Critically, with this design we were also able to examine whether a learner's WM and inhibitory control would predict his or her degree of learning (i.e., change in proficiency) across the semester as a first step at establishing the predictive validity of executive functions for L2 learning. To control for differences in general academic performance and motivation, we gathered measures of GPA, SAT, and motivation to learn an L2, which we included as covariates in a series of hierarchical and repeated-measures multiple regression analyses. If adult learners' L2 proficiency is related to individual differences in executive functioning, then we expected that WM and inhibitory control would account for unique variance in L2 proficiency at test and at retest. Furthermore, WM and inhibitory control should predict the amount of learning during the semester, as measured by the positive change in L2 proficiency between test and retest.

Method
Participants attended two separate testing sessions, as described below.

Participants
Native English speakers were recruited from language courses at Pennsylvania State University. All participants were enrolled in either a first-semester German introductory course or a third-semester Spanish introductory conversation course. Eighteen German students (eleven female, seven male) and thirty Spanish students (eighteen female, twelve male) participated in the first testing session during the sixth week of the semester. For the German students, the first testing session was conducted during class time (though students were informed of their ability to opt out of participating). The Spanish students chose one of three evening sessions for the first testing session. The second testing session was conducted in a lab outside of class time. A total of twenty-four students (eight German, sixteen Spanish) had complete data from both testing sessions (two participants' second session data were incomplete due to technical errors during testing).

Materials
Participants completed measures of L2 proficiency, motivation to learn the L2, WM, and Inhibitory Control.

L2 Proficiency Measures
The criterion measure was a multiple-choice test of grammar and vocabulary knowledge.[1] The Spanish materials included twenty items from the grammar and vocabulary section of the *Diplomas de Español como Lengua Extranjera* published by the *Instituto Cervantes* (http://diplomas.cervantes.es/candidatos/modelo.jsp). The German materials were fifteen fill-in-the-blank items taken from the University of Wisconsin language course placement exam. For both languages participants completed separate, parallel forms at the test and retest sessions. The test and retest proficiency scores involved the combination of the grammar and vocabulary questions.

Individual Difference Measures
To assess academic performance, participants reported their GPA and SAT scores. Motivation to learn the L2 was measured using thirty-three items adapted from Gardner's (2004) Attitude/Motivation Test Battery. In this battery, participants read a series of statements (e.g., "I would study a foreign language in school even if it were not required"), and for each statement they indicate the degree *to which they agree with the statement on a scale from 1 (Strongly Disagree) to 7 (Strongly Agree)*. The battery quantifies five facets of motivation: interest in foreign languages; attitudes toward learning the L2; integrative orientation (interest in learning the L2 in order to interact with native speakers of the L2); instrumental orientation (interest in learning the L2 for its pragmatic or utilitarian value); and L2 class anxiety (degree of discomfort while

participating in the L2 class). A composite score was computed as the average of all five facets, with L2 class anxiety negatively coded. In preliminary analyses, using only the composite score led to similar results as using the five individual facet scores; thus, for simplicity, only the composite score results are reported below.

Working memory was measured with the operation span task (Turner and Engle 1989), which requires simultaneous processing of simple arithmetic operations and storage of words in memory. In this task participants first view an equation (e.g., "$(7 * 2) - 5 = 9$") and indicate with a button press whether the equation is correct or incorrect, then briefly view a to-be-remembered word before the next equation is presented. Operation-word pair trials are presented in sets ranging from two to six trials. At the completion of a given set, participants must recall as many of the two to six words from that set as possible. Three sets of each set length were presented, for a total of sixty trials. Participants received one point for each correctly recalled word from trials on which a correct operation judgment was made, thereby requiring participants to adequately attend to both the processing and storage components of the task to score highly. Since the primary processing task involves solving math equations rather than processing language, this WM measure is arguably less dependent on language skills per se and thus was chosen to minimize variance due to differences in L1 language proficiency (cf. reading span task of Daneman and Carpenter 1980).

Given recent claims that inhibitory control is an important executive functioning component for L2 use (e.g., Abutalebi and Green 2007; Bialystok, Craik, and Luk 2008), the study also included the Simon task (e.g., Simon and Rudell 1967) as a measure of inhibitory control. In the Simon task, participants view a series of colored boxes on a computer screen and must respond based on the color but not location of the box. On congruent trials, the colored box appears on the same side as the required response. But on incongruent trials, the box appears on the side opposite the required response. Since participants must suppress the natural tendency to respond to the location of the stimulus, this mismatch in stimulus and response locations typically leads to slower correct responses on incongruent trials relative to congruent trials (known as the Simon effect; Simon and Rudell 1967).

Procedures
The first testing session took place either in the classroom (German) or during an out-of-class session (Spanish). After completing an informed consent form, participants completed the test form of two paper-and-pencil L2 proficiency measures and reported their GPA and SAT scores. The second testing session took place in a lab equipped with computers to administer the computerized tasks. After completing an informed consent form, participants first completed the retest form of two paper-and-pencil L2 proficiency measures. They were then seated in front of a computer and an experimenter individually administered the language history questionnaire, the Simon task, the operation span task, and the motivation questionnaire.

Analysis
A series of hierarchical multiple regression analyses were conducted separately on the L2 proficiency scores at test and retest. These analyses were performed in three

steps. The first step examined the amount of variance in L2 proficiency that was explained by GPA and SAT scores. After factoring out the explained variance, the second step of analysis identified any unique variance that could be explained by motivation. Finally, WM and inhibitory control were added in the third step to determine whether either cognitive processing measure accounted for additional unique variance in L2 proficiency.

To test the hypothesis that cognitive abilities are related to the degree of change in L2 proficiency over the semester, a difference score (retest—test) was computed for the two proficiency measures, and the same hierarchical regression approach was followed. We also jointly analyzed the test and retest proficiency data using repeated measures regression analysis within a multilevel modeling framework in order to provide a more powerful analysis of the test–retest differences (see Raudenbush and Bryk 2002).

Results

Preliminary analyses found no reliable group differences between the German and Spanish language students on any of the predictor or criterion measures. Thus, the data from the two groups were combined for all analyses reported below. Table 9.1 provides descriptive statistics for the predictor and criterion measures for the combined sample of twenty-four participants.

Performance at Test

The analysis of the first session data provided preliminary support for the hypothesis that individual differences in WM are related to L2 proficiency. In the final regression model, 60.7 percent of the variance in test scores was accounted for by the full set of

Table 9.1
Descriptive Statistics for the Predictor and Criterion Measures

Measure	Mean	*SD*
Predictor		
SAT[a]	1221.4	145.5
GPA[a]	3.4	0.6
Motivation composite	3.4	0.7
Working memory capacity[b]	46.3	8.5
Simon effect (ms)[c]	42.0	24.1
Criterion		
Proficiency at test (%)	40.0	19.3
Proficiency at retest (%)	46.0	20.8

Notes: [a]Obtained via self-report.
[b]Working memory capacity measured as the number of to-be-remembered words out of sixty possible.
[c]The Simon effect indicates the degree of interference due to the mismatch in stimulus and response locations, with lower scores indicating better inhibitory control abilities.

predictors, $F(5,18) = 5.55, p < .01$. GPA was significantly related to proficiency at test (*semipartial r* $= .35, p < .05$), whereas SAT and motivation failed to account for a significant amount of variance. Notably, after controlling for these covariates, WM but not inhibitory control was positively related to proficiency (WM: *semipartial r* = $.31, p = .052$; inhibitory control: *semipartial r* $= .16, p > .20$), and together accounted for 10 percent of unique variance, $F(2,18) = 2.29, p = .13$.

Performance at Retest

The analysis of the second session (retest) data provided further evidence of the role of WM in L2 learning. In the final regression model, 59.6 percent of the variance in test scores was accounted for by the full set of predictors, $F(5,18) = 5.30, p < .01$. As in the initial test analysis, GPA (but not SAT or motivation) was significantly related to proficiency (*semipartial r* $= .43, p < .05$). After controlling for the covariates, WM but not inhibitory control was significantly related to proficiency (WM: *semipartial r* $= .56, p = .001$; inhibitory control: *semipartial r* $= .17, p > .20$), and together significantly accounted for 31.6 percent of unique variance, $F(2,18) = 7.04, p < .01$.

Test–Retest—Changes in L2 Proficiency

To identify predictors of changes in proficiency during the semester, we first analyzed the test–retest difference score using hierarchical regression. The patterns of results parallel those found in the individual test and retest analyses reported above: WM remained a reliable predictor of L2 proficiency even after controlling for GPA, SAT, and motivation. However, inhibitory control did not account for significant variance in L2 proficiency. In the final regression model, 40.8 percent of the variance in test scores was accounted for by the full set of predictors, $F(5,18) = 2.48, p = .071$. For the covariates, changes in proficiency were significantly related to SAT (*semipartial r* $= -.43, p < .05$) but not GPA or motivation (*semipartial r* $= .17$ and $-.06$, respectively; *ps* $> .10$). After controlling for the covariates, WM but not inhibitory control was significantly related to changes in proficiency (WM: *semipartial r* $= .43, p < .05$; inhibitory control: *semipartial r* $= .03, p > .20$). Together, WM and inhibitory control explained 13.9 percent of unique variance, $F(2,18) = 3.00, p = .075$.

To provide a more powerful analysis of the change in L2 proficiency, data from both testing sessions were analyzed using repeated measures regression. Preliminary models included all predictors from the previously reported regression analyses as main effects. The main effects provide estimates of the relationship between each predictor and L2 proficiency at test. Next, more complex models were tested that included all predictors and their interactions with testing session. A significant interaction term provides evidence of a relationship between the predictor and the degree of change in L2 proficiency from test to retest. After the addition of all interaction terms to the regression model, nonsignificant interaction terms were removed and the fit of the simplified model was compared to the fit of the main effects model.[2] The results reported below are from the final best-fitting model, which included the simple effects of GPA, SAT, L2 learning motivation, WM and inhibitory control, and the interaction between WM and testing session.

See table 9.2 for the repeated measures regression model parameters. Overall, the results replicate the patterns reported in the analyses above: variance in L2 proficiency at test was accounted for by differences in GPA and WM, and changes in L2 proficiency from test to retest were accounted for by differences in WM. In these results the intercept is interpreted as an estimate of the test (session 1) performance of a participant with a 3.0 GPA and average SAT, motivation, WM, and inhibitory control. That is, the average participant correctly answered 33.4 percent of items on the criterion measure at test. The average participant improved his or her proficiency test score at retest by over 6 percent, as indicated by the significant session parameter. The significant GPA parameter suggests that a one-point increase of GPA from 3.0 to 4.0 would predict an increase of over 16 percent in test performance, holding all other variables constant. Similarly, the significant WM parameter suggests a linear increase of about 0.85 percent in proficiency with every one point increase in WM (out of sixty possible points). Importantly, the marginal WM × session interaction suggests that as WM increased, greater improvements in proficiency were found between test and retest. Indeed, the regression parameter for this interaction indicates that an individual with a WM score ten points higher than average would be predicted to show an increase in L2 proficiency nearly twice that of the average participant, that is, $(10 * 0.51) + 6.18 = 11.28$, vs. 6.18. Taken together, these results suggest that greater WM resources are related to faster L2 learning, as indicated by a higher initial level of proficiency at test and a greater improvement during the semester. See figure 9.1 for a graphical depiction of the differential impact of WM differences on test and retest scores.

Note that when the more complete information available in repeated measures regression analysis was used, SAT was no longer related to proficiency (either as a

Table 9.2
Model Parameters from Repeated Measures Regression Analysis of L2 Proficiency Data

Predictor	Parameter Estimate
Intercept (Test %)	33.37 (3.52) **
Session	6.18 (2.54) *
GPA	16.26 (6.38) *
SAT	0.02 (0.03)
Motivation	2.13 (3.88)
WMC	0.85 (0.32) *
Inhibitory control	0.15 (0.11)
WMC × session	0.51 (0.31) +

Notes: Session = change in performance from test to retest. WMC = working memory capacity. WMC × session = interaction between working memory and testing session, indicating degree of increase in WMC's effect at retest.
+ $p < .10$.
* $p < .05$.
** $p < .01$.

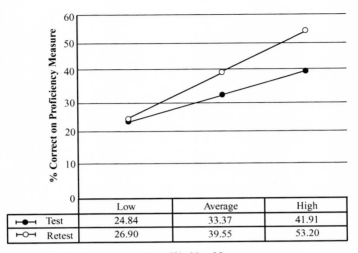

	Low	Average	High
Test	24.84	33.37	41.91
Retest	26.90	39.55	53.20

Working Memory

Figure 9.1 Regression Lines for Working Memory Predicting L2 Proficiency at Test and Retest, Based on the Repeated Measures Regression Analysis

simple effect or interacting with session), which suggests that the use of difference scores in the previous analysis may have induced a type-I error.

Discussion

The goal of this study was to provide longitudinal data on the predictive validity of two specific cognitive processing abilities, WM and inhibitory control, for L2 learning in a classroom context. Participants completed an L2 proficiency measure at the beginning and again at the end of a semester. They were also administered individual difference measures of GPA, SAT, motivation, WM, and inhibitory control. After controlling for differences in GPA, SAT, and motivation to learn the L2, WM remained a robust predictor of L2 proficiency, whereas inhibitory control did not. Specifically, greater WM resources were significantly related to greater L2 proficiency at test and retest with moderate effect sizes, and greater WM resources predicted larger gains in L2 proficiency across the semester (i.e., test–retest changes in L2 proficiency). These WM effects were found even after controlling for other relevant individual difference variables.

For over a decade, researchers have claimed that greater WM resources are related to better L2 learning (e.g., Harrington and Sawyer 1992; Miyake and Friedman 1998). Yet, to the best of our knowledge, no study in the literature has demonstrated that a learner's WM can predict L2 learning over time. The present longitudinal study provides evidence of the predictive validity of WM for L2 classroom learning, thus contributing empirical support to claims that WM is an important component of L2 aptitude (e.g., Hummel 2009; Miyake and Friedman 1998). These results also suggest that individual differences in WM may have a larger impact on learning than other cognitive processes that have been linked to L2 processing differences, such as inhibitory control (e.g., Abutalebi and Green 2007).

An examination of the regression coefficients from the three sets of analyses reported earlier suggests that WM's relation to L2 proficiency may be stronger as learners become more proficient. WM was positively related to proficiency in the initial test, and the magnitude of this relationship at retest was nearly twice as strong. Furthermore, the repeated measures analysis indicated that the slope of the WM prediction line was steeper (i.e., the predictive validity of WM was stronger) at retest than at test, as indicated by the positive WM × session parameter (see fig. 9.1). It appears that WM plays an increasingly large role in learning as L2 proficiency increases. Given the relatively short length of time (three months) between test and retest, future studies should examine whether the relationship between WM and L2 proficiency continues to strengthen across larger changes in L2 proficiency. This could be accomplished by examining specific learning contexts where rapid L2 learning is accomplished over a short time, such as in a language immersion experience during a semester abroad (e.g., Freed 1995; Linck, Kroll, and Sunderman 2009), or by extending the retest lag to a longer time interval.

Unlike WM, inhibitory control did not emerge as a robust predictor of L2 proficiency. As mentioned previously, recent research suggests that having the lifelong experience of using two languages increases inhibitory control abilities in bilinguals (e.g., Bialystok et al. 2004). The learners in our study may have been at too early a stage of L2 learning for inhibitory control effects to emerge. For example, they may not have had enough experience with controlling the two languages, or they may have still been relying heavily on their L1 to aid L2 processing (i.e., transfer from L1; see MacWhinney 2005) such that L1 inhibition was not necessary. An open question is whether inhibitory control might serve as a predictor at later stages of L2 learning or in more intensive learning contexts, such as linguistic immersion. It is possible that enhanced inhibitory control abilities in bilinguals are just a by-product of practice (Bialystok and DePape 2009). Alternatively, it is possible that at more advanced proficiency levels or with more extensive time on task, we might find that having better inhibitory control abilities may yield benefits to L2 learning. Future research will endeavor to address this issue.

Limitations
The limited or null results of the covariates (GPA, SAT, and L2 motivation) may be a by-product of characteristics of the participant sample. The final sample size of twenty-four students with complete test–retest data is smaller than ideal, especially when testing for a range of relationships using multiple regression analysis. Since the sample came from a population of students who had been preselected for university enrollment based on high school GPA and SAT (among other variables), there may be a range restriction in this sample for SAT scores, which would suppress any relationship between SAT and L2 proficiency.[3] Moreover, this preselection may have negatively skewed the distribution of SAT and GPA scores (although all measures were subjected to one-sample tests of normality, and none showed evidence of a significant deviation from a normal distribution). Nonetheless, given these concerns, the

current results should be cross-validated with a larger independent sample to verify that the reported relationships are not sample dependent.

Conclusions

This study fills a gap in the literature by providing direct evidence of claims that WM is a predictor of L2 learning (e.g., Harrington and Sawyer 1992; Miyake and Friedman 1998; cf. Juffs 2004). Using a longitudinal design, we found evidence that learners with greater WM resources were more likely to succeed in learning their L2. Future research must determine whether WM is an equally valid predictor of L2 learning at more advanced levels of language proficiency. Regardless, the results of this study indicate that measures of WM are likely to improve the predictive utility of tests of language aptitude. Given that one goal of aptitude research is to identify factors that affect an individual's ability to develop L2 proficiency over time, future studies may benefit from using longitudinal designs to determine the components of aptitude that predict subsequent learning. This line of research could also be extended to other learning contexts (e.g., immersion learning, blended learning) in order to determine whether WM and other potential components of L2 aptitude, such as inhibitory control, are differentially predictive of L2 learning outcomes across different learning contexts.

ACKNOWLEDGMENTS

The authors thank Nurcan Cile, Christina Baer, Oscar Lee, John McCormick, and Mark Minnick for their research assistance; Susan Bobb, Chris Botero, Allen Davis, Noelle Isenberg, Carrie Jackson, Nuria Sagarra, and Jorge Valdes for assisting with materials selection and preparation; Jameson Bell, Frank Poehlmann, Anke Riemann, and Tim Woolsey for supporting participant recruitment and data collection during class time; and Judith Kroll for providing financial support for this research, and the University of Maryland Center for Advanced Study of Language for financial support to the first author during the writing of this chapter. We also thank Joel Koeth for providing comments on a previous draft of the manuscript. Correspondence should be sent to Jared Linck, who is now at the University of Maryland Center for Advanced Study of Language, Box 25, College Park, MD 20742.

NOTES

1. Participants also completed a paper-and-pencil grammaticality judgment task. However, no reliable effects were found with the grammaticality judgment tasks at test or retest, thus only the grammar and vocabulary test data were included in the reported analyses.
2. Model fit is assessed by comparing the model deviance statistics for the two models, following the typical approach for model building within a multilevel modeling framework. For details on model building and assessment of model fit, see for example, Raudenbush and Bryk (2002).
3. We thank Ellen Bialystok for noting this possibility.

REFERENCES

Abutalebi, Jubin, and David Green. 2007. Bilingual language production: The neurocognition of language representation and control. *Journal of Neurolinguistics* 20:242–75.

Atkins, Paul W. B., and Alan D. Baddeley. 1998. Working memory and distributed vocabulary learning. *Applied Psycholinguistics* 19:537–52.

Baddeley, Alan D., and Graham Hitch. 1974. Working memory. In *Recent advances in learning and motivation,* ed. G. A. Bower, vol. 8, 47–90. New York: Academic Press.

Bialystok, Ellen, Fergus I. M. Craik, Raymond Klein, and Mythili Viswanathan. 2004. Bilingualism, aging, and cognitive control: Evidence from the Simon task. *Psychology and Aging* 19:290–303.

Bialystok, Ellen, Fergus I. M. Craik, and Gigi Luk. 2008. Cognitive control and lexical access in younger and older bilinguals. *Journal of Experimental Psychology: Learning, Memory, and Cognition* 34:859–73.

Bialystok, Ellen, and Anne-Marie DePape. 2009. Musical expertise, bilingualism, and executive functioning. *Journal of Experimental Psychology: Human Perception and Performance* 35:565–74.

Daneman, Meredyth, and Patricia A. Carpenter. 1980. Individual differences in working memory and reading. *Journal of Verbal Learning and Verbal Behavior* 19:450–66.

Dijkstra, Ton, and Walter J. B. Van Heuven. 2002. The architecture of the bilingual word recognition system: From identification to decision. *Bilingualism: Language and Cognition* 5:175–97.

Dörnyei, Zoltán. 2005. *The psychology of the language learner: Individual differences in second language acquisition.* Mahwah, NJ: Lawrence Erlbaum Associates.

———. 2006. Individual differences in second language acquisition. *AILA Review* 19:42–68.

Engle, Randall W. 2002. Working memory capacity as executive attention. *Current Directions in Psychological Science* 11:19–23.

Engle, Randall W., Stephen W. Tuholski, James E. Laughlin, and Andrew R. A. Conway. 1999. Working memory, short-term memory, and general fluid intelligence: A latent-variable approach. *Journal of Experimental Psychology: General* 128:309–31.

Freed, Barbara F., ed. 1995. *Second language acquisition in a study abroad context.* Philadelphia: John Benjamins.

Gardner, Robert C. 2004. Attitude/Motivation Test Battery: International AMTB Research Project. Retrieved May 16, 2007, from http://publish.uwo.ca/~gardner/.

Green, David. 1998. Mental control of the bilingual lexico-semantic system. *Bilingualism: Language and Cognition* 1:67–81.

Harrington, Mike, and Mark Sawyer. 1992. L2 working memory capacity and L2 reading skill. *Studies in Second Language Acquisition* 14:25–38.

Hernandez, Arturo E., and Gayane Meschyan. 2006. Executive function is necessary to enhance lexical processing in a less proficient L2: Evidence from fMRI during picture naming. *Bilingualism: Language and Cognition* 9:177–88.

Hummel, Kirsten M. 2009. Aptitude, phonological memory, and second language proficiency in nonnovice adult learners. *Applied Psycholinguistics* 30:225–49.

Juffs, Alan. 2004. Representation, processing and working memory in a second language. *Transactions of the Philological Society* 102:199–225.

Kroll, Judith F., and Jared A. Linck. 2007. Representation and skill in second language learners and proficient bilinguals. In *Cognitive aspects of bilingualism,* ed. I. Kecskes and L. Albertazzi, 237–69. New York: Springer.

Kroll, Judith F., Bianca M. Sumutka, and Ana I Schwartz. 2005. A cognitive view of the bilingual lexicon: Reading and speaking words in two languages. *International Journal of Bilingualism* 9:27–48.

Linck, Jared A., Noriko Hoshino, and Judith F. Kroll. 2008. Cross-language lexical processes and inhibitory control. *The Mental Lexicon* 3:349–74.

Linck, Jared A., Judith F. Kroll, and Gretchen Sunderman. 2009. Losing access to the native language while immersed in a second language: Evidence for the role of inhibition in second language learning. *Psychological Science* 20:1507–15.

Mackey, Alison, Jenefer Philp, Takako Egi, Akiko Fujii, and Tomoaki Tatsumi. 2002. Individual differences in working memory, noticing of interactional feedback and L2 development. In *Individual differences and instructed language learning,* ed. P. Robinson, 181–210. Philadelphia: John Benjamins.

MacWhinney, Brian. 2005. A unified model of language acquisition. In *Handbook of bilingualism: Psycholinguistic approaches,* ed. J. F. Kroll and A. M. B. De Groot, 49–67. New York: Oxford University Press.

Michael, Erica, and Tamar H. Gollan. 2005. Being and becoming bilingual: Individual differences and consequences for language production. In *Handbook of Bilingualism: Psycholinguistic Approaches,* ed. J. F. Kroll and A. M. B. De Groot, 389–407. New York: Oxford University Press.

Miyake, Akira, and Naomi P. Friedman. 1998. Individual differences in second language proficiency: Working memory as language aptitude. In *Foreign language learning: Psycholinguistic studies on training and retention,* ed. A. F. Healy and L. E. Bourne, 339–64. Mahwah, NJ: Lawrence Erlbaum Associates.

Miyake, Akira, Naomi P. Friedman, Michael J. Emerson, Alexander H. Witzki, Amy Howerter, and Tor D. Wager. 2000. The unity and diversity of executive functions and their contributions to complex "frontal lobe" tasks: A latent variable analysis. *Cognitive Psychology* 41:49–100.

Novick, Jared M., John C. Trueswell, and Sharon L. Thompson-Schill. 2005. Cognitive control and parsing: Reexamining the role of Broca's area in sentences comprehension. *Cognitive, Affective, & Behavioral Neuroscience* 5:263–81.

O'Brien, Irena, Norman Segalowitz, Joe Collentine, and Barbara Freed. 2006. Phonological memory and lexical, narrative, and grammatical skills in second-language oral production by adult learners. *Applied Psycholinguistics* 27:377–402.

O'Brien, Irena, Norman Segalowitz, Barbara Freed, and Joe Collentine. 2007. Phonological memory predicts second language oral fluency gains in adults. *Studies in Second Language Acquisition* 29:557–82.

Raudenbush, Stephen W., and Anthony S. Bryk. 2002. *Hierarchical linear models: Applications and data analysis methods.* 2nd ed. Thousand Oaks, CA: Sage.

Robinson, Peter. 2005. Aptitude and second language acquisition. *Annual Review of Applied Linguistics* 25:46–73.

Simon, J. Richard, and Alan P. Rudell. 1967. Auditory S-R compatibility: The effect of an irrelevant cue on information processing. *Journal of Applied Psychology* 51:300–304.

Skehan, Peter. 2002. Theorising and updating aptitude. In *Individual differences and instructed language learning,* ed. P. Robinson, 69–95. Philadelphia: John Benjamins.

Turner, Marilyn L., and Randall W. Engle. 1989. Is working memory capacity task dependent? *Journal of Memory and Language* 28:127–54.

10

The Effects of Formal Instruction and Study Abroad Contexts on Foreign Language Development: The SALA Project

CARMEN PÉREZ-VIDAL
Universitat Pompeu Fabra

MARIA JUAN-GARAU
Universitat de les Illes Balears

JOAN C. MORA
Universitat de Barcelona

THE INTEREST IN INVESTIGATING the effects of Study Abroad (SA) on linguistic outcomes and processes seems undiminishing. Whereas the main body of research to date focuses on the effect of the SA period per se, the aim of the present study is to uncover the effects of an SA period, following a formal instruction period, on the linguistic development of advanced level English major undergraduates studying for a degree in translation. The degree includes eighty hours of English tuition in the first year, prior to a three-month SA period spent in an English-speaking country (mostly in the UK and Ireland, but also in the United States, Canada, and Australia).

The data analyzed are part of the corpus gathered in the framework of a larger long-standing, state-funded research project, the Study Abroad and Language Acquisition (SALA) project, with a corpus of 63 averaged longitudinal and between 45 and 240 cross-sectional participants, according to test. They have been measured intensively, with a variety of data-collection procedures (oral and written, both with global and fine measurements) and with a comprehensively longitudinal design. Indeed, the project encompasses measurements not only during SA but before it—that is, following the AH instruction period, and also after it—in order to tap the midterm effect of SA. Participants are multilingual, Spanish/Catalan speakers learning English, their L3, and a second foreign language, their L4. Finally, these data are compared with baseline participants who are English-speaking university students on an SA program in Spain; hence, they constitute highly comparable data. The study presented here illustrates the variety of data in the SALA project by presenting analyses of written development, oral proficiency, and pronunciation in all its phonetic detail.

If we start by tackling the theoretical underpinnings underlying SA research, two key questions stand prominently for the researchers' consideration. The first and most important question concerns the interest of SA studies within the field of second language acquisition. An answer was clearly put forward by Collentine and Freed (2004, 158), in their seminal monograph edited in SSLA, where they stated: "The study of SLA within and across various contexts of learning forces a broadening of our perspective of the most important variables that affect and impede acquisition in general."

Indeed, on the one hand, SA does represent a specific context of acquisition in which specific proficiency gains can be obtained in contrast with other contexts such as formal instruction, domestic immersion, content-based teaching, or content and language integrated learning. It has been contended that an SA context may facilitate automatization of the linguistic competence practiced, whose proceduralization might have begun in an FI context (DeKeyser 2007). These are processes that to some degree involve implicit and explicit cognitive mechanisms taking place separately or at once. On the other hand, a whole set of learner variables that determine the amount of proficiency gains achieved during an SA period have been identified (see, among the seminal studies on SA, Collentine and Freed 2004; DeKeyser 1991, 2007; Freed 1995; Milton and Meara 1995; Regan 1998; Towell, Hawkins, and Bazergui 1996).

The second question concerns the actual gains obtained after SA. Research has been somewhat biased in this respect as oral production has been the winner, in terms both of the number of studies devoted to it and of conclusive results regarding the benefits derived from SA. Literacy has been the loser in both senses. Grammatical or structural competence, lexical, pragmatic, strategic, and sociolinguistic competence have also been analyzed. According to DuFon and Churchill (2006, 26) results seem to indicate the following:

- Generalized improvement in overall oral proficiency and fluency is the norm.
- Improvement in oral accuracy is not often reported.
- Even short programs seem to lend significant benefits.
- Longer programs lead to greater improvement in the area of pragmatics, pronunciation, and fluency.
- At best learner development only approaches TL norms.

When one analyzes oral communication, the skill having received the greatest attention in SA research, documentation on the development of fluency abroad abounds (see, e.g., DeKeyser 1986; Juan-Garau and Pérez-Vidal 2007; Lafford 2004; Segalowitz and Freed 2004). However, there is a dearth of SA studies focusing on oral accuracy by comparison. Moreover, findings in this domain are still far from conclusive. Thus, some scholars have reported nonsignificant progress in grammatical accuracy after an SA experience in a number of areas such as subject expression in L2 Spanish (see Isabelli 2001; López-Ortega 2002), and, similarly, little evidence suggesting that the SA context can surpass classroom learning in this domain (e.g., Collentine 2004; Torres 2003). It would thus seem that no substantial development occurs as far as accuracy is concerned after SA. However, in contrast, other comparative studies have shown SA groups to reach higher levels of accuracy than their AH counterparts (e.g., Howard 2001; Isabelli and Nishida 2005). At any rate, discrepancies in the findings evidence the need for more research in this area.

When looking at written development, a much lesser analyzed skill than oral communication, we found two studies that compared SA and AH settings and a third one that added yet an additional context, domestic immersion (IM), to the comparison. Freed, So, and Lazar (2003) reported no statistically significant differences in written fluency between the AH and SA groups. There was only a tendency toward improvement in that students in the SA context wrote longer texts that were slightly denser in lexical use in the posttest than in the pretest, two features that Polio (2001) pointed out are associated with fluency in writing after SA. Sasaki (2004, 2007) found that both groups—the English as a Foreign Language (EFL) AH in Japan and the English as a Second Language (ESL) on SA (four to nine months)—improved written quality/fluency. She followed them for three and a half years using multiple-data sources. The SA period resulted in their motivation to write well and strategy development, but the study concluded that 3.5 years was not a long enough period to allow these students to become EFL experts. The indirect effect of writing on other skills was measured in Freed, Segalowitz, and Dewey (2004). They contrasted three groups SA, AH, and IM. Reported hours per week spent writing outside of class by the IM group were significantly associated with oral fluidity. As with oral communication skills, such a lack of robust evidence points to the need for more studies on written development after an SA period.

Finally, when focusing on phonological ability as a result of SA, we notice that the differential effect of AH and SA contexts on L2 phonology remains a largely underresearched area in SLA. The main body of research has focused on oral communication skills, as already mentioned, and related cognitive processes (e.g., Segalowitz and Freed 2004; Towell, Hawkins, and Bazergui 1996) and suggests that the SA experience improves the learners' linguistic competence leading to substantial linguistic gains, particularly in the domain of oral skills. However, previous research investigating L2 speech learning and phonological acquisition in an SA setting does not consistently support the hypothesis of the SA context enhancing L2 speech production and perception (e.g., Díaz-Campos 2004; Højen 2003; Mora 2008). Such a lack of conclusive, robust evidence also calls for more research in this area.

Consequently, our study seeks to address the following research questions in relation with a three-month SA program: (a) Will the SA context with increased opportunities for interaction result in greater improvement than the FI context with regard to oral accuracy? (b) Will improvement be shown even in areas such as writing, as regards accuracy, fluency, and complexity? (c) Will phonology, both perceptive and productive, improve with increased exposure during a three-month SA period?

The Present Study

This study focuses on how linguistic development proceeds as a result of a compulsory ERASMUS-SOCRATES exchange. It taps the participants' oral accuracy in communicating, written abilities, and phonological perception and production.

Participants

The sample is largely formed by females (91.9 percent), representing the largest part of the student body at the Translation and Interpreting College in Barcelona (Universitat Pompeu Fabra) with a mean age of 18.2. In their four-year degree in translation they have two minor languages, French and German, and some of them reportedly learn other languages, such as Arabic, Chinese, Italian, or Portuguese outside university. The curriculum requires them to have a linguistic competence in English at an advanced level (a B2 CEFR) prior to the SA period. It also includes a three-month compulsory SA period in an English-speaking country, the main focus of our study.

Students were invited to collaborate with the project as paid participants. Data were elicited in quiet environments upon appointment. Participant mortality resulted in unwanted heterogeneous samples at different data collection times, particularly when midterm effect of the SA was measured. This affects the comparability of results, as discussed below.

These nonnative speakers' (NNS) performance is compared to that of a group of nineteen undergraduates from the UK and the United States who are native speakers of English (NSs) following an SA exchange program at the Universitat de les Illes Balears. Out of the nineteen NSs, fifteen come from the United States and four from the UK; three are males (17 percent) and fifteen females (83 percent). They were twenty years old on average at the time of data collection. These are clearly highly comparable data, which we used to operationalize language proficiency and as a yardstick against which to measure linguistic gain.

Design

As for the design of the study, the NNS group is followed longitudinally over the course of the first three academic years of their degree and measured at four data collection times. They allow for four different sets of measurements: FI versus SA, SA predeparture versus SA postarrival; SA midterm effects; and, finally, longitudinal development over the course of three years. Such a wealth of possible approaches to the data paves the ground for a thorough examination of SLA and context effects. The baseline group of native speakers is tested once. A total of forty-three NNSs were used in the accuracy analysis—T1 (N = 35), T2 (N = 43), T3 (N = 43), and T4 (N = 13)—and nineteen NSs. For the phonological analysis we used twenty-five NNSs and ten NSs of English. A total of thirty-seven NNNs were used in the written analysis: T1 (N = 35), T2 (N = 37), T3 (N = 37), and T4 (N = 07); and nineteen NSs.

For the EFL group the organization of the degree establishes a continuum with an initial block of FI, followed by the SA period, and then another block of FI. Data collection times are placed along this continuum at the beginning and end of each block. Thus, T1 is the pretest which takes place upon entry to the degree. T2 takes place after eighty hours of formal instruction. T3 takes place after the students' SA program. T1 is thus a pretest while T2 is both a posttest for T1 and a pretest for T3. In turn, T3 is a posttest, and T4 occurs fifteen months later, as a delayed posttest, with another block of eighty hours of FI between. Students travel to their SA destinations in groups of three to five and are distributed in about thirty different institutions. They tend to live in residences, some in flats, very seldom with families. No tutor accompanies them. The program is not a sheltered one. They sometimes find work, and they travel around as much as they can. Exposure to the TL is massive, sociolinguistically varied, and authentic (Kasper and Rose 2002).

Data Collection and Analysis

All tests were specifically designed for this study, piloted and standardized in an attempt to establish the desired level of competence, C1 (CEFR), and to capture the impact of immersion during SA. For accuracy in oral communication, a problem-solving role play was used to gather oral interaction data from peer dyads through a complex two-way negotiating task typical of conventional daily encounters. One of the students acted as a decorator and the other one as a customer. They had to discuss four different living room decorations, accompanied by illustrations, and reach an agreement. All of the digitalized speech was transcribed following CLAN conventions and codified by the researcher with the assistance of an experienced NS English teacher. Mean scores obtained by NSs and NNSs at different points in time on two accuracy indexes, errors per T-Unit (E/T-Unit) and errors per clause (E/C), were compared through ANOVAs and post hoc tests.

For the analysis of written development a composition was used. It was administered as part of a battery of four different tests (including the phonetic test mentioned below) that participants completed in an exam-like situation in the presence of two researchers. Participants were allowed thirty minutes to write on the following topic: "Someone who moves to a foreign country should always adopt the customs and way of life of his/her new country." We measured written development quantitatively in the conventional three domains in which written competence is purportedly reflected: fluency, accuracy, and complexity, both grammatical and lexical (see Celaya, Torras and Pérez-Vidal 2001; Polio 2001; Polio and Gass 1997; Torras et al. 2006; Wolfe-Quintero, Inagaki, and Kim 1998).

Regarding the measures used, words per clause (W/C) were used, as well as words per minute (W/M), a measure found to be efficient by Freed, So, and Lazar (2003). Concurrently, ratios of errors per word (E/W) and the Coordination Index (CI) were used. As for lexical complexity, Guiraud's index of lexical richness has been chosen to counteract the effct of text length (W types/W tokens). Compositions were transcribed following the Computerized Language Analysis (CLAN) conventions with the help of research assistants, and a repeated-measures ANOVA was used to calculate the variance between T3 and T2; between T2 andT1; and between T4 and T3. To contrast L3 learners' performance with NSs, a T-Test was used.

For the phonological analysis, learners' accuracy in perception was assessed through an AXB discrimination task. Three front vowel contrasts ($/i:/–/ɪ/$, $/e/–/æ/$, $/æ/–/ʌ/$), which previous studies (e.g., Cebrian 2006; Escudero and Boersma 2004; Mora and Fullana 2007) have shown to present difficulties for Spanish/Catalan learners of English were embedded in $/kl\_s/$, $/fl\_s/$, $/bl\_s/$ nonwords beginning with permissible onset clusters in Spanish/Catalan. Six realizations of every nonword were used to construct twenty-four triads for each target contrast (A vs. B) presented in four orders ($A_1B_1B_2$, $A_2A_3B_3$, $B_4A_4A_5$, $B_5B_6A_6$) and six randomizations with one-second interstimuli intervals and three-second intertrial intervals. Learners' accuracy in production was assessed by obtaining duration and frequency (Hz) measurements of tokens of the vowels in the AXB task elicited through a reading-aloud task (114-word text in English). Vowel duration and formant frequency (Hz) measurements (F0–F3) from all elicited /i:/, /ɪ/, /e/, /æ/, and /ʌ/tokens (3, 7, 4, 5, 5, respectively, embedded in the stressed syllable of lexical words) were obtained. Frequency values were subsequently converted to barks (B; an auditory scale of frequency representation), and a bark-distance normalization procedure (Syrdal and Gopal 1986) was used to obtain speaker-independent representations of vowel height (B1–B0) and frontness (B2–B1) for front vowels and to explore differences between data collection times (T1–T2–T3) and subject groups (Bohn and Flege 1990). Duration and frequency differences between the vowels making up each contrast in the AXB task were computed as a means of assessing (a) how different learners' realizations of the contrasting vowels were and (b) how such differences might change over time in the direction of native-speaker norms.

Results and Discussion

Results are displayed and discussed for accuracy in oral communication, written development, and phonological perception and production after an SA period following an FI period, and contrasted with baseline data.

Oral Accuracy Development

Mean scores corresponding to the participants' progress in oral accuracy were analyzed for E/T-Unit and E/C. In both cases NNS scores were submitted to three-factor (i.e., time, cohort, and individual) nested ANOVAs with time as the independent variable and accuracy development as the dependent variable. Post hoc paired tests were subsequently carried out. The comparisons of T1–T2 revealed that no improvement in error rate took place in the AH context. On the contrary, there was an increase in the mean number of errors, rising from 0.39 to 0.48 for E/T-Unit, which reached significance in the case of E/C, as it grew from 0.24 to 0.30 ($p = 0.029$). Significant benefits were restricted to the T2–T3 period, as indicated by a significantly lower number of E/T-Unit and E/C at T3, decreasing from 0.45 to 0.33 ($p = 0.005$) and from 0.28 to 0.19 ($p < 0.001$), respectively, after residence abroad. Improvement registered at T3 remained stable at T4, with practically no variation in mean scores; indeed, figures went from 0.31 to 0.30 and from 0.17 to 0.18, respectively.

When NNS mean accuracy scores at each time of data collection for both E/T-Unit and E/C were compared to NS ones by means of a one-way ANOVA with *time* as a between-group factor, the results were as follows: They revealed significant differences in accuracy performance for both E/T-Unit ($F[4,147] = 15.54, p < 0.001$) and E/C ($F[4,147] = 18.20, p < 0.001$). Post hoc comparisons indicated that NNS behavior significantly differed from that of NSs at all times of data collection and for both measures, as shown in table 10.1. Results revealed a tendency for NNSs to approximate the target norm after SA (i.e., at T3 and T4), although NSs continued to exhibit considerable advantage over NNSs in the area of accuracy, only making occasional performance mistakes.

Table 10.1
Mean Error Rates for E/T-Unit and E/C Measures in NS and NNS Data

	N	E/T-Unit Mean	E/T-Unit SD	E/C Mean	E/C SD
NSs	18	.045	.095	.018	.040
NNSs T1	35	.462*	.265	.297*	.188
NNSs T2	43	.479*	.249	.305*	.152
NNSs T3	43	.337*	.180	.193*	.092
NNSs T4	13	.281*	.146	.168*	.086

*Statistical significance for test figure.

These results have shown that the two contexts examined had different effects on the participants' accuracy. On the one hand, the domestic FI period did not prove beneficial, which may be accounted for by the fact that students practiced the morphosyntactic rules and vocabulary presented in class mostly through discrete-point exercises and writing tasks. This type of practice might have helped them to make the transition from declarative to procedural knowledge, but it was not specific enough to enhance their oral accuracy (DeKeyser 1997). Study abroad, on the other hand, had an overall positive effect on learners' accuracy. It might be surmised that learners were finally able to put into practice the explicitly learned knowledge accrued in the AH setting once abroad (cf. Howard 2001; Isabella and Nishida 2005; Yager 1998), hence activating the process toward a more automatic language response. On the other hand, a longer period of intensified oral practice could have helped learners to avoid errors as their L3 knowledge was advanced but not fully automatized after SA. As for stability in accuracy levels found in the midterm, results for this period, however, need to be interpreted with caution as the sample at T4 was smaller than at previous data-collection times. Finally, learners in this study came closer to NS accuracy norms after SA, suggesting that an SA period fosters a more native-like oral performance, although their performance was still quite far from that of native speakers.

Written Development Data
The analyses of written skills development report on accuracy, fluency, and grammatical and lexical complexity. Mean scores corresponding to the participants' progress in these domains of written competence are displayed in table 10.2 for W/C, W/M, E/W, CI, and GI. In all cases NNS scores were submitted to a repeated measures ANOVA with time as the within-subject factor and each of the measures as dependent variables. The analysis of variance between T1 and T2 revealed that no significant improvement took place in the AH context but rather that some significant losses appeared. Hence, fluency in terms of W/M, albeit not in W/C, yielded a significant loss, and so did the participants' lexical repertoire. Losses were also revealed for syntactic complexity, in that learners were using more coordinates than subordinates, yet not significantly. It was only in the area of accuracy that a slight improvement showed, with a decrease in the mean number of errors. As happened with oral communication, and in contrast with phonological development, as

Table 10.2
Mean Written Scores in Fluency, Accuracy, and Complexity

	T1	T2	T2	T3	T3	T4
Measures	(N = 37/37)		(N = 35/37)		(N = 07/07)	
Fluency: W/C	7.30	6.88	6.82	6.90	7.96	8.70
Fluency: W/M	8.67	6.73* ($p = 0.012$)	6.65	8.47* ($p = 0.07$)**	9.12	9.03
Accuracy: E/W	0.06	0.05	0.05	0.04	0.033	0.032
Complexity: CI	20.16	32.89	32.59	20.31	37.14	45.04
Complexity: GI	8.01	7.35* ($p = 0.013$)	7.37	7.96* ($p = 0.000$)	7.90	7.80

*$p<.05$
**$p<.01$

described below, significant benefits were restricted to the T2–T3 period, as indicated by a significantly higher number of W/M, though not significant for W/C, and a significant improvement in the participants' lexical repertoire after residence abroad. In the domain of accuracy, the tendency toward improvement, which had already started at T2, steadily continued at T3. Grammatical complexity also tended to improve, as subordinates increased, in contrast with what had happened in the T1–T2 period. Finally, and in contrast to development in oral accuracy, improvement registered at T3 did not remain stable at T4. It rather receded. T4 results, however, need to take into account the small size of the sample; hence, they have to be interpreted with the greatest caution. Fluency went down in terms of W/M; however, it kept improving as far as W/C went. This seems to indicate that the participants' efforts at clause length took place at the expense of text length. Accuracy and complexity results showed losses, although nonsignificant.

In sum, the SA period results in significant progress in written fluency and lexical complexity and likewise in considerable improvement especially in accuracy but also in grammatical complexity, in contrast with the FI period. After FI, students write less fluent texts, which are slightly more accurate yet less complex, irrespective of the fact that instruction involved specific training in writing skills. In contrast, after the SA, students write longer texts and clauses, with fewer errors per words and richer lexis. Hence, they write more fluently and in more accurate and complex language than at T2. No reported explicit training in written skills took place during SA. Hence, two interpretations might be put forward at this point. First, it could be argued that the extensive amounts of oral practice typical of SA are transferred to competence in writing. Second, it could be claimed that the predeparture writing instruction students obtain and begin to proceduralize at home starts to automatize while abroad, as DeKeyser (2007) contends. Our results are also consistent with our own measures of oral development and with a substantial body of literature on SA, as summarized above. Surprisingly, the NNS group's written performance could be compared to that of NSs' as far as fluency is concerned; conversely, the NSs proved to behave differently from expected in the use of subordination (Pérez-Vidal and Juan-Garau 2009). Regarding fluency, rhetorical verbosity is a possible explanation for these results. That is, either the verbose nature of Spanish rhetoric is transferred to English by our subjects, or "quantity" in writing is the strategy they use to enhance their written performance.

Phonological Development

We finally turn to the analyses of the impact of SA on learners' accuracy in the perception and production of the English vowel contrasts /i:/–/ɪ/, /e/–/æ/, /æ/–/ʌ/. The results obtained for perception, despite the very high scores obtained (90–96 percent), show a consistent trend (see table 10.3), discrimination scores always increasing during the FI period (between T1 and T2). This is contrary to what we expected but consistent with the results obtained by previous research (Díaz-Campos 2004; Mora 2008, for perception). A series of ANOVAs confirmed a significant overall effect for Time (T1–T2–T3) for /i:/–/ɪ/ (*F*[2, 22] = 3.65), discrimination scores significantly improving only in the FI (T1–T2) period (*p* = .043).

As for production, an analysis of the duration and frequency measurements (F1 and F2 in Barks) of the /i:/–/ɪ/, /e/–/æ/, /æ/–/ʌ/ vowel tokens revealed that most of the vowels NNSs produced differed from those of NSs both in duration and quality. As table 10.4 shows, NNSs' /i:/s present a lower (higher B1) and less front (lower B2) place of articulation than those of the NSs in this study. Similarly, whereas NSs distinguish the tense-lax pair /i:/–/ɪ/ on the basis of vowel height and frontness (/ɪ/ is lower and centralized), NNSs produce both /i:/ and /ɪ/ with almost identical frequency (B1 and B2) values, suggesting that when producing target /i:/ and /ɪ/, they were in fact producing the same vowel. This was in fact confirmed by a series of t-tests, which revealed that NNSs' /i:/ and /ɪ/ did not significantly differ in duration, height, and frontness. Similarly, /æ/ and /ʌ/ were found not to differ in height. As far as duration is concerned, NNSs produced a longer /ɪ/ than NSs and implemented the /i:/–/ɪ/ contrast with a much shorter duration difference (20 ms) than NSs (40 ms).

A series of ANOVAs on the B1, B2, and duration differences between the vowel pairs /i:/–/ɪ/, /e/–/æ/, /æ/–/ʌ/ and the B1–B0 (vowel height) and B2–B1 (vowel frontness) difference metrics yielded a general overall significant improvement in vowel height (B1–B0) and frontness (B2–B1) in the direction of native-speaker norms. Differences in duration between vowels in contrasting pairs did not undergo significant changes. However, when significant changes over time occur, they occur almost exclusively in the FI (T1–T2) period (see table 10.4), which would seem to suggest, in accordance with the perception data presented above, that the FI period had a greater

Table 10.3

Mean Percent Correct Discrimination (SD in Parentheses) in the AXB Discrimination Task

Mean %		PhC1 /ɪ/–/i:/	PhC2 /e/–/æ/	PhC3 /æ/–/ʌ/	Vs
Valid Subjects at T3 (N = 24)	T1	90.80 (9.66)	90.66 (8.15)	91.22 (7.74)	90.90 (7.46)
	T2	96.72 (4.44)	93.60 (7.97)	95.53 (6.4)	95.28 (5.36)
	T3	94 (7.6)	91.33 (8.06)	93.5 (7.89)	92.94 (4.97)

■ Table 10.4
Normalized Mean Vowel Height (B1–B0[1]) and Frontness (B2–B1[2]) Frequencies in Barks and Duration (in ms) at T1, T2, and T3.

	Time	V1 /iː/	V2 /ɪ/	V3 /e/	V4 /æ/	V5 /ʌ/
B1–B0	T1	2.83	3.12	5.04	5.38	5.70
	T2	2.49*	2.61**	4.65*	4.95***	5.22***
	T3	2.34	2.34	4.22**	4.68	4.78
	NSs	1.87	3.03	5.75	5.91	5.37**
B2–B1	T1	8.21	8.04	5.57	3.84	3.97
	T2	9.33**	8.68*	6.27*	4.13	4.28*
	T3	9.27	8.78	6.39	4.13	4.66
	NSs	10.65	7.50	4.87	4.09	4.37
Duration	T1	126	106	129	126	116
	T2	125	103	129	129	114
	T3	117	95	127	119	108
	NSs	124	84	116	135	109

Notes: 1. Lower values represent a higher tongue position.
2. Higher values represent a more advanced tongue position.
Asterisks indicate significant differences at T2 (with respect to T1) and T3 (with respect to T2): $* = p < .05$; $** = p < .01$; $*** = p < .001$.

impact on vowel-production accuracy. Furthermore, frequency changes seem to affect vowel quality in general and do not result in NNSs producing the vowel pairs /iː/–/ɪ/, /e/–/æ/, and /æ/–/ʌ/ with more distinct vowel quality and duration.

A possible explanation for the unexpected results obtained in the analysis of the perception and production data is that a short-term SA period may not provide enough experience with L2 sounds to be able to effect changes in the learners' ability to perceive and produce L2 vowel contrasts. The attentional focus of the learner may be directed toward other areas of communicative competence in an SA situation and gains in perceptual ability may need special focused practice, as the outcome of phonetic training studies suggests (e.g., Aliaga-Garcia and Mora 2009; Bradlow et al. 1999; Iverson, Hazan, and Bannister 2005).

Summary and Conclusions

Turning to our three research questions, our study indicates that an SA period results in clear benefits in oral accuracy and written competence, hence questions one and two can be answered positively. For these two domains, although benefits only became apparent abroad, it can be assumed that the AH and the SA contexts have both supported gains in oral accuracy and general written ability, albeit differentially— the former by providing learners with a solid grammatical and lexical foundation and academic written practice that would bear fruit later on, and the latter by allowing learners to participate in abundant complex communicative situations that helped them in most cases both boost their oral performance, thus making it more accurate, and improve their written skills.

A somewhat different picture is provided by the results we obtain on phonological development; hence, research question three must be answered negatively. A short-term SA period may not provide enough input or sufficient focused practice with L2 sounds for the learners' phonological competence to develop noticeably.

These findings seem to point at the importance of three variables in SA program design: initial level of competence, length of SA program, and nature of academic practice. It can be inferred that a predeparture advanced competence level allows for benefits to accrue in areas such as oral accuracy and writing during a three-month SA program. However, in domains that seem to require more focused attention, such as phonological perception and production, a longer SA period might be needed for improvement to be obtained. We can conclude by stating that our results throw new light on two areas that had received little attention and for which expectations are not generally very high, accuracy in oral proficiency and written competence. Future research must acknowledge that domains that are intrinsic to academic work, namely accuracy in oral production and writing, seem to improve from the natural immersion conditions of SA. Our findings also confirm prior results as far as pronunciation and phonological development. In such a vein, it is relevant to quote the following words by DeKeyser (2007, 212): "The skills that students have acquired abroad may be both overestimated and underestimated, depending on what is assessed and how."

ACKNOWLEDGMENTS

This research received financial support through HUM2007-66053-C02-01 and 02/FILO and ALLENCAM (2005 SGR 01086) from the Spanish Ministry of Education and the Catalan government, respectively. We would like to sincerely thank Robert DeKeyser for his unfailing encouragement and his most invaluable comments on an earlier version of this paper. We would like to acknowledge Jaume Llopis's assistance with statistics, and Teodora Mehotcheva and Margalida Valls's support.

REFERENCES

Aliaga-García, Cristina, and Joan C. Mora. 2009. Assessing the effects of phonetic training on L2 sound perception and production. In *Recent Research in Second Language Phonetics/Phonology: Perception and Production,* ed. Michael A. Watkins, Andréia S. Rauber, and Barbara O. Baptista, 2–31. Newcastle upon Tyne, UK: Cambridge Scholars Publishing.

Bohn, Ocke-Schwen, and James E. Flege. 1990. Interlingual identification and the role of foreign language experience in L2 vowel perception. *Applied Psycholinguistics* 11:303–28.

Bradlow, Anne R., Reiko Akahane-Yamada, David B. Pisoni, and Yoh'ichi Tohkura. 1999. Training Japanese listeners to identify English /r/ and /l/: Long-term retention of learning in perception and production. *Perception & Psychophysics* 61:977–85.

Cebrian, Juli. 2006. Experience and the use of non-native duration in L2 vowel categorization. *Journal of Phonetics* 34:372–87.

Celaya, María-Luz, Rosa-Maria Torras, and Carmen Pérez-Vidal. 2001. Short and mid-term effects of an earlier start: An analysis of EFL Written Production. In *EUROSLA Yearbook 1,* ed. Susan H. Foster-Cohen and Anna Nizegorodcew, 195–209. Amsterdam: John Benjamins.

Collentine, Joseph. 2004. The effects of learning context on morphosyntactic and lexical development. *Studies in Second Language Acquisition* 26:227–48.

Collentine, Joseph, and Barbara F. Freed. 2004. Learning context and its effects on second language acquisition: Introduction. *Studies in Second Language Acquisition* 26:153–71.

DeKeyser, Robert M. 1986. *From Learning to Acquisition. Foreign Language Development in a US Classroom and during a Semester Abroad.* PhD diss., Stanford, CA: Stanford University.

———. 1991. Foreign language development during a semester abroad. In *Foreign Language Acquisition: Research and the classroom,* ed. Barbara F. Freed, 104–19. Lexington, MA: D.C. Heath.

———. 1997. Beyond explicit rule learning. *Studies in Second Language Acquisition* 19:195–221.

———. 2007. Study abroad as foreign language practice. In *Practice in a second language: Perspectives from applied linguistics and cognitive psychology,* ed. Robert DeKeyser, 208–26. Cambridge: Cambridge University Press.

Díaz-Campos, Manuel. 2004. Context of learning in the acquisition of Spanish second language phonology. *Studies in Second Language Acquisition* 26:249–73.

DuFon, Margaret A., and Eton Churchill. 2006. *Language learners in study abroad contexts.* Clevedon, UK: Multilingual Matters.

Escudero, Paola, and Paul Boersma. 2004. Bridging the gap between L2 speech perception research and phonological theory. *Studies in Second Language Acquisition* 26:551–85.

Freed, Barbara F. 1995. What makes us think that students who study abroad become fluent? In *Second Language Acquisition in a Study Abroad Context,* ed. Barbara F. Freed, 123–48. Amsterdam: John Benjamins.

Freed, Barbara F., Norman Segalowitz, and Dan Dewey. 2004. Context of learning and second language fluency in French: Comparing regular classroom, study abroad and intensive domestic immersion programs. *Studies in Second Language Acquisition* 26:275–301.

Freed, Barbara F., Sufumi So, and Nicole A. Lazar. 2003. Language learning abroad: How do gains in written fluency compare with oral fluency in French as a second language? *ADFL Bulletin* 34:34–40.

Højen, Anders. 2003. *Second language speech perception and production in adult learners before and after short-term immersion.* PhD diss., University of Aarhus.

Howard, Martin. 2001. The effects of study abroad on L2 learners' structural skills. In *EUROSLA Yearbook 1,* ed. Susan H. Foster-Cohen and Anna Nizegorodcew, 123–41. Amsterdam: John Benjamins.

Isabelli, Casilda A. 2001. *The impact of a study abroad experience on the acquisition of L2 Spanish syntax: The null subject parameter.* PhD diss., University of Illinois at Urbana–Champaign.

Isabelli, Casilde A., and Chiyo Nishida. 2005. Development of Spanish subjunctive in a nine-month study-abroad setting. In *Selected Proceedings of the 6th Conference on the Acquisition of Spanish and Portuguese as First and Second Languages,* ed. David Eddington, 78–91. Somerville, MA: Cascadilla Press.

Iverson, Paul, Valerie Hazan, and Kerry Bannister. 2005. Phonetic training with acoustic cue manipulations: A comparison of methods for teaching English /r/–/l/ to Japanese adults. *Journal of the Acoustical Society of America* 118:3267–78.

Juan-Garau, Maria, and Carmen Pérez-Vidal. 2007. The effect of context and contact on oral performance in students who go on a stay abroad. *Vigo International Journal of Applied Linguistics* 4:117–35.

Kasper, Gabi, and Keith Rose 2002. *Pragmatic development in a second language.* Oxford: Blackwell.

Lafford, Barbara. 2004. The effect of context of learning (classroom vs. study abroad) on the use of communication strategies by learners of Spanish as a second language. *Studies in Second Language Acquisition* 26 (2): 201–26.

López-Ortega, Nuria. 2002. *The development of discourse competence in study abroad learners: A study of subject expression in Spanish as a second language.* PhD diss., University of Cincinnati.

Milton, James, and Paul Meara. 1995. How periods abroad affect vocabulary growth in a foreign language. *ITL Review of Applied Linguistics* 107–108:17–34.

Mora, Joan C. 2008. Learning context effects on the acquisition of a second language phonology. In *A portrait of the young in the new multilingual Spain,* ed. Carmen Pérez-Vidal, Maria Juan-Garau, and Aurora Bel, 241–63. Clevedon, UK: Multilingual Matters.

Mora, Joan C., and Natalia Fullana. 2007. Production and perception of English /ɪ/–/iː/ and /Θ/–/ʝ/ in a formal setting: Investigating the effects of experience and starting age. In *Proceedings of the 16th International Congress of Phonetic Sciences,* ed. Jürgen Trouvain and William J. Barry, 1613–16. Saarbrücken, Germany: Universität des Saarlandes.

Pérez-Vidal, Carmen, and Maria Juan-Garau. 2009. The effect of study abroad (SA) on written performance. In *Eurosla Yearbook 9,* ed. Leah Roberts, Daniel Véronique, Anna-Carin Nilsson, and Marion Tellier, 270–96. Amsterdam: John Benjamins.

Polio, Charlene G. 2001. Review of second language development in writing: Measures of fluency, accuracy and complexity. *Studies in Second Language Acquisition* 23:423–25.

Polio, Charlene G., and Susan Gass. 1997. Replication and reporting: A commentary. *Studies in Second Language Acquisition* 19:499–508.

Regan, Vera. 1998. Sociolinguistics and language learning in a study abroad context. *Frontiers: The Interdisciplinary Journal of Study Abroad* 4:61–91.

Sasaki, Miyuki. 2004. A multiple-data analysis of the 3.5-year development of EFL student writers. *Language Learning* 54:525–82.

———. 2007. Effects of Study-Abroad experiences on EFL writers: A multiple-data analysis. *The Modern Language Journal* 91:602–20.

Segalowitz, Norman, and Barbara F. Freed. 2004. Context, contact, and cognition in oral fluency acquisition: Learning Spanish in at home and study abroad contexts. *Studies in Second Language Acquisition* 26:173–99.

Syrdal, Ann K., and H. S. Gopal. 1986. A perceptual model of vowel recognition based on the auditory representation of American English vowels. *Journal of the Acoustical Society of America* 79:1086–1100.

Torras, Maria-Rosa, Teresa Navés, María-Luz Celaya, and Carmen Pérez-Vidal. 2006. Age and IL development in writing. In *Age and the rate of foreign language learning,* ed. Carmen Muñoz, 156–82. Clevedon, UK: Multilingual Matters.

Torres, Jenna P. 2003. *A cognitive approach to the acquisition of clitics in Spanish: Insights from study abroad and classroom learners.* PhD diss., Cornell University.

Towell, Richard, Roger Hawkins, and Nives Bazergui. 1996. The development of fluency in advanced learners of French. *Applied Linguistics* 17:84–119.

Wolfe-Quintero, Kate, Shunji Inagaki, and Hae-Young Kim. 1998. *Second language development in writing: Measures of fluency, accuracy and complexity. Technical Report 17.* Manoa: University of Hawai'i Press.

Yager, Kent. 1998. Learning Spanish in Mexico: The effect of informal contact and student attitude on language gain. *Hispania* 81:898–911.

11

Input Processing Principles: A Contribution from First-Exposure Data

REBEKAH RAST
The American University of Paris and UMR 7023 (CNRS)

THIS CHAPTER ADDRESSES learners' processing of linguistic input at the absolute beginning of the second language acquisition experience.[1] Its content emerges from the question: What do adult language learners *do* with the target language (TL) input they receive? In VanPatten's (2002) response to DeKeyser et al. (2002), he writes, "I would like to end where we all seem to converge: Namely, if we all agree about the fundamental role of input in acquisition, then we need to look at *what* learners do to input, *why* they do it, and *what insights* this may provide for instruction if any" (828). The data presented here, collected from French learners of Polish upon initial exposure, contribute to our understanding of these learner processes, notably how and why some TL input becomes part of the learner's language system and some does not. In addition, the data speak to the question of what helps a learner perceive, comprehend, and/or (re)produce a particular input item. VanPatten's research over the past two decades (e.g., VanPatten 1996, 2002, 2004, 2007) seeks to understand the mechanisms underlying these processes and to identify learning activities that will aid learners in processing and using information in the TL environment. His framework for doing this involves Input Processing (IP), a theoretical model, and Processing Instruction (PI), an instructional technique informed by IP. This chapter focuses on IP, and in particular on two IP principles, the Primacy of Content Words Principle and the Sentence Location Principle. It examines these principles in light of data collected within the first seconds, minutes, and hours of exposure to a novel TL.

Theoretical Background

Aspects of the question, What do adult language learners *do* with the TL input they receive?, have been scrutinized in the fields of SLA and psycholinguistics for some time. Some research programs have investigated processes in language acquisition such as detection, noticing, awareness, and attention (cf. for example Ellis 2006; Robinson 2003; Schmidt 2001), whereas others have focused on how learners extract form from the input, or rather, parse utterances when attempting to comprehend the TL speech stream (cf. Carroll 2001). VanPatten's (1996, 2004) work is largely centered on the latter. His IP model consists of principles and subprinciples that seek to explain how learners make form-meaning connections. An important aspect of his research program is the fact that his IP model informs his instructional technique (PI). For any instructional technique or method to be considered a reliable pedagogical tool, the principles it derives from must be tested and proven as sound. This is where the debate begins.

The principles of VanPatten's IP model have been tested by empirical research. Consider the Primacy of Meaning Principle: "Learners process input for meaning before they process it for form" (VanPatten 2004, 14). Cadierno (1995) argues that learners tend to rely on adverbial markers of tense (e.g., "today") as indicators of temporal reference and that this delays their processing of verb inflections of tense to make form-meaning connections. Likewise, a study by Lee et al. (1997) suggests that although beginning learners detect grammatical cues, lexical cues are more useful for processing semantic information and reconstructing propositional content. Concerning the Sentence Location Principle (SLP), by means of a sentence repetition task, Barcroft and VanPatten (1997) found that, for beginning English learners of Spanish, utterance-initial items were more acoustically salient than medial or final positions, and that stress increased the chance of a word being repeated. Similarly, Klein's (1986) study on sentence repetitions reveals a privileged role for initial and final positions. In a critique of VanPatten's IP model, DeKeyser et al. (2002) claim that in the model, key cognitive constructs are inappropriately defined and operationalized, and therefore serve as a "poor basis for interpreting the findings of the PI approach they are claimed to motivate" (806).

SLA research has offered minimal information about how learners process input at the very beginning of the L2 acquisition process, resulting in uncertainty as to how learners process *initial* input (or process input *initially*). Given that VanPatten's IP is viewed as "an initial step in the creation of a linguistic system" (2002, 242), any and all data that speak to this "initial step" should be considered, and data collected from different target and source language combinations should be added to the configuration.

One way to study what learners do with their input is to compare the input to which they are exposed with their performance on tasks in the TL. The procedures of controlling and measuring the input from the moment of first exposure to the TL become crucial in this approach. Given the methodological challenges posed by studying natural languages, artificial languages have often been developed for this means (e.g., Hudson Kam and Newport 2005; Hulstijn and DeKeyser 1997; Reber 1967). More recently, natural language data have been collected from adults at first exposure to a novel target language and/or within the first minutes and hours of acquisition (cf. Carroll 2008; Gullberg et al. 2009; Han and Sun 2009; Park and Han 2008; Rast 2008; Zwitserlood et al. 2000).[2]

In the present study the TL input was completely controlled and documented, with a view to observing its role in L2 perception, comprehension, grammatical analysis, and eventually acquisition. The term "input processing" here refers to what the learners do with this input, that is, perceive, notice, segment, convert a stimulus into a message, parse, and map form to meaning or meaning to form. It entails more than what Schmidt (1990, 129) refers to as the "necessary and sufficient condition for converting input to intake," namely noticing. It includes also subliminal or incidental perception (with no assumption as to whether or not this leads to learning) as well as comprehension. This differs from, but yet encompasses, VanPatten's use of the term Input Processing, which, in his research refers to learners' connecting a form with its meaning and/or function (VanPatten 2004, 9). The present article sets out to examine, through the lens of first-exposure data, VanPatten's IP model, namely two sub-principles of the Primacy of Meaning Principle, that is, Principle 1a, "Learners process content words in the input before anything else"; and New Principle P1f, "Learners tend to process items in sentence initial position before those in final position and these latter in turn before those in medial position" (2004, 14).

The Study

This section presents the methodology and relevant results of a study of French learners of Polish at the very early stages of adult foreign language acquisition.

Methodology

The data presented in this article were collected from two distinct types of participants:

- French learners of Polish attending a specially designed Polish course ("learners").
- French speakers for whom the only Polish input was that provided during the language task ("first-exposure participants").

All participants were university students who had had no contact with Polish at the onset of the study. Those in first-exposure groups performed no more than one test each to avoid a cumulative effect of exposure.

The specially designed Polish course was held once a week for six weeks, totaling eight contact hours not including testing time. To fully document the TL input, the Polish instructor wore a microphone, and all class sessions were recorded. Recordings were transcribed using the CHILDES programs (MacWhinney 2000); these transcriptions represent the input referred to in this article. The instructor used the communicative approach in the classroom, avoided grammatical explanations, and asked students not to consult dictionaries, grammar books, or any outside input for the duration of the project.

The data reported on here were collected by means of two tests, namely a sentence repetition test and a sentence translation test. During the sentence repetition test, participants listened to 17 Polish sentences, a total of 113 words (see appendix).[3] Sentences were spoken only once, and participants were asked to repeat them as best they could. During the sentence translation test, participants listened to the same set of sentences used for the sentence repetitions; however, in this case, participants were told to listen to the sentences and to write, in French, the translation equivalent of the words they thought they understood. They also heard the sentences only once.

The sentence repetition test was administered to a group of first-exposure participants (referred to as Period 0h00) (n = 8) and to our group of learners after four hours of exposure to Polish (Period 4h00) and again after eight hours (Period 8h00) (n = 8). The sentence translation test was taken by a group of first-exposure participants only (n = 9).

Data Analysis Procedures

We analyzed the sentence repetition data at the level of the word, examining correct repetitions of words in the sentences, as well as words that were not repeated at all. Two criteria were used to identify a correct repetition: (a) The number of syllables in the repeated word had to be the same as the number of syllables found in the original word to be repeated. (b) Only one phoneme per syllable could be repeated incorrectly. If a repetition did not meet these two criteria, as determined by a native Polish speaker, it was not counted as a correct repetition. We did not investigate in detail the words that were repeated incorrectly; however, we calculated the number of words that were not repeated at all by participants, allowing for an alternative analysis of the results.

We also analyzed the sentence translation data at the level of the word. Criteria for a correct translation were as follows: When the translation carried the same meaning as the Polish word, regardless of its grammatical form, the word was judged as a correct translation. For example, if a participant heard the Polish word *studentem*, meaning "étudiant" (student), and responded "étudie" (study), the response was coded as correct even though the word class was incorrect. False cognates were not counted as correct translations.

Hypotheses

We begin by examining VanPatten's Principle 1a, "Learners process content words in the input before anything else" (2004, 14). When considering the question of how learners make form–meaning connections upon initial contact with the TL, we need to examine all factors that could potentially aid learners in doing this. The category "content words" is one factor of interest. We understand from VanPatten (1996) that what he called content words are meaningful lexical items and that the term "noncontent words" refers to functional items such as prepositions, articles, and pronouns. Given that the categories "content word" and "noncontent word" may be irrelevant categories for a learner with no knowledge of the TL in question (with the exception of TL words that are lexically transparent with respect to another language known to the learner), we opted for analyses of the effect of word stress and word length on initial perception/repetition and comprehension/translation. These factors have been shown to affect learners' ability to perceive items in the input in that they increase the salience of the item (cf. Barcroft and VanPatten 1997; Carroll 2004a; Rast and Dommergues 2003). As VanPatten (2004, 8) points out, "In most natural languages, content lexical items tend to receive stronger stress than noncontent items." We also know that noncontent words tend to be short words, or "little words," as VanPatten (2004, 14) describes them. We therefore examined the overall effect of word stress and word length on participants' ability to repeat and translate Polish words. The words in the Polish sentences were grouped as follows: (a) unstressed (n = 55) − content and noncontent words; (b) stressed (n = 58) − content words only; (c) zero-to-one syllable (n = 48) − noncontent words only; (d) two syllable (n = 37) − content words except for one token of *ale* "but"; (e) three-to-six syllable" (n = 28) − content words only. If VanPatten's Principle 1a holds for our participants, we would expect words in the stressed group to be better repeated and translated than those in the unstressed group, and the longer two-to-six-syllable words to be better repeated and translated than the short zero-to-one-syllable words.

Also of interest to our study is VanPatten's New Principle P1f, "Learners tend to process items in sentence initial position before those in final position and these latter in turn before those in medial position" (2004, 14). Results of our two tests were analyzed with respect to the three possible word positions in a sentence: initial (n = 17), medial (n = 79), and final (n = 17). If this principle holds for our participants, we would expect words in sentence initial position to be better repeated and translated than words in final position, and words in medial position to show the most difficulty.

Results

In this section, results will be provided for three factors: word stress, word length, and position of the word in the sentence.[4] For each of these factors, three types of analyses have been conducted: (a) words repeated correctly during the sentence repetition test (more detailed information appears in Rast 2008);[5] (b) words not repeated during the sentence repetition test; and (c) words translated correctly during the sentence translation test.

Word stress. Rast and Dommergues (2003) found that more participants repeated stressed words (content words only) than unstressed words (content and noncontent words combined). As a follow-up, we analyzed the same sentence repetition data from a different perspective and investigated words that were not repeated by any participant at any period. In this case, if Principle 1a holds, we would expect to find more unstressed words not repeated than stressed words. This was precisely our result, as shown in figure 11.1. We found a significant difference between stressed and unstressed words at all periods: $F(2,224) = 43.717, p < .01$.

We asked a new group of first-exposure participants to translate our Polish sentences into their native French. We did not administer this test to our learners and, consequently, have results from Period 0h00 only. As with the sentence repetitions, correct translations were measured as a function of word stress with two stressed

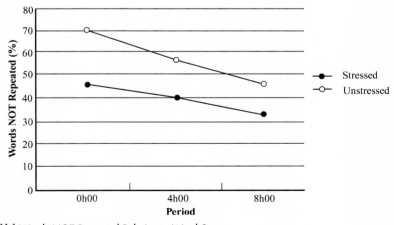

Figure 11.1 Words NOT Repeated Relative to Word Stress

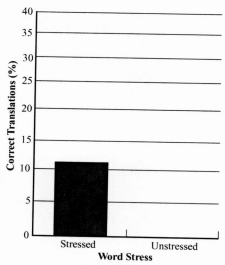

░ Figure 11.2 Words Translated Correctly Relative to Word Stress

values, stressed and unstressed. Results presented in figure 11.2 show a main effect of stress on our participants' ability to translate the Polish words, $F(1,111) = 17.557$, $p < .01$.[6]

In fact, no unstressed words were correctly translated, including the unstressed content words. Some, but not all, of the stressed words (content words only) were translated. Taken together, the results of the sentence repetition and translation tests provide partial support for VanPatten's Principle 1a in that content words are often stressed, and this stress seems to aid processing. It follows that the stress–unstressed distinction may be as necessary as the content–noncontent distinction at this early level of L2 acquisition.

Word length. We hypothesized that not only word stress but also word length would affect the processing of content vs. noncontent words. Rast and Dommergues (2003) found that the length of the word as measured in syllables did not appear to play a significant role in the ability of participants to correctly repeat the word. Using the same data, we conducted a two-way ANOVA (with word length as an intergroup factor and periods as repeated measures) to examine the effect of word length on words that were *not* repeated by our participants at any given period (figure 11.3).

Although results showed no overall effect of word length across periods, $F(2,110) = 2.4$, *n.s.*, a PLSD Fisher comparison revealed a slight effect of word length at Period 0h00 only, due to the difference between zero-to-one-syllable words and two-syllable words and between zero-to-one-syllable words and three-to-six-syllable words ($p < .05$ in both cases). Not surprisingly, the zero-to-one-syllable words showed fewer repetitions at Period 0h00 than the longer words. Given that the zero-to-one-syllable group comprised only noncontent words, these results are in line with VanPatten's Principle 1a. We then looked at the results of the sentence translation test

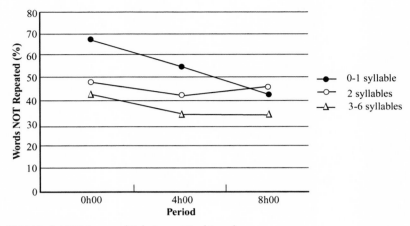

Figure 11.3 Words NOT Repeated Relative to Word Length

with regard to sentence length. Figure 11.4 shows the distribution of correct translations of the 113 words categorized into three word-length groups.

A one-way ANOVA confirmed a significant effect of word length, $F(2,110) =$ 7.2, $p < 0.01$, on correct translations. A PLSD Fisher analysis revealed no significant difference between the zero-to-one-syllable group and the two-syllable group but did show a significant difference between the zero-to-one-syllable group and the three-to-six-syllable group, as well as between the two-syllable group and the three-to-six-syllable group ($p < .01$ in both cases). In other words, the length of the word as measured in syllables appeared to play a role in the ability of our participants to

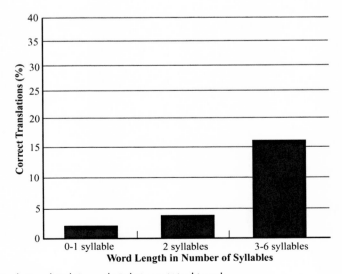

Figure 11.4 Words Translated Correctly Relative to Word Length

correctly translate a word at first-exposure, three-to-six-syllable words showing a higher success rate than two-syllable words and zero-to-one-syllable words. Given that, together, the two-syllable group and the zero-to-one-syllable group contained content and noncontent words, we are unable to comment on the effect of word length on participants' ability at first exposure to translate content and noncontent words. We highlight, however, that word length does seem to affect learners' processing at the initial stage and should, therefore, be taken into consideration in our models of input processing.

Word position. Rast and Dommergues (2003) found a significant effect of position on correct sentence repetitions due to the differences between both initial and medial, and medial and final positions ($p < .05$ in both cases), but not between initial and final. Again, using the same data, we investigated words that were *not* repeated and also found a main effect of position, $F(2,110) = 8.6, p < .01$ (see fig. 11.5).

In line with the findings from correct repetitions, a PLSD analysis revealed that this main effect was due to the difference between initial and medial, and medial and final positions ($p < .05$ in both cases). No significant difference was found between initial and final positions. These results provide support for the assumption in Van-Patten's Principle 1f that learners tend to process items in sentence initial and final position before those in medial position. They do not, however, provide support for the assumption that learners process items in sentence initial position before those in final position. With regard to sentence translations, a one-way ANOVA confirmed a significant effect of position on correct translations, $F(2,110) = 17.777, p < .01$. PLSD Fisher comparisons revealed no significant difference between words in initial and medial position but showed a significant difference between words in initial and final, and between words in medial and final positions as shown in figure 11.6; more words in final position were translated correctly.

This said, we examined the interaction between position and transparency (a measure of lexical similarity between French and Polish forms and meanings)[7] and

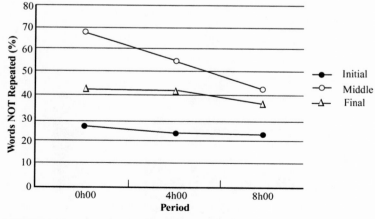

Figure 11.5. Words NOT Repeated Relative to Position in Sentence

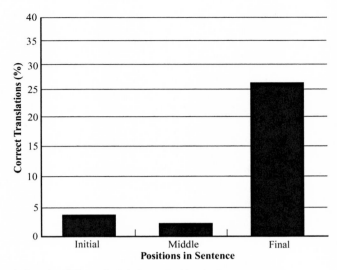

Figure 11.6 Words Translated Correctly Relative to Position in Sentence

found a significant interaction between these two factors, $F(4,104) = 39.440$, $p < .01$. As VanPatten (2004, 19) himself points out, "principles do not operate in isolation." The fact that more transparent words appeared in sentence final position than in sentence initial position in our tests may have influenced our results for initial and final positions. A future study will require more control over factors such as transparency to observe more precisely the effect that each factor has on such a task.

Under normal circumstances, learners' processing final position before initial position would be a surprising result given the amount of research that claims initial position to be the privileged position in sentence processing (cf. Barcroft and VanPatten 1997; Klein 1986). However, given the observed interaction between transparency and position mentioned above, this is less surprising. Indeed, an interesting observation is that this interaction between transparency and position affected repetitions and translations differently. It appears that the combination of very transparent and final position may be a more powerful predictor for translation (comprehension) than for repetition (perception and reproduction). It follows that when formulating theoretical principles of input processing, we need to compute the potential influence of any one factor over another, and this with respect to a given level of processing (perception, comprehension, and so on). Once we identify which factors are involved in input processing, such as position, stress, word length, and transparency, we then need to investigate the relations between these factors as they clearly operate together and not in isolation.

Discussion

Han and Peverly (2007) hypothesize that learners with no existing knowledge of the TL will adopt a form-based approach to input processing. They pose the question:

"What approach, meaning-based or form-based, do absolute beginners use when processing the target language written input for the very first time?" (25). Results of their empirical study (TL Norwegian) revealed that their learners relied more on form than on meaning to process the input, challenging VanPatten's Principle 1. A follow-up study (Han and Sun 2009) confirmed these results. The current study has limitations given the small number of participants. However, taken as a whole, results from studies of *ab initio* learners suggest that juxtaposing a meaning-based and a form-based approach may be missing the point. Beginning learners appear to rely on all of the knowledge they bring to the TL task (cf. Rast 2008; Ringbom 2007). When they are able to latch on to something meaningful, they do so. Something "meaningful" could be in the form of content words or noncontent words, and it could be forms with high or low communicative value. If the only lexical item the learner recognizes is in the middle of the sentence, it may be the only item the learner attends to. The factors we must consider are numerous. With his IP, VanPatten has given us a stimulating launching pad for these discussions. His model appears to be inadequate, however, for explaining the input processing of true beginners of a foreign language. As Carroll (in press) suggests, "Before any of the principles of IP theory can apply, some *other theory of input processing* is required which, we must assume, sets the stage for form-meaning mappings." Given that VanPatten's instructional technique PI is informed by IP and that he refers specifically to initial contact with the given input, we must consider relevant findings and their implications for teaching carefully, in particular the teaching of beginning learners.

Conclusion

This paper presents a selection of results from our study of French learners of Polish at the very first stages of L2 acquisition. By means of sentence repetition and translation tests, we examined two of VanPatten's subprinciples of IP. Analysis revealed that our findings concerning word stress, word length, and word position are not at odds with VanPatten's principles, "Learners process content words in the input before anything else" and "Learners tend to process items in sentence initial position before those in final position and these latter in turn before those in medial position." What needs to be reconsidered, however, for the initial stages of L2 acquisition, is the relevance of categories under investigation. Is it useful for us to examine the processing of content vs. noncontent words at this stage, or should we be looking at the properties of these words (stress, length, position, etc.) and observing to what extent certain properties help learners accomplish a task in the TL? Carroll (2004b, 300) claims that "the relevant properties are in the mind/brain of the learner/listener, not in the signal per se." Regardless of where these properties abide, we need to understand how learners make use of them to analyze the TL input. At first exposure to a novel TL, learners have no knowledge of the TL per se, but they are sensitive to and aided by certain factors, and they make use of knowledge they bring to the TL task. Ultimately, we seek to understand how they manage to segment the sound stream and make some sense of it. And they do manage as I have shown here, a truly phenomenal feat.

APPENDIX 11A

The sentence repetition test and the sentence translation test. (The same sentences were used for both tests.) Stressed words are underlined. Nouns are marked for case (N = nominative; A = accusative; D = dative; G = genitive; I = instrumental; L = locative)

1) Piotr, mieszka w Krakowie, i studiuje informatykę.
   Peter-N lives in Krakow-L and studies computer science-A.

2) Anna jest Włoszką, i mieszka we Włoszech.
   Anna-N is Italian and lives in Italy-L.

3) Nauczyciel zna Marka, i mój brat zna go również.
   (The) teacher-N knows Mark-A and my brother-N knows him-A also.

4) Piotra mama, wykładowcą jest na uniwersytecie.
   Peter-G mother-N teacher-I is at university-L.
   (= Peter's mother is a teacher at the university.)

5) Jestem w Warszawie, i znam ją bardzo dobrze.
   (I) am from Warsaw-L and know it-A very well.

6) Zupę Marek zje chętnie.
   Soup-A Mark-N will eat gladly. (= Mark will gladly eat the soup.)

7) Marek, zna mojego kolegę, i mojego kolegę, zna również mój brat.
   Mark-N knows my colleague-A and my colleague-A knows also my brother-N.
   (= Mark knows my colleague, and my brother also knows my colleague.)

8) Anka i Marek, nie mieszkają w Krakowie, ale znają go dobrze.
   Anka-N and Mark-N not live in Krakow-L but know it-A well.
   (= Anka and Mark do not live in Krakow, but they know it well.)

9) Juan jest Hiszpanem, i mówi świetnie po polsku.
   Juan-N is Spanish and speaks brilliantly in Polish.

10) Lekarz, nie zna mojego kolegi.
    Doctor-N not knows my colleague-G. (= The doctor does not know my colleague.)

11) Piwa napije się Piotr.
    Beer-G will drink himself Peter-N. (= Peter will drink a beer.)

12) Lekarza, zna mój kolega.
    Doctor-A knows my colleague-N. (= My colleague knows the doctor.)

13) Książkę mojego kolegi, zna Piotr bardzo dobrze.
    Book-A my colleague-G knows Peter-N very well.
    (= Peter knows my colleague's book very well.)

14) Podchodzi kelner do Jacka.
    Approaches waiter-N to James-G. (= The waiter approaches James.)

15) Mojego nauczyciela zna moja mama.
    My teacher-A knows my mother-N. (= My mother knows my teacher.)

16) <u>Piotr</u>, <u>Marii</u>, i <u>Jackowi</u>, opowiada <u>film</u>.

Peter-N Marie-D and James-D tells (about) film-A.

(= Peter tells Marie and James about the film.)

17) <u>Marek</u> jest <u>studentem</u>, i mieszka w <u>Krakowie</u>.

Mark-N is (a) student-I and lives in Krakow-L.

NOTES

1. I wish to thank ZhaoHong Han for inviting me to participate in the panel "Learner spontaneous processing of input" at *GURT 2009* and ultimately inspiring this article. I also thank other members of the panel and an anonymous reviewer for their insightful comments. I will be forever grateful to Jean-Yves Dommergues, Marzena Wątorek, and Clive Perdue for their contributions to task development, data collection, and data analysis for this extensive project. Correspondence concerning this article should be addressed to Rebekah Rast, The American University of Paris, 147 rue de Grenelle, 75007 Paris, France. E-mail: rrast@aup.fr.

2. Barcroft and VanPatten's (1997, 109) study is concerned with "the acoustic salience of L2 grammatical forms at the initial stages of input processing." It is important to note that their learners were adult native English speakers with "no more than two years of high school Spanish" (the TL for their study). This implies that some learners may have had as much as two years of exposure to the TL, much more than participants in a first-exposure study.

3. The original test comprised twenty sentences; three were eliminated from the final analysis.

4. Due to an insufficient number of types of noncontent words in our stimuli, we did not conduct statistical analyses on content and noncontent words per se.

5. Due to space constraints, we have not reprinted results of correct repetitions in the form of tables. These can be found in Rast and Dommergues (2003) and Rast (2008).

6. The first version of results shown in figures 11.2, 11.4, and 11.6 appeared in Rast (2010). Results are reprinted here with the permission of John Benjamins.

7. To rate the lexical transparency of our stimulus items, first-exposure participants listened to the Polish words of our sentence repetition/translation test in isolation and were asked to translate them. Words not translated or translated incorrectly were categorized as opaque, those translated by 1 to 50 percent of the participants were categorized as fairly transparent, and those translated correctly by 51 to 100 percent of the participants received the rating of very transparent.

REFERENCES

Barcroft, Joe, and Bill VanPatten. 1997. Acoustic salience of grammatical forms: The effect of location, stress, and boundedness on Spanish L2 Input Processing. In *Contemporary perspectives on the acquisition of Spanish*, Vol. 2: *Production, processing, and comprehension*, ed. William R. Glass and Ana Teresa Pérez-Leroux, 109–21. Somerville, MA: Cascadilla Press.

Cadierno, Teresa. 1995. Formal instruction from a processing perspective: An investigation into the Spanish past tense. *The Modern Language Journal* 79: 179–93.

Carroll, Susanne. 2001. *Input and evidence: The raw material of second language acquisition.* Amsterdam: John Benjamins.

———. 2004a. Segmentation: Learning how to 'hear words' in the L2 speech stream. *Transactions of the Philological Society* 102 (2): 227–54.

———. 2004b. Commentary: Some general and specific comments on Input Processing and Processing Instruction. In *Processing instruction: Theory, research, and commentary*, ed. Bill VanPatten, 293–309. Mahwah, NJ: Lawrence Erlbaum Associates.

———. 2008. Naming: A first exposure study. Paper presented at the Annual EUROSLA Conference 18, Aix-en-Provence, September 11–13.

———. In press. The Sentence Location Principle: A Closer Look. *International Review of Applied Linguistics in Language Teaching.*

DeKeyser, Robert, Rafael Salaberry, Peter Robinson, and Michael Harrington. 2002. What gets processed in processing instruction? A commentary on Bill VanPatten's "Processing Instruction: An update." *Language Learning* 52:805–23.

Ellis, Nick. 2006. Selective attention and transfer phenomena in L2 acquisition: Contingency, cue competition, salience, interference, overshadowing, blocking, and perceptual learning. *Applied Linguistics* 27 (2): 164–94.

Gullberg, Marianne, Christine Dimroth, Leah Roberts, and Peter Indefrey. 2009. The first seven minutes of contact with an unknown language. Paper presented at the Third A. Guiora Annual Roundtable Conference in Cognitive Neuroscience of Language, Nijmegen, the Netherlands, October.

Han, ZhaoHong. 2007. Input processing: A study of *ab initio* learners with multilingual backgrounds. *The International Journal of Multilingualism* 4 (1): 17–37.

Han, ZhaoHong, and Yayun Sun. 2009. Input Processing: A replication of Han and Peverly (2009). Paper presented at the *Georgetown University Round Table on Languages and Linguistics: Implicit/Explicit Conditions, Processes, and Knowledge in SLA and Bilingualism,* 13–15.

Hudson Kam, Carla, and Elissa L. Newport. 2005. Regularizing unpredictable variation: The roles of adult and child learners in language formation and change. *Language Learning and Development* 1 (2): 151–95.

Hulstijn, Jan, and Robert DeKeyser, eds. 1997. Special issue: Testing SLA theory in the research laboratory. *Studies in Second Language Acquisition* 19 (2).

Klein, Wolfgang. 1986. *Second language acquisition.* Cambridge: Cambridge University Press.

Lee, James, Teresa Cadierno, William R. Glass, and Bill VanPatten. 1997. The effects of lexical and grammatical cues on processing past temporal reference in second language input. *Applied Language Learning* 8 (1): 1–23.

MacWhinney, Brian. 2000. *The CHILDES project: Tools for analyzing talk,* Vol. II: *The Database,* 3rd ed. Mahwah, NJ: Lawrence Erlbaum Associates.

Park, Eun Sung, and ZhaoHong Han. 2008. Learner spontaneous attention in L2 Input Processing: An exploratory study. In *Understanding second language process,* ed. ZhaoHong Han. Clevedon, UK: Multilingual Matters.

Rast, Rebekah. 2010. First exposure: Converting target language input to intake. In *Inside the learner's mind: Cognitive processing and second language acquisition,* ed. Martin Pütz and Laura Sicola, 99–115. Amsterdam, Philadelphia: John Benjamins.

———. 2008. *Foreign language input: Initial processing.* Clevedon, UK: Multilingual Matters.

Rast, Rebekah, and Jean-Yves Dommergues. 2003. Towards a characterisation of saliency on first exposure to a second language. In *EUROSLA yearbook 3,* ed. Susan Foster-Cohen and Simona Pekarek-Doehler, 131–56. Amsterdam: John Benjamins.

Reber, Arthur S. 1967. Implicit learning of artificial grammars. *Journal of Verbal Learning and Verbal Behavior* 6:855–63.

Ringbom, Håkan. 2007. *Cross-linguistic similarity in foreign language learning.* Clevedon, UK: Multilingual Matters.

Robinson, Peter. 2003. Attention and memory during SLA. In *The handbook of second language acquisition,* ed. Catherine Doughty and Michael Long, 631–78. Malden, MA: Blackwell.

Schmidt, Richard W. 1990. The role of consciousness in second language learning. *Applied Linguistics* 11 (2): 129–58.

———. 2001. Attention. In *Cognition and second language instruction,* ed. Peter Robinson, 3–32. Cambridge: Cambridge University Press.

VanPatten, Bill. 1996. *Input processing and grammar instruction: Theory and research.* Norwood, NJ: Ablex.

———. 2002. Processing instruction, prior awareness and the nature of second language acquisition: A (partial) response to Batstone. *Language Awareness* 11 (4): 240–58.

———. 2004. Input processing in second language acquisition. In *Processing instruction: Theory, research, and commentary,* ed. Bill VanPatten, 5–31. Mahwah, NJ: Lawrence Erlbaum Associates.

———. 2007. Input processing in adult second language acquisition. In *Theories in second language acquisition,* ed. Bill VanPatten and Jessica Williams, 115–36. Mahwah, NJ: Lawrence Erlbaum Associates.

Zwitserlood, Pienie, Wolfgang Klein, James Liang, Clive Perdue, and Eric Kellerman. 2000. The first minutes of foreign-language exposure. Unpublished manuscript, Max-Planck Institute for Psycholinguistics, Nijmegen.

III

Empirical Research on L2 Phonology

12

What Is Implicit and What Is Explicit in L2 Speech? Findings from an Oral Corpus

HEATHER E. HILTON
Université Paris 8

AFTER A BRIEF INTRODUCTION clarifying the terms "implicit" and "explicit" as they apply to learning and language processing, this article investigates implicit and explicit processes in L2 speech, using different types of disfluency in an oral corpus as indicators of explicit processes at work: silent and filled pauses, retracing, word fragments, and drawled or lengthened syllables. A corpus of oral productions by native speakers and L2 learners of English and French at different proficiency levels reveals basic differences in the distribution of hesitation structures: more clause-internal hesitations and a higher rate of retracing illustrate the difficulty disfluent learners have accessing appropriate language forms in the declarative L2 base. The serial encoding of concepts by disfluent L2 learners is compared with the manipulation of six- to eight-word "runs" by the fluent speakers, and formulaic chunking of syntactically structured groups is hypothesized to account for this fluent performance, in line with conclusions formulated by Goldman-Eisler (1958), Pawley and Syder (1983), and Raupach (1984).

In SLA research, the adjectives "implicit" and "explicit" have been used to qualify knowledge, memory, learning, processes, and competence. In this article knowledge and memory systems will be qualified as "declarative" or "nondeclarative," and the terms "implicit" and "explicit" will be reserved for two domains only—learning and language processing. Data from a spoken corpus will be examined to investigate implicit/explicit processing issues in L2 speech, and I will return very briefly to questions of implicit and explicit L2 learning in my concluding remarks.

Memory Structures, Learning and Language Processing: Basic Terminology

It is generally accepted that human *memory* is composed of two distinct systems, the declarative and the nondeclarative (or procedural) systems (Broadbent 1977, cited in Berry 1994, 148–49; Cohen and Squire 1980; Squire 1992). Ullman's "Declarative/ Procedural Model" (Ullman 2001a, 2001b, 2004, 2005) attempts to identify the basic memory structures underlying verbal performance, with a focus on the particular features of L2 representation and processing. The declarative base underlying language is the "set of memorized form-meaning pairings" commonly referred to as the mental lexicon (Ullman 2001a, 38). Kormos hypothesizes that one of the major differences between the L1 and L2 declarative base is the presence of declarative knowledge of L2 morphosyntactic forms learned in the L2 classroom (Kormos 2006, 167). The declarative system is sometimes referred to as "explicit memory," because its elements can be consciously recalled or verbalized, but I consider the term to be ambiguous, and will limit myself to the more conventional "declarative" memory. The nondeclarative system underlying language use consists of the long-established motor and cognitive skills or habits (Ullman 2001b, 106), the procedures that make online language processing possible: articulatory routines, subconscious processing of facial expressions and social situations, syntactic assembly, and possibly certain morphological routines—although there is a good deal of debate on the subject, as evidenced in the exchange between MacWhinney (2005), and Ullman and Walenski (2005). Nondeclarative routines and procedures are "committed" to specific processing contexts or functions, and difficult to verbalize.

Explicit learning involves attentional effort, "conscious problem-solving and deduction" (Ellis 2002, 170), where "various mnemonics, heuristics, and strategies are engaged to induce a representational system" (Reber 1976, 93). Implicit learning is learning without awareness of what is being learned (DeKeyser 2003, 314), "an abstraction of information from the environment . . . without recourse to explicit systems for encoding the stimuli" (Reber 1976, 88). Implicit learning involves neocortical sensori-motor conditioning, which is incremental, highly dependent on the frequency of stimulus occurrence (Broeder and Plunkett 1994; Ellis 2002, 143, 175), and slow—the result of hundreds (or, for language, thousands: Ellis 2005, 215) of hours of processing. Explicit learning involves the hippocampal system, which "binds together disparate cortical representations into a unitary representation that can then be recalled by partial retrieval cues at a later time" (Ellis 2002, 175); the explicit addition of a new form-meaning pair to the mental lexicon can occur relatively quickly.

In terms of language processing, the qualifiers "implicit" and "explicit" can be considered equivalents of, respectively, "automatic" and "effortful" (Hasher and Zacks 1979) or controlled (Shiffrin and Schneider 1977). By definition, an automatic process requires "only minimal attentional capacity" in working memory (Hasher and Zacks 1979, 357) and can therefore be considered implicit; an effortful process requires the mobilization of attentional resources in the executive component of working memory and can therefore be qualified as explicit. Automatic processes are extremely rapid and unstoppable once triggered; controlled or explicit processes consume not only attentional resources but also more processing time. Extensive research into the precise nature of language processing has, of course, revealed that fluent or efficient language skill depends on the automatic processing of so-called lower-level formal elements, with attentional resources devoted to higher-level processes of discourse organization, and strategic management of encoding or decoding challenges and of the social aspects of the exchange.

Early research into first-language spoken production established a link between various disfluencies (forms of hesitation) and nonautomatic or higher-order, explicit processes: "Pauses were conceived of as . . . involving acts of choice. They were expected to occur where linguistic solutions fitting the speech intentions are not readily available, or where automatic verbalization is rejected in favor of 'newer', more specifically selected verbal expression" (Goldman-Eisler 1957, 1497; see also Lounsbury 1954). If, like Goldman-Eisler and her contemporaries, we consider the hesitation phenomena of spoken production—silent and filled pauses, retracing, stutters, and drawls[1]—as indicators of explicit attentional processes, then careful scrutiny of the distribution of these disfluencies in L1 and L2 speech should provide useful information about what is implicit and what is explicit in native and non-native speech.

The PAROLE Corpus

The *Langages* research team at the Université de Savoie has constituted an oral corpus of productions by sixty-eight learners in three different L2s: English, French, and Italian (Hilton, Osborne, and Derive 2008). The corpus was designed to include samples of spoken language by learners at different levels, performing comparable tasks in different languages, and is therefore entitled PAROLE (*PARallèle, Oral en Langue Etrangère*). Initially, our objectives in designing the corpus were linguistic: we wanted to examine the phonological, lexical, morphological, and syntactic characteristics of different L2 proficiency levels and to identify cross-linguistic and language-specific phenomena. Participants in the project were not selected through proficiency testing but were simply recruited (on a volunteer basis) from student groups that were hypothesized to have differing levels of oral competence (newly arrived freshmen in an Applied Language program, compared with postgraduate language majors preparing for the highly competitive teacher recruiting examinations in France, for example). Each subject completed five short production tasks; a corpus of productions by twenty-seven native speakers (NS) performing the same tasks as our learners was also compiled, to provide benchmark values for the analyses carried out on the L2 corpus. All the contributors to the corpus were enrolled at the Université de Savoie; all the learners completed a battery of tests and questionnaires, and were paid minimum wage for the three hours devoted to the data collection procedure (see Hilton 2008b for details). The findings presented here are compiled from two summary tasks, in which the subjects described a short video sequence immediately after viewing, with minimal intervention from the interviewer. Due to the fact that the transcriptions for Italian have not yet been completed, I will be reporting data for the productions in English (thirty-three learners and nine native speakers) and in French (twelve learners and eight native speakers). The English–French subset of the L2 corpus totals 9,087 words (one hour and fifteen minutes of L2 speech), and the NS subset 3,732 words (twenty-two minutes of L1 speech).

PAROLE was not designed to elicit particular behaviour from a temporal point of view, yet this has become a major focus in our analyses to date. From the beginning of the transcription process, we were struck by various hesitation phenomena in the L2 corpus and decided to code these meticulously. PAROLE has been transcribed using the Child Language Data Exchange System (CHILDES), which includes the CHAT transcription conventions (Codes for the Human Analysis of

Transcripts), and the CLAN (Computerized Language Analysis) package of programs for the analysis and editing of the transcriptions. The version of PAROLE currently online follows the 2007 CHILDES guidelines (MacWhinney 2007), which we
adapted for the systematic coding and timing of hesitations. According to standard
CHAT procedure, an utterance in PAROLE is defined as an independent clause and
all its dependent clauses (basically, a T-unit); all errors, word fragments (stutters),
drawls, and retracings, as well as silent and filled pauses and other hesitation phenomena have been transcribed conventionally. We coded four different types of retracing: simple repetitions, reformulations (in which only one element of the
repeated material has been changed), restarts (more than one element changed), and
false starts (Hilton 2008b, 20–21). All hesitations of 200 ms or more (Butterworth
1980, 156) are coded and carefully timed, using the waveform in the "Sonic Mode"
of CLAN; millisecond totals for each hesitation are entered directly in the main transcription line, at the precise location of the pause in the speech stream. In the learner
corpus, chains of silent and filled pauses (between two words or attempted words)
are frequent. Despite the fact that fluency research has traditionally considered silent
and filled pauses separately, we decided to "scope" these complex hesitation groups
in CHAT, and enter the total duration of the hesitation in the transcription line (see
Hilton [2009] for a detailed description of disfluency coding in PAROLE). In an offline version of the corpus, the position of each hesitation has been coded, according to three possible locations: at an utterance, clause boundary, or within a clause.
The syntactic components of each utterance have also been coded manually: as a
main clause (simple, coordinate, or superordinate), subordinate clause (finite or non-
finite), nonverbal phrase, or what we are calling a "support clause" (a complement
clause or an existential clause).

Fluency Subgroups

In first-language-acquisition research, mean length of utterance (MLU, measured in
words or morphemes per utterance) is a classic indicator of developmental level, and
speech rate (measured as words, syllables, or phonemes per minute) is the standard
temporal fluency measure. In L2 research, pause rate, mean length of pause, and mean
length of run (or MLR, the number of words or syllables produced between two
pauses) have been shown to be effective fluency indicators (Towell, Hawkins, and Bazergui 1996; Trofimovich and Baker 2006). The programs provided with CLAN calculate MLU as well as total speaking time; the timing of hesitations in PAROLE has
therefore enabled us to establish, for each subject, total hesitation time, percentage
of production time spent hesitating, average length of hesitation, words per minute,
and mean length of run. Raw numbers of retracings and errors have been converted
to relative frequencies of retracing and error (per 1,000 words).

Since we do not have (reliable, cross-linguistic) proficiency ratings for the PA-
ROLE subjects, we have established a quantitative "fluency index" (FI) to enable us
to identify learner subgroups of different fluency levels for comparison. Three basic fluency indicators—speech rate (in words per minute), percentage of production
time spent hesitating, and mean length of run—have been given a coefficient value
(in relation to the NS average for each measure) and combined in the FI (Osborne

2007). In the analyses that follow, I examine two extreme learner groups—those subjects with the lowest FI scores (n = 12, first quartile), and those with the highest FI scores (n = 12, fourth quartile)—whose performance can be compared to the NS control group.

Findings: Production and Hesitation in PAROLE

Table 12.1 gives the basic production and fluency measures for all the L2 learners and native speakers in PAROLE, as well as for the low-FI and high-FI learner subgroups. The median values presented in the table illustrate the differences between the learner and the NS corpus, between low-FI and high-FI learners, and between

Table 12.1
Production and Fluency Findings in PAROLE

Production Indicator (median value given, unless otherwise indicated)	All Learners (n = 45)	Low FI Learners (n = 12)	High FI Learners (n = 12)	Native Speakers (n = 17)	Kruskall-Wallis Analyses of Variance (low-FI/ high-FI/ NS; where appropriate)
Words per Minute	105.5	56.6	136.5	183.5	$H(2) = 32.53$, $p < .0001$
Mean Length of Run (in words)	3.70	2.35	5.60	8.30	$H(2) = 30.46$, $p < .0001$
Variance, MLR	2.146	0.119	1.370	3.687	—
% Production Time Hesitating	40.6%	58%	29.5%	21.2%	$H(2) = 28.15$, $p < .0001$
Median Length of Hesitation	697 ms	976 ms	575 ms	499 ms	$H(2) = 26.66$, $p < .0001$
Variance, Length Hesitations	1.734	3.715	0.296	0.191	—
Maximum Hesitation	21.34″	21.34″	6.37″	5.56″	(all minima 200 ms)
Mean Length of Utterance	11.1	7.6	13.4	16.3	$H(2) = 27.97$, $p < .0001$
Rate of Retracing (per 1,000 words)	83.3	130.1	50.8	39.8	$H(2) = 17.04$, $p < .001$
Stutter Rate (per 1,000 words)	27.9	31.3	27.3	12.1	$H(2) = 14.14$, $p < .001$
Rate of Error (per 1,000 words)	93.2	164.9	74.1	10.6	$H(2) = 34.30$, $p < .0001$
Syntactic Units per Utterance	1.78	1.32	2.19	2.82	$H(2) = 29.52$, $p < .0001$
Syntactic Units per Minute	14.6	8.2	22.1	29.3	$H(2) = 31.77$, $p < .0001$

fluent learners and native speakers. For all of the measures where Kruskall-Wallis analyses of variance show significant between-group differences, post hoc (Mann-Whitney) comparisons between subgroup pairs are all significant (at the $p < .01$ level at most), unless stated otherwise below. There are, of course, significant differences between the two learner subgroups on the three temporal measures used to establish the fluency index; more precisely, the low-FI learners' speech rate—as measured in words per minute and mean length of run—is less than half of the rate of the high-FI learners and less than one-third the rate of the native speakers, with a hesitation every two or three words. The low variance in MLR for the low-FI subgroup illustrates that this hesitant, word-by-word encoding process is a constant of disfluent production; L1 speech appears to be characterized by more individual variation in length of run.

Further investigation of between-group differences in the frequency of occurrence of different types of hesitations, retracings, or syntactic units has been carried out, using chi-square tests (along the lines of Pawley and Syder 1983). A test comparing the location of hesitations produced by the subgroups, according to the three possibilities we coded (utterance boundary, clause boundary, or within-clause), reveals that the proportions of hesitations at these three locations differ according to fluency level: $\chi^2(4, 2001) = 98.99, p < .0001$. Members of the low-FI subgroup hesitate more within clauses (57 percent of their hesitations), and only 43 percent of the time at syntactic or discursive boundaries. This distribution is reversed for the high-FI subgroup, 56 percent of whose hesitations are situated at a boundary, 44 percent within a clause. Corroborating earlier research in L1 production (Hawkins 1971), we find that our native speakers hesitate 70 percent of the time at a boundary, and only 30 percent within a clause. Complex hesitation groups (comprising at least one silent and one filled pause) are also characteristic of L2 production, which contains significantly fewer isolated silent pauses, and more hesitation groups than L1 speech: $\chi^2(1, 3366) = 20.9, p < .0001$. 77 percent of the hesitations produced by the low-FI learners are hesitation groups, compared with 58 percent and 54 percent, respectively, for the high-FI learners and native speakers.

Although table 12.1 shows a significant difference in the rate of retracing between the three subgroups, post hoc comparisons reveal the difference to lie primarily between the disfluent learners and the other two subgroups, the difference between the fluent learners and the native speakers being nonsignificant (U[12, 17] = 73, $p = .20$). Chi-square tests of the occurrence of the four different types of retracing (repetitions, reformulations, restarts, and false starts) show that the three subgroups differ ($\chi^2[4, 667] = 13.52, p < .01$): the disfluent learners produce proportionally more simple repetitions, the fluent learners fewer restarts, and the native speakers more restarts and false starts than the learners. Corpuswide, simple repetitions involve function words 72 percent of the time; this appears to be a constant, for both learners and NS.

Table 12.1 shows a significant difference in stuttering rate between the three fluency subgroups, but post hoc analysis reveals the difference to lie between the native speakers and the learners (U[45, 17] = 141.5, $p < .0001$), since the two learner groups are statistically equivalent in their rates of stuttering (U[12, 17] = 51.0, $p = .23$). Error rates are, obviously, higher for L2 learners than for native speakers, although our median of ten errors per thousand words for the NS subjects is higher than findings by other researchers—Levelt cites one slip of the tongue per 1,000 words (1989, 199). We have tabulated as errors not just slips with content words but also missing function words, which increases the tally considerably. A chi-square test of the distribution of the four different types of syntactic unit coded in PAROLE (main clauses, subordinate clauses, phrases, and support clauses) reveals significant differences between the three subgroups in the use of these different syntactic structures: $\chi^2(6, 1432)$ = 35.18, $p < .0001$. The NS subjects in PAROLE produce proportionally more main clauses and phrases than the learners, and both learner subgroups produce proportionally more support clauses (with the disfluent subgroup twice as reliant on these clauses as the fluent subgroup); the fluent learners produce more subordinate clauses and distinctly fewer phrases. So although fluent learners and native speakers both produce more syntactically dense utterances than disfluent learners, they tend to do so in different ways: the learners by incorporating more subordinate clauses and the NS by expanding their clauses with nonverbal phrases.

Discussion

Various aspects of spoken production are illustrated in these findings, but I will focus here on those that shed light on the processing characteristics of fluent and disfluent L2 speech, and especially on the implicit or explicit nature of these processes. Our analyses show that L2 production (whether fluent or disfluent) is characterized by a higher proportion of hesitations within clause boundaries; disfluent L2 speech is characterized not only by longer, more frequent, and more complex hesitations, but also by more simple repetition. In L1 research clause-internal hesitations and the repetition of function words have both been linked to problems of lexical retrieval (Maclay and Osgood 1959; Fathman 1980). In analyses reported elsewhere (Hilton 2008a, 158–59), I did indeed find that disfluent clause-internal hesitations in PAROLE (clause-internal hesitations lasting three seconds or more) were followed 78 percent of the time by a lexical error, a lexical approximation, or an overt declaration of inability to find the right word. The lexical encoding of conceptual information is largely automatic in L1 speech, and much more frequently effortful—an explicit process—in a less familiar language.

Simple repetition (coded "[/]" in CLAN) also appears to be connected with issues of lexical encoding in PAROLE; most repetition in the corpus also involves a lengthened syllable (coded ":"), which furnishes a few extra milliseconds for lexical retrieval. Repetition is frequently accompanied by other hesitation phenomena, the presence of which appears to signal a slightly more effortful search of the declarative base—in examples 1a–b, the word immediately following the repeated determiner is a lower-frequency noun:

(1a) *015: uh we can see **a: [/]** #1_034 **a** skyscraper↑ +/. (repetition including a drawled function word and a silent pause lasting 1.034)

(1b) *N46: [...] donc on voit en fait **une [/] u:h [#0_348] une grue** [...] (NS repetition, including a drawled filled pause lasting 348 ms; *so in fact we see a u:h a crane*)

Explicit grammatical encoding generates similar patterns of hesitations, drawls, and repetitions (although hesitations lasting over a second are rare). Characteristically, explicit morphological processes also generate reformulation (coded "[//]"), since the speaker is manipulating different word forms:

(2a) *020: [...] the elephant actually **slap [/]** #0_220 **slap [//] slaps** hi:m [...].

(2b) *012: [...] **<(h)e: show> [//]** <uh #> [#0_529] **he shows** [...].

Not surprisingly, L2 learners produce proportionally more morphological reformulations than the native speaker subjects: 32 percent of all reformulations produced by NS involve morphological changes, compared with 37 percent by the high-FI learner group, and 47 percent by the low-FI group ($\chi^2[6, 237] = 33.97, p < .0001$). There also appears to be a qualitative difference in the function of reformulation according to fluency level. For L2 learners, morphological reformulation attests to a grammatical monitoring process, in which learners are apparently accessing a declarative base of inflectional rules, as in example 2. Morphological reformulation by our native speakers seems more closely linked to lexical retrieval processes than to explicit grammatical processes; in example 3, the reformulated syllable is drawled, but there are no pauses or other hesitations:

(3a) *N43: [...] donc il arrive **<au dernie:r> [//] à la dernière** partie [...] de la barre de chocolat. (*so he gets to the la:st the last part of the chocolate bar*, adjective adjusted to match the noun *partie*)

(3b) *N15: [...] well a: higher storey on **a: [//] an** apartment complex [...]

Reformulation may also involve lexical or semantic adjustments in the encoding process, 50 percent of the time for the native speakers, and from 27 percent to 39 percent of the time for the low-FI and high-FI subgroups, respectively. These reformulations attest to an explicit monitoring of the nature (social register in 4c) or quantity (4a–b) of information being communicated:

(4a) *019: a:nd #0_517 the fridge falls **<on a car> [//] on a green car** [...].

(4b) *022: [...] **<the elepha:nt> [//] the baby elephant** [...]

(4c) *N46: [...] **<le gars** d' en dessous> [//] (en)fi:n #0_459 le: [/] **le monsieur** du dessous (*the guy down below well the: the man from downstairs*)

Restarts (coded "[///]") and false starts (coded "[/-]") found in more fluent productions also appear to reflect discursive-level monitoring processes:

(4d) *N13: #0_348 it's a &b **[/-]** #0_279 the: other one was when he was just a little boy now he's about thirty↑ [...]

The higher proportion of restarts and false starts found in our NS corpus no doubt illustrates that speakers explicitly focusing on lower-level processes have less working memory capacity available to monitor discourse construction in this fashion.

It is difficult to say to what extent stuttering or word fragments (coded "&" in CHAT, as in example 4d above) reflect implicit or explicit processes; they appear to play a different role in fluent and disfluent speech. Stuttering by more fluent speakers may be associated with errors in the phonological assembly of readily available linguistic information (examples 5a–b), or changes in discursive plans, when accompanied by lexical or syntactic reformulation (5c–d):

(5a) *021: […] and <**the &fring>** [**//**] **the fridge is being** [///] […] <going up> [*].

(5b) *N10: […] there's a: [//] an **&obj obnoxious** apparently little boy […]

(5c) *N47: […] <**le &ga le:>** [**//**] **donc l' enfant** […] . (*gars* or *garçon* [kid or boy] replaced by *enfant* [child])

(5d) *N44: […] ensuite **la** [**/**] **&g la:** [**//**] **ça coupe**. (*then the g- the: it cuts to a new scene*)

By contrast, the stuttering produced by the less fluent learners may be connected with problems in the articulation of inhabitual phonetic groups (example 6a), or with more explicit lexical (6b) or morphological (6c) encoding:

(6a) *407: […] c' est le **&propret #0_348 &pri #0_488 propri(é)taire** [*] de la voiture […] . (*It's the owr- ow- owner of the car*; NS of Mandarin Chinese)

(6b) *008: […] people are **&m #0_284 moving**↑.

(6c) *413: […] qui <**le &f>** [**//**] **lui** [***] **frappe** […] (*which hi- him hits him*; change from the direct to the indirect object pronoun form)

Of course, many idiosyncrasies in the formal aspects of L2 encoding occur without generating surface disfluency, illustrating the automatic nature of the processing of these interlanguage forms. Up to 80 percent of the morphological errors in the high-FI subcorpus are smoothly integrated into the L2 speech stream, as in example 7:

(7a) *032: #0_273 suddenly it fall [*] down onto the car.

(7b) *418: […] #0_847 e:t il est dans une [*] défilé. (*a:nd he's at a parade*)

These forms may have initially been generated strategically, but use of the form appears to have become automatic, since no disfluency is generated. This is also true of the vast majority of phonological "errors" in the learner corpus, which do not cause disfluency, perhaps because they are not technically errors but nonstandard articulatory routines.

Conclusions

It is tempting to interpret the hesitation differences we have just summarized as examples of different processes at work in L1 and L2 oral production. I interpret the data differently, however, in an attempt to bring SLA processing models into line with more unified theories of cognition (as advocated by Segalowitz 2003, 395). Fluent speech in PAROLE is characterized by a far greater proportion of hesitations occurring at discursive and syntactic boundaries, which I think illustrates two important processing characteristics. First, these hesitations may illustrate the "higher-order" attentional processes taking place during fluent speech; "pausology" research conducted in the

1950s and 1960s attributes syntactic and discursive planning functions to pauses situated at boundaries (Goldman-Eisler 1958). The second phenomenon illustrated by the boundary location of the majority of hesitations in fluent speech may be the formulaic or prefabricated nature of much of the material that is assembled during encoding. Proficient speakers appear to encode their ideas in syntactically structured word groups—the six- to eight-word "runs" that the most fluent PAROLE subjects (whether NS or L2 learners) produce on average. In contrast, the most disfluent speakers produce extremely short runs, of two or three words, with low variance in this measure across the low-FI group (table 12.1). If we compare two examples from the corpus of explicit manipulation of linguistic material, as evidenced through various retracing processes, we can see that the less-fluent speaker (example 8a) is encoding her ideas one content word at a time, whereas the native speaker (example 8b) is substituting and exchanging what appear to be prefabricated multiword units (notice the absence of pauses, despite multiple retracings):

(8a) *003: […] but the [/] the fridge <u:h #> [#3_846] 0aux fallen [//] #0_952
     non@l1 falls <u:h #> [#1_684] on u:h [#0_488] a car↑ .
(8b) *N13: […] (be)cause I guess they don't want (t)o: [///] it won't fit up [///] they
     won't [//] don't want to take it <up the elevator> [//] up the stairs so +/.

All speakers, presumably, perform the same explicit processes when they speak: discourse planning, adjusting for the reactions of their conversation partner, compensating for eventual encoding difficulties. The implicit processes of oral production are surely the same, too, whether one is speaking in a language practiced since birth or a language learned later in life: the concept one wishes to express automatically activates memory structures. If the memory structures needed to express the concept are difficult to activate (L1), or even lacking (L2), an explicit, effortful process will be necessary to compensate for the missing information or routine. It is my hypothesis, therefore, that the difference between fluent and disfluent speech is not primarily a difference in the processes at work (although on the surface this may appear to be the case); the difference lies more precisely in the nature of the declarative base available for the linguistic encoding of ideas. A novice learner, or a learner having had little processing contact with the L2 will be accessing a declarative base containing a few hundred words, memorized grammar and pronunciation rules, and a few stock phrases or idiomatic expressions. The implicit processes activating the declarative L2 base will frequently fail to find preassembled chunks of language ready for speedily encoding ideas, and an effortful, serial assembly process will ensue (Kormos 2006, 166). Effortful retrieval can even become a morpheme-by-morpheme process, as the speaker consults the special declarative base of "rules and exceptions" learned in the L2 classroom; in example 8c, three retracings are necessary for a learner to assemble the correct French verb structure for (the irregular verb) *he saw:*

(8c) *406: […] <il v:oir> [//] u:h [#0_528] <il a voir> [/] <uh #> [#0_394] […]
     <il a voir> [//] <uh #> [#0_470] <il a vu> […].

Conceptual and syntactic organization also seem to fall prey to the serial condition that characterizes effortful language production, as evidenced by the proportionally greater numbers of existential support clauses in the low-FI group's summaries; the attentional effort devoted to lower-level encoding in disfluent speech appears to limit discursive planning to the serial enumeration of events.

By contrast, implicit activation processes in the brain of an advanced learner or native speaker will activate a rich declarative base, consisting of tens of thousands of prefabricated word groups—the "chunks" of associated items upon which expert performance depends (Miller 1956): "[Chunking] is the development of permanent sets of associative connections in long-term storage and is the process that underlies the attainment of automaticity and fluency in language" (Ellis 2000, 38–39). The notion that fluent oral production depends on the availability of multiword units isn't exactly new (Goldman-Eisler 1958, 67; Pawley and Syder 1983; Raupach 1984), but the full significance of a formulaically structured "mental lexicon" has not yet been explored (or even acknowledged) in much psycholinguistic research. The hypothesis that the declarative base for language is formulaically structured provides an interesting explanation for the development of automaticity in language processing, compatible with memory-based theories of automaticity, such as Logan's instance theory: "Performance is automatic when it is based on single-step direct-access retrieval of past solutions from memory" (1988, 493). The formulaic hypothesis also tallies with Paradis's conviction that representations in long-term memory are either declarative or nondeclarative and that declarative knowledge does not eventually "become procedural" (Paradis 2004, 41). Of course, a formulaic account for fluency differences in L2 production remains a working hypothesis, which needs to be tested and pitted against proceduralization models (Anderson 1996), in carefully controlled experimental paradigms (Dąbrowska 2004).

A formulaic explanation for some aspects of temporal fluency in spoken production would have major implications for language learning and teaching, in addition to its importance for language acquisition research. Despite extensive research on the L2 "mental lexicon" over the past twenty years, we still know relatively little about how this complex language base is constructed in long-term memory (Meara 2006). The syntagmatic associations between words in our L1 are certainly acquired implicitly, during the thousands of hours of oral and written processing we perform every year. Normal L2 classrooms do not provide enough input and contact time with the language to enable this sort of implicit associative learning to take place, and as a result, most L2 learners lack the type of formulaic knowledge that native speakers possess (Wray 2000, 168). Is the memorization of formulaic sequences an area of L2 learning where explicit memorization could replace the thousands of hours of contact necessary for the implicit learning of these sequences in the L1? Would explicitly acquired formulaic sequences behave in similar fashion to implicitly acquired chunks in online communicative processing? In an instructed L2 learning context, multimedia training materials could provide the type of meaningful repetitive processing necessary to attain a speeded-up, explicit (or semi-explicit) chunking of the L2 declarative base, which could then be solicited for real communication tasks during contact time with the teacher and fellow learners.

NOTE
   1. Defined as "non-phonemic lengthening of syllables" (Raupach 1980, 266).

REFERENCES

Anderson, John R. 1996. *The architecture of cognition*. Mahwah, NJ: Lawrence Erlbaum Associates.

Berry, Dianne C. 1994. Implicit and explicit learning of complex tasks. In *Implicit and explicit learning of languages*, ed. Nick Ellis, 147–64. London: Academic Press.

Broadbent, Donald E. 1977. Levels, hierarchies and the locus of control. *Journal of Experimental Psychology* 29:181–201.

Broeder, Peter, and Kim Plunkett. 1994. Connectionism and second language acquisition. In *Implicit and explicit learning of languages*, ed. Nick Ellis, 421–54. London: Academic Press.

Butterworth, Brian. 1980. Evidence from pauses in speech. In *Language Production* Vol. 1 *Speech and Talk*, ed. Brian Butterworth, 155–75. London: Academic Press.

Cohen, Neal J., and Larry R. Squire. 1980. Preserved learning and retention of pattern-analyzing skill in amnesia: Dissociation of knowing how and knowing that. *Science* 210 (10/10): 207–10.

Dąbrowska, E. 2004. Rules or schemas? Evidence from Polish. *Language and Cognitive Processes* 19 (2): 225–71.

DeKeyser, Robert. 2003. Implicit and explicit learning. In *The handbook of second language acquisition*, eds. Catherine J. Doughty and Michael H. Long, 313–48. Oxford: Blackwell.

Ellis, Nick C. 1995. *Implicit and explicit learning of languages*. London: Academic Press.

———. 2000. Memory for Language. In *Cognition and second language instruction*, ed. Peter Robinson, 33–68. Cambridge: Cambridge University Press.

———. 2002. Frequency effects in language processing: A review with implications for theories of implicit and explicit language acquisition. *Studies in Second Language Acquisition* 24 (2): 143–88.

———. 2005. At the interface: Dynamic interactions of explicit and implicit language knowledge. *Studies in Second Language Acquisition* 27 (2): 305–52.

Fathman, Ann K. 1980. Repetition and correction as an indication of speech planning and execution processes among second language learners. In *Towards a cross-linguistic assessment of speech production*, ed. Hans W. Dechert and Manfred Raupach, 77–86. Frankfurt: Peter Lang.

Goldman-Eisler, Frieda. 1957. Speech production and language statistics. *Nature* (December 28): 1497.

———. 1958. Speech analysis and mental processes. *Language and Speech* 1:59–75.

Hasher, Lynn, and Rose T. Zacks. 1979. Automatic and effortful processes in memory. *Journal of Experimental Psychology: General* 108:356–88.

Hawkins, P. R. 1971. The syntactic location of hesitation pauses. *Language and Speech* 14:277–88.

Hilton, Heather E. 2008a. The link between vocabulary knowledge and spoken L2 fluency. *Language Learning Journal* 36 (2): 153–66.

———. 2008b. *Corpus PAROLE: Architecture du corpus et conventions de transcription*. In *BilingBank* of *TalkBank*. Pittsburgh: Carnegie Mellon University.

———. 2009. Annotation and analyses of temporal aspects of spoken fluency. *CALICO Journal* 26 (3): 644–61.

Hilton, Heather E., John Osborne, and Marie-Jo Derive. 2008. *Corpus PAROLE*. Chambéry, France: Université de Savoie. In *BilingBank* of *TalkBank*. Pittsburgh: Carnegie Mellon University. http://talkbank.org/BilingBank/.

Kormos, Judit. 2006. *Speech production and second language acquisition*. Mahwah, NJ: Lawrence Erlbaum Associates.

Levelt, Willem J. M. 1989. *Speaking: From intention to articulation*. Cambridge, MA: MIT Press.

Logan, Gordon D. 1988. Toward an instance theory of automatization. *Psychological Review* 95 (4): 492–527.

Lounsbury, Floyd G. 1954. Transitional probability, linguistic structure and systems of habit family hierarchies. In *Psycholinguistics: A survey of theory and research*, ed. Charles E. Osgood and Thomas A. Sebeok, 93–101. Bloomington: Indiana University Press.

Maclay, Howard, and Charles E. Osgood. 1959. Hesitation phenomena in spontaneous English speech. *Word* 15:19–44.

MacWhinney, Brian. 2005. Commentary on Ullman et al. *Brain and Language* 93:239–42.

———. 2007. *The CHILDES Project: tools for analysing talk, electronic edition*. Pittsburgh: Carnegie Mellon University. http://childes.psy.cmu.edu/manuals/.

Meara, Paul. 2006. Emergent properties of multilingual lexicons. *Applied Linguistics* 27:620–44.

Miller, George A. 1956. The magical number seven, plus or minus two: Some limits on our capacity for processing information. *Psychological Review* 63:81–97.

Osborne, John. 2007. Measuring fluency in an oral learner corpus. Paper presented at the Corpus Linguistics Biannual Conference. Birmingham, UK: University of Birmingham.

Paradis, Michel. 2004. *A neurolinguistic theory of bilingualism.* Amsterdam: John Benjamins.

Pawley, Andrew, and Frances Hodgetts Syder. 1983. Two puzzles for linguistic theory: Nativelike selection and nativelike fluency. In *Language and Communication,* ed. Jack C. Richards and Richard W. Schmidt, 191–225. London: Longman.

Raupach, Manfred. 1980. Temporal variables in first and second language speech production. In *Temporal Variables in Speech,* ed. Hans W. Dechert and Manfred Raupach, 263–70. Den Haag, Netherlands: Mouton.

————. 1984. Formulae in second language speech production. In *Second Language Productions,* ed. Hans W. Dechert, Dorothea Möhle, and Manfred Raupach, 114–37. Tübingen, Germany: Gunter Narr.

Reber, Arthur S. 1976. Implicit learning of synthetic languages: The role of instructional set. *Journal of Experimental Psychology: Human Learning and Memory* 2 (1): 88–94.

Segalowitz, Norman. 2003. Automaticity and second languages. In *The handbook of second language acquisition,* ed. Catherine J. Doughty and Michael H. Long, 382–408. Oxford: Blackwell.

Shiffrin, Richard M., and Walter Schneider. 1977. Controlled and automatic human information processing II: Perceptual learning, automatic attending and a general theory. *Psychological Review* 84:127–90.

Squire, Larry. 1992. Memory and the hippocampus: A synthesis from findings with rats, monkeys, and humans. *Psychological Review* 99 (2): 295–331.

Towell, Richard, Roger Hawkins, and N. Bazergui. 1996. The development of fluency in advanced learners of French. *Applied Linguistics* 17:84–115.

Trofimovich, Pavel, and Wendy Baker. 2006. Learning second language suprasegmentals: Effects of L2 experience on prosody and fluency characteristics of L2 speech. *Studies in Second Language Acquisition* 28 (1): 1–30.

Ullman, Michael T. 2001a. The declarative/procedural model of lexicon and grammar. *Journal of Psycholinguistic Research* 30 (1): 37–69.

————. 2001b. The neural basis of lexicon and grammar in first and second language: The declarative/procedural model. *Bilingualism: Language and Cognition* 4 (1): 105–22.

————. 2004. Contributions of memory circuits to language: The declarative/ procedural model. *Cognition* 92 (1–2): 231–70.

————. 2005. A cognitive neuroscience perspective on second language acquisition: The declarative/procedural model. In *Mind and context in adult second language acquisition,* ed. Cristina Sanz, 141–78. Washington, DC: Georgetown University Press.

Ullman, Michael T., and Matthew Walenski. 2005. Moving past the past tense. *Brain and Language* 93 (2): 248–52.

Wray, Alison. 2000. Formulaic sequences in second language teaching: Principle and practice. *Applied Linguistics* 21:463–89.

13

Explicit Training and Implicit Learning of L2 Phonemic Contrasts

FRED R. ECKMAN
University of Wisconsin–Milwaukee

GREGORY K. IVERSON
University of Wisconsin–Milwaukee and University of Maryland Center for Advanced Study of Language

ROBERT ALLEN FOX AND EWA JACEWICZ
The Ohio State University

SUE ANN LEE
Texas Tech University

THE PURPOSE OF THIS CHAPTER is to report preliminary findings of an ongoing investigation into constraints on the acquisition of L2 phonemic contrasts. We elicited production and perception data in two of the three logically possible ways in which a NL and a TL can differ with respect to a two-way phonemic contrast, as listed in (1).

(1) NL–TL Differences in a Two-Way Phonemic Contrast

   (a) The NL lacks sounds corresponding to either of the two TL phonemes.

   (b) The NL has sounds corresponding to one, but not both, of the two TL phonemes.

   (c) The NL has sounds corresponding to both of the TL phonemes, but in complementary distribution as allophones of the same phoneme.

This chapter considers only the latter two language-contact situations, those depicted in (1b) and (1c), and reports on the elicitation of both production and perception data to investigate these two NL–TL combinations.

A language-contact situation that illustrates (1b) as well as (1c) arises with respect to Korean as the NL and English as the TL. Thus, exemplifying (1b), Korean has [p], as does English, but Korean lacks [f] altogether, a sound that stands in phonemic contrast to /p/ in English. At the same time, both Korean and English have [s] and [š], but whereas these sounds contrast in English, they are in complementary distribution in Korean, because [š] occurs only before a (phonological) high front vowel or glide, and [s] occurs elsewhere. In Korean these two sounds are related by a principle or rule such as that in (2).

(2) Korean Allophonic Rule

/s/ is realized as [š] before the high front vowel or glide, elsewhere as [s].

The task of a Korean learner of English in acquiring these two contrasts seems straightforward: on the one hand, the learner must acquire the phoneme /f/ to differentiate words such as *pan* and *fan,* and, on the other hand, the learner must suppress the application of the NL allophonic rule so as not to render *see* the same as *she.* If the early stages of the interlanguage (IL) grammar are tied closely to the NL phonological patterns, then the learner will err on TL words containing /f/, most likely substituting /p/ (*fan* = *pan*), the phonetically closest segment in the NL inventory, and the learner will also transfer (2) into the IL grammar, erring on TL words containing [s] before a high front vowel (*see* = *she*).

However, general principles of phonology, to be discussed below, constrain the application of (2) in the IL and thus restrict the errors that the second-language learner makes, depending on whether the learner is at a stage in which [š] represents the phoneme /š/ rather than /s/ in the IL, at least for some words. Through the hypotheses developed in detail below, we predict that L2 learners who acquire a contrast such as that in (1c) in what we term morphologically derived environments will necessarily generalize that contrast to morphologically basic environments but not vice versa. Employing these general phonological principles as the basis for an intervention strategy, we attempted to manipulate the learning and generalization of the /s/–/š/ and /p/–/f/ contrasts.

The remainder of the chapter is structured as follows. The next section outlines the background for the study, setting the theoretical basis for the work and connecting it to previous research in the area. The section concludes with the statement and rationale of the hypotheses. We then lay out the methodology used to elicit the data. The two sections following deal with the findings, reporting them in the results section and interpreting them in the discussion section. The final section concludes the chapter.

Background

This section sets the context for the study by reviewing the literature in the two areas where the findings impinge on previous work. The discussion is followed by a description of the theoretical grounding for, and the statement of, the hypotheses.

The results of this research can be seen as a contribution to the discussion of two areas of L2 phonology, the first a long-standing issue dating back to the times of the Contrastive Analysis Hypothesis (CAH) (Lado 1957), the second a more-recent question on the relationship between a second-language learner's perception versus production of a TL phonemic contrast. We consider each in turn.

As far back at least as the CAH, allophones have played a significant role in hypotheses about L2 learning difficulty. The central claim of the CAH is that differences between the NL and TL are the major source of difficulty in L2 acquisition (Lado 1957, 2). A corollary of this claim is that the degree of difficulty associated with any given NL–TL difference is a function of the degree of difference between the NL and TL. Thus, the area of maximum difficulty in Lado's terms would result from structures where the NL and TL are maximally different. Although it may be possible to interpret the notion of maximal difference between the NL and TL in several ways, a reasonable interpretation in terms of the present discussion would be that of an NL–TL combination as in (1a) or (1b), where the NL is lacking one or both of the TL phonemes in question. However, instead of adopting this conclusion as characterizing maximum difficulty, Lado states that "when one significant unit or element in the native language equates bilingually with two significant units in the foreign language we have maximum learning difficulty" (1957, 15).

This statement depicts the language contact situation exemplified for (1c), in which Korean learners of English must split the allophones [s] and [š] into separate phonemes. In fact, the example that Lado uses to illustrate his claim about maximum difficulty is that of a learner whose NL is Spanish, which has the sounds [d] and [ɾ] as allophones of /d/, who then must split the categorization of these sounds into two phonemic units in English.

In addition to the seminal work by Lado, allophones have played an important role in the description and explanation of L2 phonological difficulty up through recent work. Considerations of space allow discussion of only one such work, viz., that of Hammerly (1982), who conducted a pronunciation study in which he proposed a six-level hierarchy of difficulty. Allophones figured into the four highest degrees of difficulty, the highest of all being NL allophones that fall into a different (including contrastive) distribution in the TL, supporting on empirical grounds the above claim about maximum difficulty.

Allophonic distribution is also part and parcel of more recent proposals regarding L2 phonological difficulty. The first two hypotheses of Flege's (1995) Speech Learning Model (SLM) can be construed in terms of Lado's claim. Specifically, the SLM's first hypothesis asserts that NL and TL sounds are related to each other at the allophonic level. The second hypothesis claims that, in the process of L2 acquisition, new phonetic categories are set up if a phonetic difference is perceived between the sounds in question. As allophones are outside of the lexicon and therefore unlikely to be perceived by the learner, the hypothesis predicts that TL sounds that correspond to NL allophones of the same phoneme are unlikely to be perceived as different and thus not likely to be set up as different categories, that is, as distinct phonemes.

Whereas it is clear that the role of NL and TL allophones has been prominent in various proposals regarding L2 phonological difficulty over the decades, what is equally apparent is that no one has been able to suggest an explanation for this fact. The findings of the present study have a bearing on this question, and we will speculate on a possible place to look for an explanation.

We now turn to the second area of L2 phonology that forms part of the context for this study, specifically, the relationship between a L2 learner's perception of a TL phonemic contrast and the production of that contrast.

One of the overarching questions in this respect is whether learners have to perceive contrasts before they can produce them. Although it would seem to be intuitively clear that a learner must perceive any given contrast before being able to implement it in production, the literature in fact attests all four logical possibilities: a contrast can be neither perceived nor produced; it can be both perceived and produced; it can be produced but not perceived; and it can be perceived but not produced.

Two of these possibilities are straightforward and require little or no elaboration: there are numerous documented examples of learners who can neither perceive nor produce a TL contrast that is absent in the NL, as well as instances in which L2 learners can both perceive and produce TL contrasts that happen to match up with NL distinctions (e.g., Bion et al. 2006). The other two logical possibilities are not as straightforward and therefore require discussion.

The first of these two, the one that is more intriguing, is that L2 learner productions of certain contrasts can exceed their ability to perceive those contrasts, which has been reported in Sheldon and Strange (1982), who replicated and extended earlier work. Sheldon and Strange tested native speakers of Japanese learning English on their ability to perceive and produce the distinction between /r/ and /l/, a contrast lacking in Japanese. Specifically, it was found that native speakers of English, when listening to recordings of the subjects' productions of minimal pairs containing /r/ and /l/, could successfully distinguish /r/ from /l/ better than the subjects themselves could distinguish this contrast in their own productions.

It is these results from Sheldon and Strange (1982) that clearly render the relationship between phonological perception and production not straightforward and that raise the question of how L2 learners can produce a contrast unless they know that a contrast has to be produced.

The answer, it seems, lies in the fact that the L2 subjects in the Sheldon and Strange study cited above received written input on the contrasts in question. The subjects did not have to hear the difference between /r/ and /l/ in order to know that they had to produce this contrast; they could discern that a contrast existed between /r/ and /l/ from the spelling of the words. Therefore, in language acquisition by preliterate children, it can still be maintained that perception of a contrast will precede its successful production; however, in L2 acquisition, if the learner is provided with written access to the contrast, or at least with some nonauditory way to discern the distinction, it is possible that production approximating a contrast may precede its perception.

The final logical possibility with respect to perception and production of a TL contrast is the one in which the learners can perceive the contrast in question but are unable successfully to produce it. As outlined above, Flege's (1995) SLM is predicated on the notion of "equivalence classification," according to which an L2 learner sets up phonetic categories for TL phones on the basis of the learner's perception of the TL segments in terms of the established NL categories. In a review of the literature on the relationship between L2 learners' perception and production of TL contrasts on both consonants and vowels, Flege (1999) found that perception and production are correlated but only weakly so. The works examined by Flege included selected studies on the perception and production of consonants as well as vowels; however, due to space limitations, we will limit ourselves to the studies on consonants.

Aoyama et al. (2004) investigated Japanese-speaking learners of English on the perception of English /r/ and /l/. Because English /r/ (a rhotic vocoid without tongue contact) is perceptually less similar to Japanese /r/ (an alveolar tap) than is English /l/ (an alveolar lateral, also with tongue contact), the SLM predicts that English /r/ should be acquired by Japanese learners faster than English /l/. The results supported this. More recently, Kluge et al. (2007) studied the production and perception of English /m/ and /n/ in coda position by native speakers of Brazilian Portuguese, for whom these are merged in the NL. The results showed a positive correlation between the perception and production tests. Given this background, we now turn to the theoretical context for the four hypotheses forming the basis for this study.

The assumption underlying the general research program to which this study belongs is that IL grammars are the way they are, in part, because they are constrained by general grammatical principles. Specific to the research being reported here is the hypothesis that two of these principles, listed below in (3) as adapted from work by Kiparsky (1982, and elsewhere), can also form the basis for intervention strategies regarding the IL grammars.

(3) Phonological Principles
   (a) Structure Preservation
      Representations within the lexicon consist only of elements drawn from the phonemic inventory.
   (b) Derived Environment Constraint
      Structure-preserving rule applications are restricted to derived environments (i.e., rule applications that involve phonemes of the language apply only across morpheme boundaries).

Structure Preservation states that words and morphemes in the lexicon of a grammar comprised only phonemes; no allophones are part of the lexicon. The Derived Environment Constraint claims that rules that apply to, or produce, phonemes must apply in environments that arise from putting two morphemes together. That is, such rules must produce morphemic alternations. Rules that produce allophones are not restricted in this way and so can apply everywhere, in morphologically simple and morphologically composite environments.

As outlined in Eckman, Elreyes, and Iverson (2003), Structure Preservation and the Derived Environment Constraint have important implications for learnability, in general, and for the acquisition of the English contrast between /s/ and /š/, in particular. It follows from these principles that the acquisition of a TL phonemic distinction whose contrasting segments correspond to allophones of the same phoneme in the NL will take place in stages. At the beginning, when the IL grammar lacks the contrast, the transferred NL rule will apply across the board in both basic and derived environments. As the learner begins to acquire the contrast in question, the two segments take on the status of phoneme, and therefore become part of the IL lexicon. As a consequence, the Derived Environment Constraint permits the rule to apply only in derived contexts, that is, only across morpheme boundaries. The last stage would be one in which the contrast has become acquired to the point where the rule is suppressed altogether.

Thus, if a native speaker of Korean learning English transfers the NL allophonic rule to the IL grammar and is subject to the two constraints in (3), then the following stages of acquisition for the /s/–/š/ contrast are predicted.

(4) Acquisition sequence

Stage I, No Contrast: not able to make the relevant target language contrast, applying the NL rule in both derived and basic environments (e.g., a Korean learner says the pairs *sea–she* and *messing–meshing* homophonously, as [ši] and [mɛšɪŋ]);

Stage II, Partial Contrast: able to make the contrast in some words, applying the NL rule only in derived environments (a Korean learner says *sea–she* correctly but errs by producing *messing–meshing* homophonously);

Stage III, Contrast: able to make the contrast in all words, applying the NL rule in neither derived nor basic environments (a Korean learner says the pairs *sea–she* and *messing–meshing* correctly);

Excluded stage: able to make the contrast in some words, applying the NL rule only in basic contexts (a Korean learner says the pair *sea–she* homophonously, but says *messing–meshing* correctly).

Of importance is that the stages of acquisition in (4) would not be predicted for learning a contrast such as (1b) because there is no allophonic rule involved.

Within this context, we now posit the hypotheses in (5).

(5) Hypotheses

a. Acquisition of the production of a contrast such as (1b) will not be sensitive to morphological structure.

b. Acquisition of the perception of a contrast such as (1b) will not be sensitive to morphological structure.

c. Acquisition of the production of a contrast such as (1c) will exhibit a derived environment effect sensitive to morphological structure.

d. Acquisition of the perception of a contrast such as (1c) will not exhibit a derived environment effect sensitive to morphological structure.

The rationale for (5a) is that there is no rule involved in the contrast; the rationale for (5b) and (5d) stems from the fact that virtually all (if not truly all) generalizations about L2 grammars have been made on the basis of data from production, not perception. The hypothesis in (5c) has its roots in the two general principles of phonology, Structure Preservation and the Derived Environment Constraint, given in (3).

Before concluding this section, we wish to emphasize the claims underlying the hypotheses in (5). As the consonantal phonemic inventory in (6) shows, Korean has lax, tense, and aspirated contrasts among its bilabial, alveolar, and velar stops, the same contrast in its postalveolar affricates, and a lax versus tense contrast in its coronal fricatives. And in addition to a three-way point of articulation contrast in nasals, Korean also has a liquid phoneme (rendered here as /l/, though it has both central and lateral allophones) and /h/. Yet the claim embodied in the hypotheses in (5) is that, despite the possibility that a Korean learner of English may be able to perceive a number of different contrasts on the basis of the inventory in (6), the explanation for the staged learning outlined in (4) for the /s/–/š/ contrast—as opposed to /p/–/f/— is that the principles in (3) constrain the application of the NL allophonic rule after it is transferred to the IL grammar.

(6) Phonemic Inventory of Korean Consonants

p pʰ p'   t tʰ t'   k kʰ k'   c cʰ c'
s s'
m n ŋ
l
h

Given this background along with the above hypotheses, we turn now to a description of the elicitation methods used to gather our production and perception data.

Methods

In a test of the hypotheses in (5), we elicited baseline productions and perception judgments from 10 participants on the /p/–/f/ contrast and from twenty different participants on the /s/–/š/ contrast and elicited perception judgments from the thirty participants on their respective contrast. We then trained the participants on their respective contrast using nonce words that showed the contrast either in the basic environment or in the derived environment. After the training, the baseline productions were elicited again to serve as a posttest. Of the thirty native speakers of Korean serving as participants for the study, ten were students at the City University of Incheon, Korea, ranging in age from nineteen to twenty-five years, and twenty were students in the Intensive English Program at the University of Wisconsin–Milwaukee, ranging in age from eighteen to thirty-six. A group of eight native-speaker controls was used for the perception stimuli for each contrast.

Two sets of stimuli were used in the study, one for the production of the target sounds and one for their perception. These two sets were used twice to collect subject responses at two points in time: (1) as a pretest (or baseline), at the beginning of the study before each subject entered the training phase, and (2) as a posttest, after the training had been completed. For the baseline pretest, sixty target words and thirty fillers was selected, all existing lexical items in English, each target word containing either /p/ or /f/, or /s/ or /š/, in three different positions in a morphologically basic word: initial before a high front vowel (e.g., *sip/ship*), medial (e.g., *lesson/ocean*), final (e.g., *pass/crash*) and in one additional position (medial, at the juncture with another morpheme) in morphologically composite words containing either the suffix *-ing* or *-y,* (e.g., *passing/brushing* or *messy/bushy*).

The perception stimuli consisted of naturally produced, single words recorded by a male native speaker of American English. All words were existing minimal pairs in English, in which either /p/ or /f/, or /s/ or /š/, occurred in initial and final positions in basic words and in medial position followed by the suffix *-ing* or *-y,* e.g.,

fan/pan, laugh/lap, cuffing/cupping; seep/sheep, plus/plush, classing/clashing. The
stimulus set consisted of seventy-two items (four stimuli × two contrastive segments
× three positions in a word × three repetitions).

Experimental Procedures

Several custom programs were written in MATLAB for the purposes of the present
study. For the production of the baseline pretest and the posttest, a program controlling the recordings displayed on a computer screen a set of pictures, clues, and com-
mands such as "Wait" or "Speak" designed to guide the subject and the experimenter
in order to elicit the word in question. The stimuli were presented in a random order,
recorded directly onto a hard disc drive at the sampling rate of 44.1 kHz. Subjects
spoke into a head-mounted microphone at a distance of one inch from the lips.

A second program controlled the perception experiment, employing a single-in-
terval two-alternative forced choice (2AFC) identification procedure, with the two response choices, /s/ and /š/, displayed on the computer monitor. After hearing the
stimulus word, the subject indicated with the press of a mouse button whether the
word contained a /p/ or an /f/, or an /s/ or an /š/, depending on the contrast being tested.
The stimuli were presented in a random order over Sennheizer HD600 headphones
at a comfortable listening level (~70 dB HL). Each subject was tested individually.
To make the perception task more demanding, the stimuli were presented in masking white noise at two different levels of sound-to-noise (S/N) ratios: 0 dB and −4

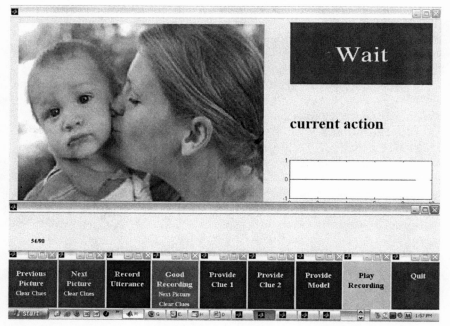

Figure 13.1 Computer Screen Display for Baseline for Eliciting the Baseline Production of the Derived-
Environment Word, "Kissing."

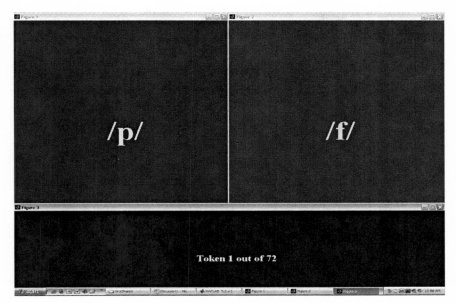

Figure 13.2 Computer Screen Display Used in the Perception Task for the /p/–/f/ Contrast.

dB. The use of masking noise is not uncommon in perception tasks because it is often necessary, as in the present study, to determine not simply whether the learner has acquired the contrast perceptually, but also the degree to which the perceptual contrast has been learned.

A third program guided the training of the participants on the production of the /p/–/f/ or /s/–/š/ contrast, depending on which baseline the person produced. The training program took the participants through a series of steps that were somewhat similar to the baseline production task in which pictures and verbal models that were presented to, and were to be learned by, the participant. Only nonce words (e.g., *nafe, kefing, hosing, hisi*) were used in the training phase.

After the training sessions the same production and perception tasks were conducted to elicit subjects' responses to the /p/–/f/ and /s/–/š/ contrast in the form of posttraining tests to assess the effects of learning.

The data were collected at Milwaukee and then transferred to Ohio State where they were transcribed by research assistants who were blind to the hypotheses. The transcriptions were then returned to Milwaukee, where they were scored. A subject's performance on a task had to reach the 80 percent criterion, the threshold that has been invoked in L2 research for several decades, in order for the subject's interlanguage grammar to be credited with having the contrast in question.

Results

In this section we describe the results according to how they bear on each of the hypotheses in (5). In production of the baselines and the posttest of the /p/–/f/ contrast, we observed no pattern of sensitivity to morphological structure (see fig. 13.3). On

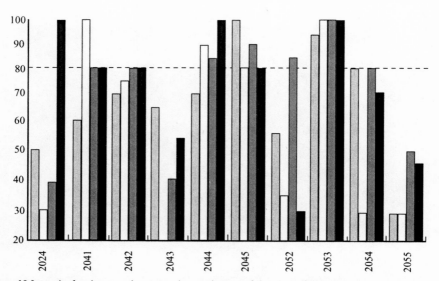

Figure 13.3 Results for the L2 Subjects on the Production of the /p/–/f/ Contrast on the Pretest and Posttest in Basic and Derived Environments

either the pretest or the posttest, the subjects' performance on the contrast evinced all four of the logical possibilities. Three of the subjects (2024, 2041, 2044), on either the pretest or posttest, crossed the threshold in the morphologically composite words without doing so on the morphologically basic words; four of the subjects (2024, 2043, 2052, 2055) did not reach the criterial threshold in either environment on one or both of the tests; two of the subjects (2045 and 2053) showed that they had the contrast in both environments on both pre- and posttests; and finally, two of the subjects (2052 and 2054) showed the contrast in the morphologically basic environment without having the contrast in the morphological-composite words on the posttest. Thus, hypothesis (5a) was supported because there is no morphologically sensitive pattern in the participants' production of the /p/–/f/ contrast. Within our framework, this is because there is no NL allophonic rule associated with the /p/–/f/ contrast, and therefore the general phonological principles in (3) above do not predict the stages of acquisition shown in (4).

The results of the perception task involving the /p/–/f/ contrast are shown in table 13.1. The subject identification numbers are shown at the head of the rows in the tables, and the columns indicate whether the performance was on the pretest or posttest, whether the environment was basic or derived, and the amount of the signal degradation. As can be seen from table 13.1, the performance of only one subject (2044) reached the criterial threshold on either the pre- or posttest; the scores of all the others were much lower and showed no morphologically sensitive pattern. The control subjects performed better overall than did the L2 participants on the perception task; however, they also showed no morphologically sensitive pattern in their performance. Therefore, hypothesis (5b) was supported.

We now turn to the /s/–/š/ contrast, where we see different results than those for the /p/–/f/ contrast. In the production of the baselines and the posttest on this

Table 13.1
Results of Perception for Subjects on /p/–/f/

	Pretest 0 dB		Pretest −4 dB		Posttest 0 dB		Posttest −4 dB	
	Basic	Derived	Basic	Derived	Basic	Derived	Basic	Derived
2024	60.42	62.5	62.5	33.33	79.17	50	75	58.33
2041	54.17	45.83	62.5	62.5	60.42	37.5	54.17	45.83
2042	62.5	58.33	60.42	50	64.58	41.67	47.92	66.67
2043	54.17	25	60.42	45.83	58.33	50	60.42	33.33
2044	83.33	54.17	81.25	45.83	75	50	68.75	58.33
2045	68.75	37.5	56.25	62.5	64.58	62.5	60.42	58.33
2052	68.75	41.67	70.83	58.33	60.42	75	60.42	41.67
2053	66.67	50	58.33	58.33	58.33	58.33	62.5	54.17
2054	56.25	58.33	37.5	41.67	54.17	66.67	66.67	54.17
2055	62.5	62.5	50	62.5	83.33	66.67	70.83	62.5

contrast, five subjects lacked the contrast in both basic and derived environments (see fig. 13.4); the performance of eight subjects showed that their IL had the contrast by reaching the 80 percent criterial threshold in both basic and derived environments (shown in fig. 13.5); and seven subjects evinced a derived environment effect by having the contrast in basic environments only, on the pretest, the posttest,

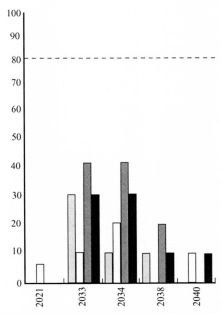

Figure 13.4 Results for the Production of the /s/–/š/ Contrast by the L2 Subjects That Lacked the Contrast in Both Basic and Derived Environments on both the Pretest and the Posttest

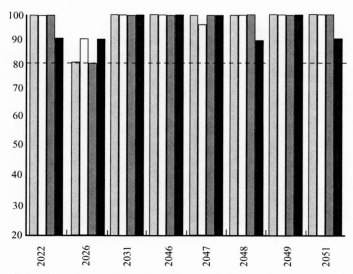

▓ Figure 13.5 Results for the Production of the /s/–/š/ Contrast by the L2 Subjects That Exhibited the Contrast in Both Basic and Derived Environments on Both the Pretest and the Posttest

or both (depicted in fig. 13.6). No subjects evidenced an IL that had the contrast in derived environments but lacked it in basic environments. Therefore hypothesis (5c) was supported.

Table 13.2 presents the results for the L2 subjects on the perception task for the /s/–/š/ contrast. The rows and columns of the table show the same information as that

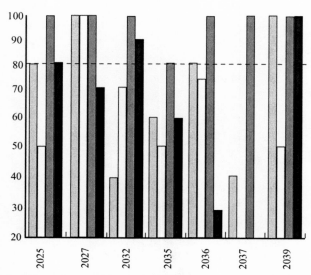

▓ Figure 13.6 Results for the Production of the /s/–/š/ Contrast by the L2 Subjects That Evidenced the Contrast in the Basic Environment but Not in the Derived Environment on Either the Pretest or the Posttest

Table 13.2

Results of Perception for Subjects on /s/–/š/

	Pretest 0 dB		Pretest −4 dB		Posttest 0 dB		Posttest −4 dB	
	Basic	Derived	Basic	Derived	Basic	Derived	Basic	Derived
2031	77.82	87.5	79.17	88	100	95.83	85.42	95.83
2032	77.08	91.67	70.83	87.5	77.08	75	68.75	83.33
2033	72.92	54.17	68.75	54.17	89.58	79.17	81.25	79.17
2034	97.92	87.5	83.33	95.83	95.83	100	89.58	95.83
2035	79.17	100	70.83	91.67	91.67	83.33	72.92	79.17
2036	83.33	83.33	87.5	91.67	97.92	100	95.83	100
2037	70.83	62.5	70.83	79.17	91.67	79.17	75	83.33
2038	75	54.17	58.33	54.17	87.5	75	72.92	75
2047	87.5	87.5	83.33	79.17	93.75	91.67	70.83	100
2048	66.67	87.5	70.83	95.83	83.33	75	79.17	70.83
2049	81.25	87.5	72.92	75	91.67	100	72.92	91.67

for table 13.1. Using once again the 80 percent threshold for acquisition of a contrast, we see that there was no patterned sensitivity to morphological structure in either the 0 dB or −4 dB SNR degradation level on either the pretest or posttest. In fact, seven of the subjects performed contrary to what would be expected for a derived environment effect. Once again, the controls performed better overall on this task than did the L2 participants, but there was no pattern of morphological sensitivity. Therefore, hypothesis (5d) was supported.

To recapitulate this subsection, the results from the study support the four hypotheses. The acquisition of the /s/–/š/ contrast by Korean-speaking L2 learners of English attests the three permissible stages in (4) above, while showing no evidence of the excluded stage. Moreover, this derived environment effect was relevant only in the case where an NL allophonic rule was involved, that is, not in the acquisition of the /p/–/f/ contrast, where no allophonic rule was applicable. Thus, our general claim that IL grammars are subject to general constraints was supported, as were the hypotheses concerning the perception of the contrasts in question.

Discussion

Our discussion of the results will reprise each of the major points described in the beginning of the chapter. The first is that our findings suggest a possible line of investigation that could shed light on why it has been reported over several decades that the splitting of NL allophones into separate TL phonemic categories is so difficult. The second point of discussion is to suggest why it may be the case that the perception and production of L2 phonemic contrasts are only weakly, rather than strongly, correlated. The third point is that general principles of phonology constrain IL grammars in such a way that L2 contrasts are acquired according to different paths, some following staged development through basic and derived environments, and others not. Finally, we take up the claim that these general principles can be the basis for intervention strategies. We begin with the question of maximum difficulty.

As the findings of our study show, acquiring a contrast between two sounds that are allophones of the same phoneme in the NL will take place in stages whereby the contrast is acquired first in morphologically simple words and then proceeds to include words that are both morphologically simple and morphologically complex. No such staging is predicted for the acquisition of contrasts where the NL lacks one or both of the sounds. Thus, past observations that splitting NL allophones into TL phonemes is more difficult than learning other kinds of phonemic distinctions may be due to the fact the learners have two stages to pass through to reach full acquisition in the case of the former, but not in the case of the latter. Of course, our claim at this point can be only suggestive until there is empirical work to address the question.

The explanation of the second point, the finding by Flege (1999) that perception and production of L2 contrasts are only weakly correlated, may also be related to the stages of acquisition associated with the production, but not the perception, of TL contrasts involving allophonic splits. Our findings suggest that the stages of acquisition in (4) hold for the production of a contrast such as in (1c) but not for the perception of that contrast. Thus, it would seem that the correlation between L2 learners' production and perception of contrasts involving allophonic splits would pattern in a way that is distinct from the correlation between the production and perception of other L2 phonemic contrasts. As with the first point above, the status of this suggestion as an explanation for the weak correlation is ultimately an empirical question and therefore must await further study.

The third point of discussion is that IL grammars are the way they are because they are constrained, at least in the case at hand, by general phonological principles. This was shown through the three stages of acquisition in (4) being attested by the production patterns of the L2 learners for the /s/–/š/ contrast, where an NL allophonic rule is involved but not in the case of the acquisition of the /p/–/f/ contrast, where no such NL rule is motivated. This point leads in turn to the final topic to be discussed, the general claim that the principles described in (3) can form the basis of a strategy for intervening in the IL; we therefore take these two point together.

We return to the results from the seven subjects whose IL grammar showed a derived environment effect (fig. 13.6), where we can observe some interesting results with respect to the effect of the training. Of these seven subjects, whose performance on the contrast in either the pretest or the posttest was at stage 2 in (4) above, four subjects were trained using nonce words with the contrast in the basic environment (2025, 2027, 2036, and 2039) and three were trained using nonce words with the contrast in a derived environment (2032, 2035, 2037). With the exception of 2027, all the subjects improved their performance between the pretest and posttest on the production of the contrast in at least one of the environments. Subject 2027 produced 100 percent of the contrasts in both basic and derived environments on the pretest, but then on the posttest scored 100 percent in the basic environment, but 70 percent in the derived environment. We have no explanation for why subject 2027 did worse on the posttest in the derived environment; however, we note that the IL pattern of contrast on the posttest nevertheless conforms to one of the predicted stages in (4).

Now let us consider the pattern of generalization of learning for the other subjects. Subjects 2025 and 2039 were trained using words with the contrast in the basic environment, and were able to generalize this training to the derived environment. This type of generalization from basic to derived environment is possible according to the principles in (3) but not necessary.

What is more interesting, we believe, in terms of the patterns of generalization of the contrast are the three cases in which the subjects were trained on words with the contrast only in derived environments. Subject 2032 lacked the contrast in both basic and derived environments on the pretest but, after training, evinced the contrast in both environments. Thus, this subject was able to generalize the contrast from the derived environment, on which training took place, to the basic environment, which was not trained. Similar results were obtained for subjects 2035 and 2037, except that on the posttest the contrast was not evidenced in the derived environment but was shown only in the basic environment, despite the fact that the contrast was not trained on the basic environment.

Thus, if a subject that lacks the contrast in both the basic and derived environments is trained on the contrast in only the derived environment and in fact learns the contrast in only that environment, the result would be an IL grammar that represents the excluded stage in (4) and is not licensed according to the principles in (3). According to our results, what happens in this case is that the contrast seems to be generalized to the basic environment, thereby producing an IL grammar that is allowed according to the principles in (3).

Conclusion

This chapter has reported findings that support the conclusion that the acquisition of L2 phonemic contrasts is constrained by general grammatical principles, which, in turn, lead to different paths of learning and can be used as the basis for intervention strategies.

ACKNOWLEDGMENTS

An earlier version of this paper was presented at the 2009 Georgetown University Round Table conference, March, 15, 2009. We would like to thank the members of the audience for their questions, comments, and general feedback. As always, any remaining errors or inconsistencies are our own. We also wish to express our appreciation to the following for their assistance with this research: Cara Campbell, Anne Hoffmann, Samantha Lyle, John Olstad, Heather Povletich, and Julia Sammet.

This work was supported in part by a grant from the National Institutes of Health 1 R01 HD046908-03. The positions expressed in this paper are those of the authors and do not necessarily reflect those of NIH.

REFERENCES

Aoyama, K., James Flege, S. Guion, R. Akahane-Yamada, and Y. Tsuneo. 2004. Perceived phonetic dissimilarity and L2 speech learning: The case of Japanese /r/ and English /l/ and /r/. *Journal of Phonetics* 23:233–50.

Bion, R. A. H., Paula Escudero, Andreia Rauber, and Barbara Baptista. 2006. Category formation and the role of spectral quality in the perception and production of English front vowels. *Proceedings of Interspeech* 2006:1363–66.

Eckman, Fred, Abdullah Elreyes, and Gregory Iverson. 2003. Some principles of second language phonology. *Second Language Research* 19:169–208.

Flege, James. 1995. Second language speech learning: Theory, findings and problems. In *Speech production and linguistic experience: Issues in cross-language research,* ed. W. Strange, 233–77. Timonium, MD: York Press.

———. 1999. The relation between L2 production and perception. *14th International Congress of Phonetic Sciences* 99:1273–76.

Hammerly, Hector. 1982. Contrastive phonology and error analysis. *International Review of Applied Linguistics* 20:17–32.

Kiparsky, Paul. 1982. Lexical phonology and morphology. In *Linguistics in the morning calm,* ed. I. S. Yang, 3–91. Seoul: Hanshin.

Kluge, C. D., Andreia Rauber, M. S. Reis, and R. A. H. Bion. 2007. The relationship between perception and production of English nasal codas by Brazilian learners of English. *Interspeech* 2007:2297–2300.

Lado, Robert. 1957. *Linguistics across cultures.* Ann Arbor: University of Michigan Press.

Sheldon, Amy, and Winifred Strange. 1982. The acquisition of /r/ and /l/ by Japanese learners of English: Evidence that speech perception can precede speech production. *Applied Psycholinguistics* 3:243–61.

IV

Empirical Studies on Key Issues in Bilingualism: Aging, Third Language Acquisition, and Language Separation

14

English Speakers' Perception of Spanish Vowels: Evidence for Multiple-Category Assimilation

LESLIE S. GORDON
The University of Georgia

RESEARCH IN SECOND LANGUAGE PHONOLOGY in general and L2 perception in particular has historically lagged behind research in other areas of L2 acquisition. However, the last two decades of the twentieth century saw an increased amount of research in L2 perception, work that culminated in some new and influential models. While work in L2 perception during this period was both theoretical and empirical, collectively addressing multiple variables, one constant underlies the vast majority of the work: the influence of the first language (L1) phonology upon L2 phonology. Since even the earliest days of second language acquisition (SLA) research, the influence of the L1 upon the acquisition L2 phonology has been widely accepted and empirically supported (Eckman 2004).

The research in L2 phonology that began in the middle of the last century was centered on production and, more specifically, predicted points of difficulty based upon L1–L2 phonological and allophonic differences (for the Contrastive Analysis Hypothesis [CAH] see Lado 1957; see also Ioup 1984; Stockwell and Bowen 1965). In these early studies the popular focus was the native English-speaking learner of an L2. Some years later, studies in L2 phonology shifted their focus and examined production problems on the basis of L1–L2 similarities rather than differences (for the Crucial Similarity Measure, Wode 1976, 1978). Eventually criticism of both the CSM and the CAH arose due to the lack of a clear definition for what constituted similarities and differences (Rochet 1995).

Findings from studies conducted in the later years of the twentieth century helped further clarify the definition of L1–L2 similarities and differences. The Speech Learning Model (SLM) (Flege 1995) proposes that L2 learners rely on a mechanism called equivalence classification when confronting L2 sounds. Equivalence classification describes the listener's perception of L2 sounds as being "similar" to L1 sounds, falling within a crucial similarity range of an L1 sound and thus judged as being equivalent to that sound, or as being "new" sounds, which are sounds without a clear counterpart in the L1 falling outside the crucial range of equivalency to L1 categories (Wode

1978). Studies of equivalence classification have shown that L2 sounds deemed by the learner to be equivalent to L1 sounds are harder to acquire because the learner is likely to assign both sounds to one L1 category rather than create a new L2 category (Flege 1995). Much of Flege's body of work on the SLM examines data from non-native English speakers and the patterns they exhibited when confronting L2 English sounds (Flege 1987a, 1987b, 1988, 1991; Flege and Eefting 1987; Flege and Liu 2001). The Perceptual Assimilation Model (PAM) (Best 1994, 1995; Best, McRoberts, and Goodell 2001; Best, McRoberts, and Sithole 1988), like the SLM, holds that the difficulty of nonnative contrast discrimination can be predicted based on the perceived similarity or discrepancy between L1 and L2 categories. More specifically, the PAM cites the role of phonetic-articulatory similarities between L1 and L2 sounds in L2 perception. Furthermore, a key tenet of the PAM is the task facing the learner of perceiving not only L1–L2 difference but also the difference between two L2 sounds. The PAM proposes different levels of categorization of L2 sounds depending on the degrees of similarity or differences previously described.

The goal of the present study is to contribute to the discussion of the role that L1–L2 similarities and differences play in L2 perception. The comparative nature of the English and Spanish vowel inventories makes them an interesting vehicle by which to further study the topic at hand. The literature on cross-language perception studies involving English and Spanish tends to be focused upon the perceptual ability or difficulties faced by native Spanish speakers of L2 English, a scenario in which the L2 vowel inventory is much larger and includes some categories that have no counterpart in the L1. For instance, Spanish-speaking learners of English must acquire the lax vowels, for instance /ɪ/, which do not exist in Spanish (Flege 1991). English speakers face the opposite scenario, and perception of Spanish vowels seems superficially to be a much easier task, as the five vowels of Spanish do have near equivalents in the English vowel inventory. However, for reasons discussed in the ensuing sections of this paper, English speakers' perception of L2 Spanish vowels may not be as simple as it seems, and at the present time there is a need in the perception literature for more empirical studies that directly assess the perceptual ability of English-speaking speakers of L2 Spanish.

The effect of time on L2 development is another variable that perception research has not yet clearly explained. That the L1 phonological system can be so influential in the perception of L2 phonology is underscored by studies that have shown that even prolonged exposure to the L2 (Sanz 2000) and early age of acquisition of the L2 (Flege, Munro, and MacKay 1995; Pallier, Bosch, and Sebastian-Galles 1997) do not ensure acquisition of native-like L2 perception. A common focus of research in L2 perception has been the end state of phonological acquisition rather than the stages of perceptual acquisition throughout L2 development, where learners of often mixed skill levels are compared to native L2 speakers. Furthermore, different constructs have been used to measure the effect of time of exposure to L2. Some research has measured age of arrival and degree of continued use (Flege, Schirru, and MacKay 2003; MacKay, Meador, and Flege 2001), while others have examined learners who collectively had many years of exposure to the L2 (Pallier, Bosch, and Sebastian-Galles 1997). Few have examined the effects of formal instruction at precisely defined intervals (Escudero and Boersma 2002). Are L2 learners with multiple semesters or even years of exposure more skilled in their L2 vowel perception than beginners? Do patterns of L2 perception change steadily with increase in L2 exposure? These questions merit empirical study for the implications they have on popular current assumptions regarding if, when, and how to teach second language phonology. An additional goal of the present study is to examine the vowel perception of English-speaking learners of L2 Spanish at different levels of instruction in order to determine the effects of continued instruction on L2 perceptual development.

Review of the Literature
The Effect of L1 on L2 Categorical Perception

Categorical perception, as its name implies, recognizes stimuli as belonging to one phonological category or another. Experimental research into listener capacity for categorical perception of L1 and L2 categories has revealed the high degree of sensitivity of human phonological perception. By six to twelve months of age the perceptual system of the human infant becomes biased in favor of the native language (Best, McRoberts, and Sithole 1988; Kuhl and Iverson 1995; Polka and Werker 1994; Werker and Tees 1984). Kuhl's (1991) model of the "perceptual magnet effect" describes the perceptual behavior of the infant acquiring L1. According to this model, the perceptual system matches the categories present in speech input to established L1 categorical prototypes (the "magnets") and draws the good instances of a category from the input toward the prototypes. The benefit of categorical perception is the speed with which incoming stimuli can be parsed and categorized (Wode 1994, 1995). The essence of the magnet model has also been extended to the perceptual system of the adult L2 learner and is echoed in Flege's SLM (1995). If the L2 category falls within a crucial similarity range to an underlying L1 category in the listener's phonological space, the "magnet" will pull that L2 sound toward the L1 prototype and the listener will equate the L2 category to the L1 category. Though categorical perception is advantageous, it can also result in errors, and the SLM predicts that L2 sounds deemed by the learner to be equivalent to L1 sounds are harder to acquire because the learner is likely to assign both sounds to one L1 category rather than create a new L2 category.

Phonological Inventory Size and L2 Perception

The probability that a listener will equate an L2 sound to one or more L1 sounds may be influenced by the size and shape of the phonological inventories involved, both the L1 and the L2. Commonly reported in the perception literature are cases where the L2 is larger than the L1 and in some such cases the learner is faced with problems associated with assimilating, or equating two L2 categories to just one L1 category, what Best (1995) refers to as single category assimilation (Best 1995; Flege 1995; Flege, Schirru, and MacKay 2003). By contrast, a limited number of studies to date have examined cases in which the L1 is larger and, furthermore, features extraneous native sounds not present in the L2.

Recent research has taken up this issue. An experiment by Escudero and Boersma (2002) examined Dutch speakers' perception of L2 Spanish, a scenario in which the

L1 had a larger vowel inventory than the L2. The authors describe a pattern of multiple-category assimilation (MCA) by Dutch learners of Spanish, showing that MCA causes categorization problems in L2 perceptual development. Dutch speakers in that study manifested MCA in their perception of the Spanish front vowels /i/ and /e/. Because Dutch has three front vowels /i/, /ɪ/, and /ɛ/, Dutch speakers sometimes perceived Spanish /i/ as Dutch /i/ but sometimes as /ɪ/ and still other times as /ɛ/.

The English-speaking learner of Spanish faces a very similar scenario. Research by Morrison (2003), following the experimental design of Escudero and Boersma (2002), found that the English-speaking learner of Spanish faces a scenario similar to the Dutch learners previously described. Morrison found support for the existence of MCA for native English learners of Spanish for some Spanish vowels. The English listeners overwhelmingly assimilated Spanish /i/, /e/, and /o/ to English /i/, /e/, and /o/, respectively. Morrison's English listeners manifested MCA in their perception of low central Spanish /a/ as English /æ/, /ʌ/, /a/, and /ɛ/ and in their assimilation of Spanish /u/ to English /ʊ/ and /u/.

The basic English vowel inventory (fig. 14.1), like the Dutch vowel inventory, is at least twice the size of the Spanish vowel inventory (fig.14.2). Varieties of English differ in terms of the number of categories and the position of those categories in the vowel space, yet most will feature eleven to fifteen distinct vowel categories. The basic inventory shown in figure 14.1 is representative of American English and is the relevant point of reference for the speakers in the present study.

The English vowel categories /i/, /e/, /o/, /u/, and /a/ are near equivalents to the five Spanish vowel categories /i/, /e/, /o/, /u/, and /a/ (variants excluded). The fact that English, with a larger vowel inventory, contains a subset of vowels often judged as "equivalent" to the Spanish vowels, may make the English speaker's perception of Spanish a seemingly easy task and may be the reason that perception research to date has largely excluded a detailed investigation of the English-speaking learner of L2 Spanish, as in the early stages of L2 acquisition lexical storage and retrieval may be

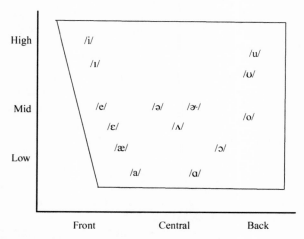

▓ Figure 14.1 The American English Vowel Inventory

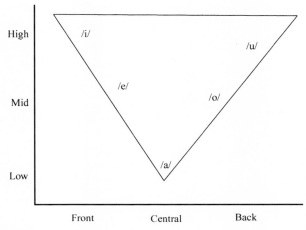

Figure 14.2 The Spanish Vowel Inventory

aided by the presence of similar vowels (Escudero and Boersma 2002). English also features lax vowels—/ɛ/, /ɪ/, /ʊ/, /ɔ/, to name a few—that do not exist in L2 Spanish. The position of these lax vowels relative to the /e/ and /i/ categories that have counterparts in L2 Spanish has been shown to interfere with perception of L2 Spanish /e/ and /i/. An acoustic study of perception by Bradlow (1996) showed a strong effect of the native English /ɪ/ and /ɛ/ categories upon perception of Spanish /i/ and /e/. Bradlow's English listeners tended to judge the Spanish stimuli with reference to their native vowel categories. The result of that tendency was the strong effect of the /ɪ/ and /ɛ/ categories, vowels present in English but not in Spanish. When listening to Spanish vowels, English speakers' area of uncertainty corresponded to the acoustic space corresponding to these English vowels.

Furthermore, the near equivalency between the Spanish vowels and a subset of English vowels does not obscure the inherent acoustic and base-of-articulation differences between these vowels in the two languages (Bradlow 1995). The English tense vowels and their near equivalents in Spanish differ along several parameters such as tongue height, backness, tenseness, duration, and diphthongization. Previous studies have shown these parameters to be important for perception and that English and Spanish speakers differ in their reliance upon certain cues, such as duration, when distinguishing between the vowels of these languages (Flege 1991; Flege, Bohn, and Jang 1997).

Because of the need for more research on perceptual patterns of English-speaking learners of Spanish, and in consideration of recent empirical data on the effects of extraneous L1 categories on the perception of L2 sounds, further investigation of the MCA pattern for English-speaking learners of Spanish is warranted. The present study investigates English speakers' perception of Spanish front vowels /e/ and /i/;[1] do these listeners map Spanish /e/ and /i/ to multiple L1 English categories? Furthermore, whether patterns of perception change as a result of increased exposure to L2 Spanish is also a question that must be explored empirically; therefore, the effect of level of L2 exposure is also examined here. The present study addresses the following research questions:

1. Does L1 English vowel inventory size have an effect upon listener perception of L2 Spanish vowels? Specifically, do English speakers demonstrate MCA for Spanish front vowels /e/ and /i/?
2. Does increased exposure to L2 Spanish have an effect upon listeners' L2 vowel perception?

Methodology
Participants
Participants were adult college-level students from three levels of Spanish. Participant profile questionnaires ensured that participants were native speakers of English, exposed to Spanish during or after adolescence, with no previous explicit instruction in Spanish phonetics. Profile questionnaires also verified participants' level of L2 exposure, measured in weeks or semesters of previous Spanish study. This information was used to eliminate any between-subject inconsistency that might be overlooked or disregarded in the course of placement in college-level Spanish courses and to ensure proper matching of participants to level. Cases of partial or complete data loss during the experiment due to computer program failure were eliminated from the study. Details on the final participant pool are given with the description of the experimental tasks that follows.

Stimuli and Procedure
To test the hypothesis that English speakers at multiple levels of instruction will demonstrate MCA for Spanish front vowels, the targeted stimuli were the Spanish front vowel categories /e/ and /i/ embedded in CVCV tokens. The remaining three Spanish vowels /a/, /o/, and /u/, also embedded in the same CVCV, provided data to which to compare listeners' performance on target vowel stimuli. The decision to use CVCV syllable shapes was made in consideration of Spanish phonotactics, as CVCV syllable shapes are highly frequent in Spanish and are permissible in English as well. The consonants used in the CVCV stimuli, initial /b/ and intervocalic /s/, as well as the final vowel, /a/, were also carefully selected in order to ensure phonotactically permissible syllable shapes in both languages. Distractors of a slightly different shape (C/r/VCV, for example /prasa/) were also included among the stimuli. The stimuli used in the listening tasks can be seen in tables 14.1 and 14.2. The CVCV stimuli for the listening tasks in both conditions were obtained from the naturally produced tokens of one female native Spanish speaker. Minor acoustic editing was done to ensure that tokens were balanced with regard to volume, intonation, and duration of vowels. Acoustic measurement and editing ensured that both vowels of each stimulus were of appropriate duration for Spanish (as calculated from repeated productions of ten native Spanish speakers) and also to ensure balanced vowel duration between stimuli.

Two listening tasks, which followed in part the tasks used in Escudero and Boersma (2002), required listeners to attend to the CVCV stimuli but under different conditions to elicit different perceptual modes.

Perceptual condition 1. The first task assessed the degree to which English speakers perceive a binary contrast in Spanish (/e/ and /i/, for example) as more than two categories in English and therefore demonstrate MCA. Participants heard Spanish vowels in CVCV items and were asked to classify the vowels according to the English vowel categories. They were not told that the items contain Spanish vowels. In this condition the CVCV stimuli were embedded in an English sentence of the type "Hear the word _____." Participants identified the vowel they heard by choosing from ten English response options (appendix 14A) written orthographically rather than phonetically transcribed due to the requirement that participants be untrained in phonetics. Listeners heard ten repetitions of each CVCV stimulus and six repetitions of each distractor for a total of sixty-eight stimuli, randomly presented, in the first condition of the MCA task. The final participant pool for the /e/ stimuli consisted of the following: Beginners, N = 39; Intermediate, N = 49; Advanced, N = 34. The final pool for the /i/ stimuli included: Beginners, N = 39; Intermediate, N = 37; Advanced, N = 24. This information is also shown in tables 14.1 and 14.2.[2]

Perceptual condition 2. The second phase of the MCA pretest was a test of Spanish perceptual proficiency. Listeners were told that they were hearing Spanish vowels and were told to match the items they heard to the five Spanish response options shown on the screen. In phase 2 the same Spanish CVCV items used in Perceptual Condition 1 were delivered in the Spanish carrier phrase "*Escucha la palabra* _____." As this phase of the MCA task asked participants to choose only from Spanish vowels categories, the selection set was reduced to only those items that matched the Spanish target vowels, in the same CVCV stimuli frame, plus distracters (appendix 14B). Once again, listeners heard ten repetitions of each CVCV stimulus and six repetitions of each distractor for a total of sixty-eight stimuli, randomly presented, in the second condition of the MCA pretest. The final participant pool for the /e/ and /i/ stimuli consisted of the following: Beginners, N = 64; Intermediate, N = 72; Advanced, N = 46. This information is also shown in tables 14.1–14.3.[3]

Testing Procedure
Before beginning the experimental phase all participants were familiarized with the screen and response procedure on day 1 during a brief (fifteen to twenty minutes) familiarization session designed to introduce participants to the look of the experiment, the response method and most important, to ensure that they would make the correct association between the vowels they heard and the orthographically spelled response options in the experiment. In the familiarization session participants first heard the target vowel sounds and were given real English examples of words containing those sounds. They then completed a ten-item quiz in which they heard nonsense syllables containing the target vowels embedded in nonsense CVCV shapes. In these familiarization stimuli the vowel sounds were spelled with the same orthography used in the full experiment, but these were embedded between consonants that were unique to those used in the stimuli in the full experiment. Wrong answers to or questions about the quiz were discussed between the researcher and individual participants before they continued on to the first task. The computer-delivered listening tasks in the

full experiment were created with E-Prime software. The experiment was run in a language classroom equipped with PCs at individual learning stations. All participants were equipped with earphones at their individual stations to prevent disturbance from other PC stations or from ambient noise.

Results

To determine whether English speakers demonstrate MCA for Spanish vowels /e/ and /i/, analysis of the results must involve two steps. The first step is to examine listeners' pattern of categorization of Spanish target vowels and specifically, the frequency with which, in Perceptual Condition 1, listeners mapped L2 Spanish vowels to L2 English near-equivalent vowels (Spanish /e/ to English /e/; Spanish /i/ to English /i/). Table 14.1 lists the descriptive statistics for Perceptual Condition 1. The means given in table 14.1 indicate the percentage of instances (out of a possible ten repetitions) in which listeners perceived a Spanish vowel stimulus as its English equivalent. For example, in Perceptual Condition 1 when a listener heard "besa" and selected response option "baysa," this was counted as one instance of mapping the L2 vowel to the equivalent L1 vowel (mapping Spanish /e/ to English /e/). Glancing across the means for Perceptual Condition 1 one notes the higher means for /basa/, /busa/, and /bosa/, and conversely, lower means for /besa/ and /bisa/, the target stimuli in this study. These means tell us that listeners assimilated Spanish /a/, /u/, and /o/ to the English equivalents more frequently than they assimilated Spanish /e/ and /i/ to English /e/ and /i/. Figure 14.3 provides a visual representation of these data to better illustrate the difference between listener

Table 14.1
Perceptual Condition 1: Front Vowel L2 → L1 Mapping

Stimulus Mapping	Level	N	Mean	S.D.
L2 /a/ → L1 /a/ (/basa/)	Beg	12	.74	.07
	Interm	7	.57	.29
	Adv	3	.63	.11
L2 /e/ → L1 /e/ (/besa/)	Beg	39	.33	.29
	Interm	49	.3	.29
	Adv	34	.24	.26
L2 /i/ → L1 /i/ (/bisa/)	Beg	39	.47	.24
	Interm	37	.46	.27
	Adv	24	.43	.27
L2 /u/ → L1 /u/ (/busa/)	Beg	26	.58	.22
	Interm	24	.55	.2
	Adv	16	.61	.17
L2 /o/ → L1 /o/ (/bosa/)	Beg	11	.71	.11
	Interm	9	.47	.3
	Adv	13	.6	.22

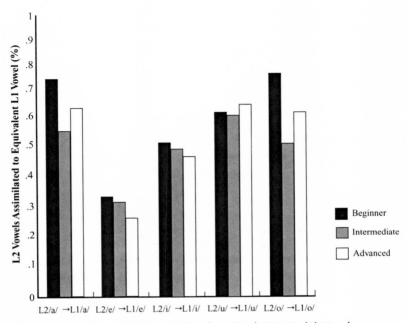

Figure 14.3 Listener Assimilation of L2 Spanish Vowels to "Similar" L1 English Vowels

perception of the target vowels and the remaining Spanish vowels. If listener perception of Spanish /e/ and, to a lesser extent Spanish /i/, is more challenging, to what should this be attributed? If listeners do not assimilate Spanish /e/ and /i/ to the equivalent English categories, what, then, are the categories to which they are mapping these vowels?

To answer this question and to determine whether English speakers demonstrate MCA for Spanish front vowels /e/ and /i/, a second step must be taken. In the organization and coding of data collected in this study, special care was taken to tally the number of times participants mapped Spanish /e/ and /i/ to English /e/ and /i/, respectively, but even more important, when they mapped those vowels to other native categories. In other words, when listeners did not map Spanish /e/ to English /e/ or when they did not map Spanish /i/ to English /i/, how frequently did they choose the response category of English /ɛ/ or /ɪ/, respectively? The paragraphs that follow review the results for these specific response patterns.

Table 14.2 displays the descriptive statistics for MCA for participants at all levels. Once again, these results indicate the number of times that listeners, when *not* mapping Spanish /e/ or /i/ to English /e/ or /i/, mapped the Spanish vowels to English /ɛ/ or /ɪ/ instead. It is notable that listeners demonstrated this perceptual pattern a minimum of 86 percent and in some cases a maximum of 95 percent of the time. In the case of Spanish /e/ the results are striking; listeners mapped the vowel to English /ɛ/ at least 95 percent of the time when they did not map it to English /e/.

There were a few cases in which these Spanish front vowels were mapped to other categories among those offered by the response options in the task; however, these

▓ Table 14.2
Percentage of Listener Assimilation of L2 Spanish Vowels /e/ and /i/ to English Lax Vowels /ɛ/ and /ɪ/ When *Not*
Assimilated to English Tense Vowels /e/ and /i/

Mapping	Level	N	Mean	S.D.
Spanish /e/ to English /ɛ/	Beg	39	.94	.17
	Interm	49	.95	.15
	Adv	34	.94	.13
Spanish /i/ to English /ɪ/	Beg	39	.86	.24
	Interm	37	.93	.15
	Adv	24	.93	.16

instances were few, and in some cases the responses given were for vowels so unrelated to the target vowels as to raise the supposition that perhaps those participants simply miskeyed their responses. Regarding listener perception of Spanish /i/, listeners once again demonstrated MCA with high frequency, mapping Spanish /i/ to English /ɪ/ as much as 93 percent of the time. The results for these two target vowels, taken together, are suggestive of two important points. First, that Spanish /e/ and /i/ are likely to incite patterns of MCA for English speakers, as evidenced by the lower means for these vowels in Perceptual Condition 1. Second, that MCA for these listeners means that they are likely to assimilate Spanish /e/ and /i/ to English /ɛ/ and /ɪ/, respectively.

The method for collecting and coding the data in Perceptual Condition 1 was also used in Perceptual Condition 2. However, this task differed from Perceptual Condition 1 in that listeners were not required to categorize stimuli according to English vowel categories but rather to Spanish vowel categories. Therefore, Perceptual Condition 2 represented a rather straightforward test of L2 Spanish perception. For example, if a listener heard /bisa/ and selected "bisa," this was an instance of correct L2 vowel perception. Table 14.3 gives descriptive statistics of listener perception of Spanish /e/ and /i/, as well as the other three Spanish vowels, for comparative purposes.

The descriptive statistics for Perceptual Condition 2 show that participants at all levels achieved high accuracy for categorizing all Spanish vowels. While the results for /e/ and /i/ do show slightly lower means among beginners, means are nevertheless very high, showing that listeners had virtually no difficulty categorizing the Spanish vowels they heard. By comparing results from the two perceptual conditions, it is clear that straightforward Spanish vowel perception is not problematic for most listeners, while perception of Spanish vowels amid the background of multiple L1 English categories is difficult, with particular regard to the /e/ and /i/ vowels.

The second research question addressed the effect of different levels of L2 exposure on learners' perception of L2 Spanish vowels and, in particular, their demonstration of MCA. Categorization means by learner level are included in tables 14.1–14.3. A glance back at those data reveals that listeners at all levels perform similarly. Two separate one-way ANOVAs were run on the data collected in Perceptual Condition 1 order to determine any difference that might exist between participants

Table 14.3
Perceptual Condition 2: Spanish Vowel Perception

Stimulus	Level	N	Mean	S.D.
/basa/	Beg	64	.98	.65
	Interm	72	.99	.02
	Adv	46	.99	.02
/besa/	Beg	64	.93	.19
	Interm	72	.98	.08
	Adv	46	.98	.05
/bisa/	Beg	64	.95	.13
	Interm	72	.97	.08
	Adv	46	.99	.03
/busa/	Beg	64	.9	.2
	Interm	72	.98	.04
	Adv	46	.98	.03
/bosa/	Beg	64	.99	.01
	Interm	72	.99	.01
	Adv	46	1	0

at different levels. The first one-way ANOVA was run on the front vowel categorization data in which listeners matched Spanish /e/ and /i/ to English equivalent /e/ and /i/, respectively (table 14.1). Results revealed listeners at all three levels to be comparable, as there was no significant difference between groups on the /besa/ stimulus ($F[2, 119] = 1.046, p = .354$) nor on the /bisa/ stimulus ($F[2,97] = .153, p = .858$). In short, statistical results confirm that all listeners perform similarly when assimilating target L2 vowels to L2 equivalent vowels, and that level of exposure to L2 has no significant effect on learner's ability to make this mapping. A second one-way ANOVA was run on the MCA data, or the instances in which listeners assimilated the target Spanish vowels to the additional native categories of /ɛ/ or /ɪ/ (table 14.2). Results again reveal no significant effect of learner level on MCA of Spanish /e/ [$F(2,119) = .113, p = .893$], or on MCA of Spanish /i/ ($F[2.97] = 1.469, p = .235$). In other words, although all participants frequently demonstrated MCA for these vowel categories, level of exposure is not a significant predictor of the occurrence.

Discussion

One of the aims of this study has been to add to our knowledge of how L1 perception influences L2 perception. Listeners in this study showed a high frequency of mapping Spanish /e/ and /i/ to English /ɛ/ and /ɪ/, respectively, vowel categories absent in the standard Spanish phonemic inventory. The current results are similar to patterns found in Escudero and Boersma (2002), where Dutch speakers mapped L2 /e/ and /i/ categories to more than one L1 category, and again, the direction of that mapping was frequently the lax vowels /ɛ/ and /ɪ/. The results differ, however, from patterns exhibited by Morrison's (2003) English listeners who mapped English /e/ and /i/ to Spanish /e/ and /i/. The low frequency with which Morrison's listeners mapped /e/ and /i/ to /ɛ/ and /ɪ/ may, by the author's admission, be due to the fact that English disfavors lax vowels in final open syllables where all target stimuli were situated in that experiment. In the present study all target vowels were in word-internal stressed syllables. Therefore this study, while not exactly replicating the results of previous experiments of a similar design, yields further evidence that the presence of L1 vowels not found in the L2 does in fact influence L2 perception.

The second research question addressed whether learners' level of Spanish exposure had an effect on listener instances of MCA. Descriptive and statistical results indicate that listeners at all levels performed similarly. A widely held assumption, independent of empirical research, is that L2 perception evolves naturally with continued input. The data from this study do not support the assumption that increased L2 exposure, at least of the type offered in a formalized learning environment, improves a listener's categorical perception. Second language perception research has to date little to offer regarding the developmental nature of speech perception. Even the widely cited SLM and PAM, reviewed earlier, do not attempt to explain how perceptual abilities evolve as a listener progresses beyond the early stages of L2 learning. Escudero and Boersma (2004) investigated the perceptual development of Spanish learners of British and Scottish English and offer a formal grammar in probabilistic Optimality Theory that demonstrates a plasticity that allows the learner to move toward a more and more native-like L2 perception grammar. Their model showed the behavior of a simulated L2 learner who received one thousand instances of vowel input per month. A slight change in vowel boundary shift was seen for this listener at ten months, but real change in the direction of L2-like vowel perception was seen after one hundred virtual months of L2 vowel input. Data from the current experiment with real listeners also indicate that such plasticity requires a considerable amount of time and input, as even the advanced listeners, some with as many as three years of exposure to L2 Spanish, show virtually no greater perceptual ability than beginners. More will be said regarding the nature of L2 input in the section devoted to research limitations.

The fact that listeners at different levels of L2 exposure performed similarly on the measures in this experiment has some important pedagogical implications. Explicit instruction on L2 phonology generally occurs in the first year of instruction and perhaps on occasion at the higher levels of instruction. Current data indicate that continued instruction, even at the higher levels, might be warranted. Phonological instruction is often production oriented, however, emphasizing the similarities between some L2 and L1 phones, and may not address listeners' ability to perceive those similarities. Furthermore, phonological instruction typically does not broach the subject of which native phonemes might interfere with accurate L2 perception.

Limitations and Future Research
The first commentary regards the nature of the experimental task. The methodology used in the present study follows in part the methodology used in a previous study that yielded informative results (Escudero and Boersma 2002). However, the task design in itself is not free from disadvantages. The data from Perceptual Condition 1 reveal patterns of L2 perception against the background of L1 and reveal the effects

of the additional L1 categories on L2 perception but do not simulate a natural language perceptual processing; in natural communication, a speaker of an L2 is not asked to listen to L2 input and explicitly compare it to native categories. Perceptual Condition 2 is a far simpler task in that it only requires listeners to correctly identify L2 vowel categories, but does not provide insight into how perception of those L2 categories might be influenced by long-established L1 categories. In short, the use of separate tasks in this way yields useful data but allows for only limited claims regarding the nature of L2 (here, Spanish) perception.[4] Future research should strive for a design that accesses both types of perception in a single task.

A second drawback concerns the stimuli used in the experiment. It is difficult to create nonsense stimuli in a CVCV frame that does not result in items that are meaningful or are similar to meaningful words in Spanish given the prevalence of that shape for Spanish nouns. In the current study the item *besa* is a meaningful lexical item (*kiss,* third-person singular) in Spanish. Experimentation with multiple other combinations of consonants and vowels produced similar problems. The set of possible combinations was even further limited by the possible acoustic impact that certain vowels have on the vowel preceding or following them. To control for this, participants were told in the task instructions that all items were nonsense items and instructed not to make any meaningful associations between test stimuli and English or Spanish. A debriefing questionnaire addressed this point, and no subject reported being influenced by items that matched or almost matched meaningful English or Spanish lexical items.

Last, there are drawbacks to addressing the effects of increased L2 exposure in a formalized learning environment. In an experiment such as this, requiring large numbers of participants, it was necessary to draw from multiple classes, a strategy that introduces a number of potentially confounding factors such as type and amount of teacher and student input in each class, the native language of the instructors of those classes, and the differing degrees to which participants sought additional opportunities to speak the language, to name but a few factors. Furthermore, as one anonymous reviewer suggested, the typical college language class does not provide truly consistent exposure; students are exposed for only three to five hours per week on average. Finally, the typical classroom environment does not duplicate the naturalistic learning that takes place in contexts of full immersion or when the learner lives in an L2-dominant area, as did the real and virtual listeners in the Escudero and Boersma study (2004) previously cited.

Future research should investigate other factors involved in English speakers' perception of similar Spanish vowels. The present analysis does not address the inherent acoustic distinctions between perceptually similar English and Spanish vowels. English and Spanish speakers rely on different spectral cues in their perception of native vowels (Escudero and Boersma 2004; Flege, Bohn, and Jang 1997; Fox, Flege, and Munro 1995). Some studies have investigated the effects of explicit perceptual training designed to shift attention from familiar (L1) cues to unfamiliar (L2) cues (Francis, Baldwin, and Nusbaum 2000). Would such training improve the English speaker's perception of L2 Spanish vowels? Data collected from acoustic and perceptual training with the participants described in this study are currently being analyzed and are expected to yield useful data for a future report and subsequent research. Further research could also explore the possibility that English speakers demonstrate MCA for the back vowels /u/ and /o/, as they are closely positioned in the vowel space to the /ʊ/ and /ɔ/ categories, categories that were also found to present challenges to English speakers in Bradlow's (1996) study.

Conclusion

The goal of the present study was to test the findings of the small number of empirical studies that have sought to describe the perceptual abilities and patterns of native English-speaking learners of Spanish. Results from this study corroborate previous findings, showing that English speakers do assimilate L2 Spanish front vowels to more than one native English vowel. This study has also provided further support for previous findings that in their perception of similar Spanish vowels English speakers perception is affected by the presence of additional native categories not present in Spanish. Ideally, at some point during L2 exposure, the English speaker will learn that some native categories do not exist in Spanish. This study demonstrates that for learners at multiple levels of exposure, the native phonology continues to influence L2 perception. A logical question for future research, both empirical and theoretical, is how that knowledge is integrated into the L2 perceptual system. Given the ever-increasing popularity of the study of Spanish as a second language both in the United States and in other areas, continued empirical research into the challenges faced by this population is highly warranted.

APPENDIX 14A
Perceptual Condition 1 Instructions and Response Options

"In this task you will hear a series of invented words. These words have been extracted from <u>English</u> sentences. As you hear each word, listen carefully to the <u>FIRST</u> vowel of the word. Identify that vowel by finding the same sound in one of the English words that you see at the bottom of the screen. Indicate your choice by clicking on the word which contains the same vowel as the word that you hear. The words on your screen are very much like the words you learned in the short practice session."

Click above to play sound

| prasa | beesa | bissa | baysa | krasa |

| buhssa | trasa | bowsa | bessa |

| bahssa | boosa |

APPENDIX 14B
Perceptual Condition 2 Instructions and Response Options

"In this task you will hear a series of invented words extracted from <u>Spanish</u> sentences. As you hear each word, listen carefully to the <u>FIRST</u> vowel of the word. Identify that vowel by finding the same sound in one of the Spanish words on your screen. Indicate your choice by clicking on the word which matches what you hear."

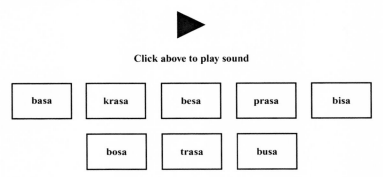

Click above to play sound

basa	krasa	besa	prasa	bisa

bosa	trasa	busa

NOTES

The author wishes to thank Alfonso Morales-Front, Cristina Sanz, and Lisa Zsiga for their many insightful suggestions throughout the course of this study. Special thanks also to Ru San Chen for assistance with statistical analyses.

1. The data reported here for front vowels were obtained from a larger experiment that examined English listeners' perception of all Spanish vowels and, in addition, examined other variables affecting those perceptual patterns. Data for the remaining back and low central vowels /o/, /u/, and /a/ are currently in late-stage analysis.

2. The larger experiment referred to in the previous note utilized a pre-, post-, and delayed posttest design and included a treatment phase of perceptual training. After the pretest (Perceptual Conditions 1 and 2), participants performing above a predetermined cutoff of 80 percent were eliminated from analysis in an effort to avoid ceiling effects. Participants did not exhibit the same variation in their responses for the /basa/, /bosa/, and /busa/ stimluli as they did for /besa/ and /bisa/. That more participants remained in the analysis for the /bisa/ and /besa/ stimuli than for the other stimuli reflects the fact that these target stimuli presented listeners with more challenges than the nontarget stimuli.

3. Participant numbers in Perceptual Condition 2 were larger than in Perceptual Condition 1 because Spanish vowel perception was highly accurate for all participants, and applying the cutoff measure described in the previous note would have not have been feasible.

4. My thanks to an anonymous reviewer for suggestions on clarifying claims made in an earlier version of this chapter.

REFERENCES

Best, Catherine T. 1994. The emergence of native-language phonological influences in infants: A perceptual assimilation model. In *The development of speech perception: The transition from speech sounds to spoken words*, ed. Judith C. Goodman and Howard C. Nusbaum, 167–224. Cambridge, MA: MIT Press.

———. 1995. A direct realist view of cross-language speech perception. In *Speech perception and linguistic experience: Issues in cross-language research*, ed. Winifred Strange, 171–204. Timonium, MD: York Press.

Best, Catherine T., Gerald W. McRoberts, and Elizabeth Goodell. 2001. Discrimination of non-native consonant contrasts varying in perceptual assimilation to the listener's native phonological system. *The
Journal of the Acoustical Society of America* 109 (2): 775–94.

Best, Catherine T., Gerald W. McRoberts, and N. M. Sithole. 1988. Examination of perceptual reorgani-
zation for non-native speech contrasts: Zulu click discrimination by English-speaking adults and infants. *Journal of Experimental Psychology: Human Perception and Performance* 14 (3): 345–60.

Bradlow, Ann R. 1995. A comparative acoustic study of English and Spanish vowels. *The Journal of the
Acoustical Society of America* 97 (3): 1916–24.

————. 1996. A perceptual comparison of the /i/–/e/ and /u/–/o/ contrasts in English and Spanish: Universal and language-specific aspects. *Phonetica* 53:55–85.

Eckman, Fred R. 2004. From phonemic differences to constraint rankings: Research on second language
phonology. *Studies in Second Language Acquisition* 26 (4): 513–49.

Escudero, Paola, and Paul Boersma. 2002. The subset problem in L2 perceptual development: Multiple-
category assimilation by Dutch learners of Spanish. *Proceedings of the Annual Boston University
Conference on Language Development* 26 (1): 208–19.

————. 2004. Bridging the gap between L2 speech perception research and phonological theory. *Studies
in Second Language Acquisition* 26 (4): 551–85.

Flege, James Emil. 1987a. Effects of equivalence classification on the production of foreign language
speech sounds. In *Sound patterns in second language acquisition,* eds. Allan James and Jonathan
Leather, 9–39. Dordrecht: Foris.

————. 1987b. The production of "new" and "similar" phones in a foreign language: Evidence for the effect of equivalence classification. *Journal of Phonetics* 15 (1): 47–65.

————. 1988. The production and perception of foreign language speech sounds. In *Human communication and its disorders: A review 1988,* ed. H. Winitz, 244–401. Norwood, NJ: Ablex.

————. 1991. Orthographic evidence for the perceptual identification of vowels in Spanish and English.
Quarterly Journal of Experimental Psychology 43:701–31.

————. 1995. Second language speech learning: Theory, findings, and problems. In *Speech perception
and linguistic experience: Issues in cross-language research,* ed. Winifred Strange, 233–77. Timonium, MD: York Press.

Flege, James Emil, Ocke-Schwen Bohn, and Sunyoung Jang. 1997. Effects of experience on non-native
speakers/production and perception of English vowels. *Journal of Phonetics* 25 (4): 437–70.

Flege, James Emil, and Wieke Eefting. 1987. Cross-language switching in stop consonant perception and
production by Dutch speakers of English. *Speech Communication* 6 (3): 185–202.

Flege, James Emil, and Serena Liu. 2001. The effect of experience on adults' acquisition of a second language. *Studies in Second Language Acquisition* 23 (4): 527–52.

Flege, James Emil, Murray J. Munro, and Ian R. A. MacKay. 1995. Factors affecting strength of perceived
foreign accent in a second language. *The Journal of the Acoustical Society of America* 97 (5):
3125–34.

Flege, James E., Carlo Schirru, and Ian R. A. MacKay. 2003. Interaction between the native and second
language phonetic subsystems. *Speech Communication* 40 (4): 467–91.

Fox, Robert Allen, James Emil Flege, and Murray J. Munro. 1995. The perception of English and Spanish vowels by native English and Spanish listeners: A multidimensional scaling analysis. *The Journal of the Acoustical Society of America* 97 (4): 2540–51.

Francis, Alexander L., Kate Baldwin, and Howard C. Nusbaum. 2000. Effects of training on attention to
acoustic cues. *Perception & Psychophysics* 62 (8): 1668–80.

Ioup, Georgette. 1984. Is there a structural foreign accent? A comparison of syntactic and phonological
errors in second language acquisition. *Language Learning* 34 (2): 1–17.

Kuhl, Patricia K. 1991. Human adults and human infants show a "perceptual magnet effect" for the prototypes of speech categories, monkeys do not. *Perception & Psychophysics* 50 (2): 93–107.

Kuhl, Patricia K., and Paul Iverson. 1995. Linguistic experience and the "perceptual magnet effect." In
Speech perception and linguistic experience: Issues in cross-language research, ed. Winifred
Strange,121–54. Timonium, MD: York Press.

Lado, Robert. 1957. *Linguistics across cultures; Applied linguistics for language teachers.* Ann Arbor: University of Michigan Press.

MacKay, Ian R. A., Diane Meador, and James Emil Flege. 2001. The identification of English consonants by native speakers of Italian. *Phonetica* 58 (1–2): 103–25.

Morrison, Geoffrey Stewart. 2003. Perception and production of Spanish vowels by English speakers. In *Proceedings of the 15th International Congress of Phonetic Sciences: Barcelona 2003*, eds. M. J. Solé, D. Recansesn, and J. Romero, 1533–36. Adelaide, South Australia: Causal Productions.

Pallier, Christophe, Laura Bosch, and Nuria Sebastian-Galles. 1997. A limit on behavioral plasticity in speech perception. *Cognition* 64 (3): B9–B17.

Polka, Linda, and Janet F. Werker. 1994. Developmental changes in perception of non-native vowel contrasts. *Journal of Experimental Psychology: Human Perception and Performance* 20 (2): 421–35.

Rochet, Bernard L. 1995. Perception and production of second-language speech sounds by adults. In *Speech perception and linguistic experience: Issues in cross-language research,* ed. Winifred Strange, 379–410. Timonium, MD: York Press.

Sanz, Cristina. 2000. Bilingual education enhances third language acquisition: Evidence from Catalonia. *Applied Psycholinguistics* 21 (1): 23–44.

Stockwell, Robert P., and J. D. Bowen. 1965. *The sounds of English and Spanish.* Chicago: University of Chicago Press.

Werker, Janet F., and Richard C. Tees. 1984. Phonemic and phonetic factors in adult cross-language speech perception. *Journal of the Acoustical Society of America* 75 (6): 1866–78.

Wode, Henning. 1976. Developmental sequences in naturalistic L2 acquisition. In *Second language acquisition,* ed. E. Hatch, 101–17. Rowley, MA: Newbury House.

———. 1978. The beginnings of non-school room L2 phonological acquisition. A survey of problems and issues based on data from English as L2 with German as L1. *IRAL, International Review of Applied Linguistics in Language Teaching* 16 (2): 109–25.

———. 1994. Nature, nurture, and age in language acquisition: The case of speech perception. *Studies in Second Language Acquisition* 16 (3): 325–45.

———. 1995. Speech perception, language acquisition, and linguistics: Some mutual implications. In *Speech perception and linguistic experience: Issues in cross-language research,* ed. Winifred Strange, 321–47. Timonium, MD: York Press.

15

Early Phonological Acquisition in a Set of English–Spanish Bilingual Twins

DAVID INGRAM AND VIRGINIA DUBASIK
Arizona State University

JUANA LICERAS
University of Ottawa

RAQUEL FERNÁNDEZ FUERTES
University of Valladolid

THIS IS THE FIRST ATTEMPT to examine the early phonological development of bilingual twins. It sought to determine the extent to which the phonological acquisition of twins was similar, and the extent to which the phonological acquisition of the two languages was similar. Language samples from twin boys acquiring English and Spanish simultaneously were taken at eighteen, nineteen, and twenty months of age, in English and Spanish. The samples were analyzed using nine measures of phonological acquisition. A scale of phonological similarity was developed to quantify comparisons between the languages and between the children. The results indicated that the phonologies of the twins were 92 percent similar in each language, showing highly similar but not identical systems. The phonologies of the languages were 71 percent similar, indicating that being twin did not impede early language separation.

Introduction

The study of twins has a long and extensive history dating back a century. Researchers have examined similarities between twins and nontwins, in terms both of the properties of language being acquired and the extent to which twin language acquisition is delayed relative to nontwin (singleton) children. Most generally, it has been found that twins tend to be more similar than nontwins and that twins show more language delay in comparison to typically developing nontwin children. Likewise, there has been an extensive literature on bilingual language acquisition, addressing similar questions. Researchers have been interested in whether or not bilingual children acquire language in similar ways to monolingual children, in terms both of the specific aspects of language being acquired and the rate of language acquisition. For the early stage of bilingual acquisition, a particular interest has been in language separation, that is, when do bilingual children begin to show signs of separating the languages? Most generally, it has been found that bilingual children show early language separation, as early as the second year of life.

Despite this diverse and active range of research on twin and bilingual language acquisition, no studies have addressed the topic of this study, which is the early phonological acquisition of bilingual twins. In particular, the present study is concerned with whether or not twin children show early separation of their phonological systems in the same way as monolingual children. Much of the literature on twin acquisition is not directly relevant for this study. For example, the study is not addressing issues of similarity between twins and nontwins, or issues about the rate and course of their language acquisition. Likewise, the relevant literature in bilingual acquisition is also limited, consisting of a small number of studies on early bilingual phonological acquisition. The following sections briefly review relevant studies on phonological acquisition in twins and bilingual children, respectively.

The studies on phonological acquisition in twins have addressed the same questions as twin studies on language acquisition as mentioned above. They have found that twins are delayed in relation to nontwins in their speech acquisition (e.g., Matheny and Bruggemann 1972), and that monozygotic twins are more similar than dizygotic twins (Lewis and Thompson 1992). A series of studies by Dodd and colleagues has shown that twin phonologies are not only delayed but also show disordered characteristics (e.g., McEvoy and Dodd 1992). While twins may show similarities to each other, no studies have found identical acquisition. In fact, despite similarities in group studies, case studies have also shown how nonalike twins can be. Leonard, Newhoff, and Mesalam (1980) found phonological differences in their case study of two-year-old twin girls. Clements and Fee (1994) reported on a set on twins in which one was developing typically but the other was phonologically impaired. The results have found that twins may show some similarities in their speech development but are by no means identical.

The first studies on early bilingual acquisition proposed that bilingual children start out with a single linguistic system, then begin to separate the languages (Volterra and Taeschner 1978). This point of view was extended to early phonological acquisition in Vogel (1975). One of the first studies to challenge this position was Ingram (1981–82). In a case study of a two-year-old English–Italian child, Ingram found some emerging differences in the early phonetic inventories, and differences in preferences for syllables. More recent research has supported this result or early language separation, though the ways in which this takes place are far from understood (Bunta, Davidovich, and Ingram 2006; Johnson and Lancaster 1998; Keshavarz and Ingram 2002; Paradis 2001).

The present study was conducted to provide preliminary results on the interaction of being twin and being bilingual, by conducting a case study of bilingual twins. Given previous research on twin phonology, it was hypothesized that the twins would show similar, but not identical, phonological systems. It was more difficult to determine a hypothesis regarding language separation. If bilingual twins acquire language like monolingual children, one would expect the twins to show early language separation. Given the shared genetic and environmental properties of being twins, however, it was equally possible that the twins would show delayed language separation. Both possibilities, therefore, were considered equally possible.

Method
Participants
The participants were twin boys Leo and Simon, who acquired Spanish and English simultaneously. Their mother was a native English speaker, and their father was a native Spanish speaker. The boys were spoken to in both languages according to the parental native language. Their language acquisition was followed in an extensive longitudinal study from the ages of 1; 0 to 6; 0. The present study examined the period of early word acquisition, using language samples of each language at eighteen, nineteen, and twenty months of age.

Language Samples
The English/Spanish bilingual data were recorded on audio and videotapes as well as on DVDs. Sessions occurred in English or Spanish contexts where the interlocutors were native speakers of English (i.e., one of the researchers or the twins' mother or their maternal grandmother) or Spanish (i.e., one of the researchers or the twins' father or Spanish-speaking visitors). The language samples were obtained in naturalistic settings, usually in the home, and the boys appeared together in the majority of the sessions. They were mostly engaged in normal household and play activities with the interlocutor(s). They were recorded in Spain during the school year and in the United States, mostly in California, during the summer months. Samples were recorded every two to three weeks, approximately thirty minutes in length. At each sample point, the twins were recorded separately in Spanish and in English.

Language Sample Analysis
Each language sample was transcribed into computerized language analysis (CLAN) format (MacWhinney and Snow 1985), written in either English or Spanish orthography. Subsequently, the transcripts were used to identify utterances in the original audio recordings. Each child utterance was extracted into an individual sound file (.wav format) for a total of 1,415 sound files. Leo produced 280 English word tokens and 252 Spanish word tokens, while Simon produced 323 English word tokens and 307 Spanish word tokens. Other sound files were excluded because the child speaking was not identifiable.

The extracted sound files were then examined for transcribable words, that is, words that were clear enough to be transcribed phonetically. Nontranscribable words were the result of limited amplitude, ambient noise, another speaker (sibling or adult interviewer) speaking concurrently, or any combination of those factors. There were 254 words identified by this process, consisting of 124 words for Leo (64 English words and 60 Spanish words), and 130 words for Simon (67 English words and 63 Spanish words). The transcribable words were subsequently transcribed independently by two phonetically trained transcribers, with differences resolved by a third transcriber.

Phonological Analyses

The final transcriptions were then phonologically analyzed using an adaptation of the Basic Analysis system in Ingram and Ingram (2001), developed in turn from other work found in Ingram (1989) and Ingram (1981). This system examines four aspects of a child's early phonological system: whole word properties (Ingram 2002), word shapes (syllables), independent consonantal inventories, and relational analyses of consonants.

Whole word properties examine the overall complexity of a child's word through two measures, the phonological mean length of utterance (pMLU) and the measure of whole-word proximity (Proximity). The pMLU assigns a score to each target word and each child production. The target word receives a point for each segment, and an additional point for each consonant. For example, a word such as "cookie" receives six points since there are four segments and two consonants. The child pMLU is calculated by assigning a point for each segment, and an additional point for each correct consonant. If a child says "cookie" as [gugi], the child receives a score of four, since there are four segments but no correct consonants. The scores for all target words and all child words are then averaged for a final pMLU score for each set of words. Proximity measures the fit between the child pMLU and the target pMLU by dividing the latter into the former. The example above yields a Proximity of .67 (or 67 percent), by dividing the child score of four by the target score of six.

Word shapes are the syllabic structures that children use in their words. Research on early phonological acquisition has shown that children select from a small number of word shapes in their first words, particularly CV and CVC for monosyllables; and CVCV, CVCVC, and VCV for multisyllabic words. Each child's words were broken down into their respective word shape from the five given above and any other ones that occurred, e.g., V, VC. Two measures were then determined from this analysis. One was the proportion of monosyllables, determined by dividing the number of monosyllabic word shapes by the overall number of words. The second measure was the number of preferred word shapes. A preferred word shape was one that was found in at least 10 percent of the total number of word shapes.

Independent analyses concern the consonants that children are using separately in onset and coda positions in words, without reference to the target sounds. Onsets were determined as either consonants used at the beginning of a word, or used intervocalically. Coda consonants were determined to be consonants either used at the end of a word, or intervocalically before an onset consonant. Once the frequencies of occurrence were determined for each consonant, a frequency criterion was used to separate the infrequently occurring consonants from the frequently occurring ones (Ingram 1981). Consonants occurring two or three times as onsets or codas were considered marginal, those occurring four to six times were considered used, and those occurring seven or more times were considered frequent. The Articulation Score (Ingram 1981) was calculated separately for onset and coda consonants. A child received two points for each consonant that was used or frequent, and one point for each consonant that was marginal.

A relational analysis was used to determine the use of the consonants in the independent analysis in relation to their targets in the adult words being produced (Ingram

1989). For example, a child might use [t] frequently, and it might be used both for the correct production of /t/, and as a substitute for another phoneme such as /k/. The relational analysis identified phonemes that were being used correctly, that is, matches, and those that were being produced by substituted sounds, that is, substitutions. A match was defined as a phoneme attempted at least three times and produced correctly in more than 50 percent of words attempted. Articulation scores were calculated separately for onset and coda consonants. A child received two points for each match.

In summary, nine measures were calculated for each child's Spanish and English. The nine measures were: pMLU of target words, pMLU of child words, proximity, proportion of monosyllables, number of preferred word shapes, articulation scores for onset and coda consonants in the independent analysis, and articulation scores for onset and coda consonant matches in the relational analysis.

A Measure of Phonological Similarity

The phonological analyses above provide an overview of a child's emerging system but only indirectly provide a comparison between children. Children may be more similar in certain areas than others, but drawing conclusions from the analyses alone would involve subjectivity. To make these comparisons more objective, a measure of phonological similarity was developed to measure similarities across the four areas of phonology that were analyzed. For each of the nine measures the children were assigned points along a continuum. A problem arises at the onset concerning the determination of what differences should be considered within a normal range of variation and which differences should be considered true variance. The final system used was the result of the first author's intuitions about how such variation occurs based on his experience in conducting such analyses (see appendix 15A).

Results

Phonological Analyses

The results of the phonological analyses for the whole-word and syllable-shape measures are given in table 15.1. Concerning the whole-word measures, the target pMLU measures ranged from 6.1 to 6.7, with the higher values occurring for the Spanish words. The child pMLUs ranged from 3.9 to 4.9, with the higher values again occurring with Spanish. Last, Proximity ranged from .63 to .78, with Spanish words showing the higher proximities.

The word-shape analysis showed similarities between the children and differences across the languages. The children showed a relatively equal use of monosyllables and multisyllables for English words but a very high rate of multisyllabic words for Spanish. The preferred syllable shapes likewise showed a language difference. The shape VCV was not frequent for English, but it was for Spanish. Conversely, CVC was the most common form for English but was uncommon in the Spanish samples. There was a within-language difference for the children in English, with Leo preferring CVCV word productions while Simon showed a higher preference for CVC productions.

The results of the independent and relational analyses are given in table 15.2. The independent analysis showed larger inventories for onsets than codas, especially so for Spanish. The onset stop consonants superficially appear to be different, with

▓ Table 15.1
Phonological Analyses for Leo and Simon in English and Spanish

	Leo's English	Simon's English	Leo's Spanish	Simon's Spanish
Whole Word Measures				
pMLU Targets	6.2	6.1	6.3	6.7
PMLU Child	3.9	4.1	4.9	4.8
Proximity	.63	.67	.78	.71
Word Shape				
Proposition Monosyllables	.52	.54	.22	.22
Preferred Syllables				
CVCV	.27	.19	.47	.36
CV	.21	.19	—	.17
CVC	.20	.29	—	—
VCV	—	—	.16	.22

[b, d, g] appearing in the English inventory while [p, t, k] appear in the Spanish inventory. These two sets, in fact, are phonetically similar, that is, an unaspirated stop that sounds to English speakers more similar to the ten voiced rather than voiceless stops. The existence of an early stage of stop production in English when there is not voice contrast and both /b, d, g/ and /p, t, k/ are produced as closer to a voiced vari-

▓ Table 15.2
Results of Independent and Relational Analyses

	Independent Analyses										
	Leo's English			Simon's English			Leo's Spanish			Simon's Spanish		
Onsets	m*	n		m	(n)		m*	n*		m*	n*	
	b*	d*	g*	b*	d*	g*	p*	t*	k*	p*	t*	k*
	f	(s)	(ʃ)*	f*	(s)	(ʃ)	(f)	s*	x		s*	(h)
		l	(j)	(w)		j		l	j*	w	(l)	j
Codas	n*			n*			n			(n)		
			(k)		(t)	k						
	(f)	s*		s*				s			s*	

*Sounds marked with * are frequent; those in parentheses are infrequent, but occur.

	Relational Analyses			
	Leo's English	Simon's English	Leo's Spanish	Simon's Spanish
Onsets	/m,n,b,d,f,(ʃ),(l),(j)/	/m,n,b,d,g,f,s,(w)/	/m,n,p,t,k,f,s,x,j/	/m,n,p,t,k,v,(f)s,l,(j)/
Codas	/n,(f)/	/n,t,k,f/	/n,s/	/n,s/

ant has been reported in Macken and Barton (1980a). These were thus recorded in that way. For Spanish, however, the early unaspirated stops are perceived as productions of voiceless stops, due to the differences in voice onset time between English and Spanish (Deuchar and Clark 1996; Macken and Barton 1980b). The use of unaspirated stops for Spanish voiced stops, therefore, is perceived as an error and was scored as such. In this sense the children's inventories are similar in their acquisition of this class of consonants, and the transcription represents the role of these as shown in the relational analysis. Differences in the children's inventories also appear among the fricatives, where [f] occurs in the English inventories while [s] is more prevalent in the Spanish inventories. All inventories show some productions of postalveolar fricatives, though these vary from [ʃ] to [x] to [h]. An impressionistic assessment would be that the inventories are similar but not the same and that the inventories look more similar within languages than across them.

The relational analyses showed similarities between the children in that they both acquired nasals, a class of stops with three places of articulation, some voiceless fricatives, and at least one approximant (glide or liquid) consonant. Simon's English words showed the most advanced acquisition of coda consonants, though his inventory is smaller in Spanish.

Phonological Similarity
The analysis of phonological similarity applied the criteria from appendix 15A to the data in tables 15.1 and 15.2 to quantify more explicitly the similarities between the children and languages. It provides two comparisons, one between the children in each language, and one between the languages within each child.

The first column of table 15.3 compares Leo's English with Simon's English. The children scored 80 percent or greater on eight of nine comparisons, which indicates an overall similarity of 88 percent. The primary difference between the children was in the matching of coda consonants, where Simon matched four consonants compared

Table 15.3
Similarities within Languages (Leo's English vs. Simon's English and Leo's Spanish vs. Simon's Spanish)

Measure	Leo vs. Simon English (%)	Leo vs. Simon Spanish (%)
pMLU Targets	100	90
pMLU Child	100	100
Proximity	90	70 (Leo)
Proposition Monosyllables	100	100
Preferred Syllables	100	100
Articulation Scores Onsets	80	100
Articulation Scores Codas	90	90
Number of Matches Onsets	90	100
Number of Matches Codas	50 (Simon)	100
Overall Similarity	88	94

Note: Child with higher score is given in parentheses for measures under 80 percent similar.

■ Table 15.4
Similarities between Languages (Leo's English vs. Leo's Spanish and Simon's English vs. Simon's Spanish)

Measures	Leo (%)	Simon (%)
pMLU Targets	100	80
pMLU Child	60 (Spanish)	70 (Spanish)
Proximity	30 (Spanish)	80
Proposition Monosyllables	50 (English)	40 (English)
Articulation Scores Onsets	100	70 (Spanish)
Articulation Score Codas	80	60 (English)
Number of Matches Onsets	60 (Spanish)	60 (Spanish)
Number of Matches Codas	90	60 (English)
Overall Similarity	73	68

Note: Language with higher score is shown in parentheses for measures under 80 percent similar.

with Leo who matched two. The Spanish comparisons yielded a percentage of 94 percent similarity, again with only one measure below 80 percent. Leo's Proximity was higher for Spanish than was Simon's (.78 vs. .71).

The comparisons between the languages for each child yielded lower percentages (see table 15.4). Leo showed a similarity of 73 percent, while Simon's rate of similarity was 68 percent. For Leo, there were four measures that were below 80 percent similar, while Simon had six measures below 80 percent similar. Leo's languages differed especially in the whole-word measures, with Spanish having higher child pMLUs and Proximity scores. His English, however, was much more monosyllabic. Simon's English and Spanish showed differences across all the measurement categories. He showed higher child pMLU scores and more monosyllables, as did Leo. In addition, he showed larger inventories of onset consonants in Spanish as well as a higher rate of matches. Conversely, he used more coda consonants in English, with more matches.

Discussion

It was hypothesized that the twins would show highly similar phonological acquisition, given their genetic similarity and shared environment. They did not show identical phonological acquisition. Three of the eighteen measurements used in their English and Spanish showed similarities of less than 90 percent. One of these was the area on whole-word Proximity, where Simon's Proximity was higher in English than Leo's, while the reverse was true for Spanish. Another difference was with coda consonants, where Simon's coda consonants were more advanced than Leo's. The third area of difference was in their preferences for word shapes. While both children used an equal percentage of CV words (21 percent vs. 19 percent), they differed in their most preferred word shapes. Whereas Leo demonstrated a preference for CVCV words (27 percent), Simon demonstrated a preference for CVC (29 percent). The latter is further evidenced by Simon's greater use of coda consonants.

Other differences can be identified by looking more closely at the consonantal inventories in the independent and relational analyses. When onsets are considered, Leo showed a preference for the use of alveolar consonants compared with labial consonants, while Simon showed the reverse. This difference can be captured by calculating the Articulation Score in the independent analysis for labial versus alveolar onset consonants. Leo's score for labials was eleven compared with fifteen for alveolars. Simon's score, however, was thirteen for labials, and eleven for alveolars. There were specific differences in the inventories themselves. Leo used an [l] at criterion in both English and Spanish, whereas Simon only used it marginally in Spanish. Additionally, Leo used the velar fricative [x] in his Spanish, while Simon used [h] in similar contexts.

Turning now to the issue of bilingual acquisition, no hypothesis was formulated as to whether the children would show delayed language separation as a consequence of being twins. The results found language differences suggestive of early language separation in that the similarities between the languages were less than those between the children. Leo's English and Spanish phonologies were 73 percent similar, and Simon's were 68 percent similar.

The language differences were most noticeable with regards to the whole-word measures and word-shape measures. In the whole-word measures, the Spanish target words were more complex as defined by pMLU. Also, the child pMLU measures were higher for Spanish, nearly a single point. Similarly, the Proximity scores were higher for Spanish by nearly 10 percentage points. These overall differences reflect the fact that the children produced more complex forms for Spanish, along with closer approximations to the adult target words, despite the fact that the target words were longer. The differences in word shapes concerned both the syllable structures of words and the preferred syllables. The twin's English words were equally divided between monosyllables and multisyllables, with a slight preference for monosyllables. Their Spanish words, however, were highly multisyllabic. Second, there were differences in syllable preferences. VCV syllables occurred over 10 percent of the time in Spanish but not in English. Conversely, CVC syllables were highly used by both children in English, but by neither in Spanish.

Language differences were not as striking for the independent and relational analyses but were found nonetheless. There were more coda consonants in English than in Spanish. The Articulation Score for English coda consonants in the independent analysis was thirteen, as compared with seven for Spanish. The inventories did overlap to quite a degree. For example, both languages contained the nasal consonants [m], [n], and three stop consonants. There were also similar numbers of fricatives, liquids, and glides. The preferred fricatives, however, did vary by language. The labio-dental [f] was more used than [s] in English, but [s] was highly frequent and more preferred in Spanish. This was true for both onsets and codas. There were also two language specific fricatives, with [ʃ] appearing in the English samples and [x] in the Spanish samples.

Previous research has found that twins tend to show delayed phonological acquisition (Matheny and Bruggemann 1972), and in some instances disordered phonological systems (McEvoy and Dodd 1992). While not the focus of the present study, the results for this particular set of twins did not show this. The children were following expected patterns of early lexical and phonological acquisition, based on general observations on early language acquisition (Ingram 1989). Both children had acquired over one hundred words by twenty months of age and were using early speech sounds and syllable shapes found in early phonological systems. The results did support previous research that twins show highly similar but not identical patterns of acquisition (Lewis and Thompson 1992). It contributes further to this finding by developing an explicit measure of phonological similarity. In particular, the measure covers four distinct aspects of phonological acquisition, while other studies have used more restricted measures (e.g., McEvoy and Dodd 1992).

Research on phonological acquisition in bilingual children has found early language separation. This was also the case in the present study. For both children the phonologies of Spanish and English were different, especially on the whole-word measures. There was no twin effect, that is, a tendency to maintain a common phonological system for both languages due to being twin. Since this is the first study of its kind, it is not possible to say whether the children are representative of bilingual twins in general. Future research on a much wider range of children is obviously necessary to see if this is in fact the case.

APPENDIX 15A
The Measurement of Phonological Similarity Criteria
General Calculation
All scores are out of ten possible points. Each point assigned to a difference drops the overall similarity 10 percent. Final results are given in percentages, so eight out of ten points is 80 percent.

Whole-Word Measures
Target pMLUs, and child pMLUs, are considered the same if they are within ±.3 of each other. Differences greater than that receive one point for each .3 difference. Proximities are considered the same if they are within ±.03 of each other. Differences greater than .03 receive 1 point for each .03 difference.

Word Shapes
Proportions of monosyllables are considered the same if they are ±.05 of each other. Differences greater than that receive one point for each .05 difference. Preferred syllable shapes are considered the same if they are the same in number. Differences greater than that are given one point for each difference.

Independent Analysis
Children are considered the same if their Articulation Scores are the same. If they are different, one point is assigned for each two-point difference. The score is calculated separately for onsets and codas.

Relational Analysis
The score for the relational analysis is done in the same manner as the Independent Analysis and is restricted to matches.

REFERENCES

Bunta, Ferenc, Ingrid Davidovich, and David Ingram. 2006. The relationship between the phonological complexity of a bilingual child's words and those of the target languages. *International Journal of Bilingualism* 10:71–88.

Clements, Albertine, and E. Jane Fee. 1994. An intra-twin phonological study: Phonologies of a SLI twin and her normally developing brother. *First Language* 14:213–31.

Deuchar, Margaret, and Angeles Clark. 1996. Early bilingual acquisition of the voicing contrast in English and Spanish. *Journal of Phonetics* 24:351–65.

Ingram, David. 1981. *Procedures for the phonological analysis of children's language.* Baltimore, MD: University Park Press.

———. 1981–82. The emerging phonological system of an Italian-English bilingual child. *Journal of Italian Linguistics* 2:95–113.

———. 1989. *Child language acquisition: Method, description, and explanation.* Cambridge: Cambridge University Press.

———. 2002. The measurement of whole word productions. *Journal of Child Language* 29:1–21.

Ingram, David, and Kelly Ingram. 2001. A whole word approach to phonological intervention. *Language, Speech and Hearing Services in Schools* 32:271–83.

Johnson, Carolyn E., and Paige Lancaster. 1998. The development of more than one phonology: A case study of a Norwegian-English bilingual child. *International Journal of Bilingualism* 2:265–300.

Keshavarz, M., and David Ingram. 2002. The early phonological development of a Farsi–English bilingual child. *International Journal of Bilingualism* 6:255–69.

Leonard, Laurence, Marilyn Newhoff, and Linda Mesalam. 1980. Individual differences in early child phonology. *Applied Psycholinguistics* 1:7–30.

Lewis, Barbara, and Lee A. Thompson. 1992. A study of developmental speech and language disorders in twins. *Journal of Speech and Hearing Research* 35:1086–94.

Macken, Marcy, and David Barton. 1980a. The acquisition of the voicing contrast in English: A study of voice onset time in word-initial stop consonants. *Journal of Child Language* 7:41–74.

———. 1980b. The acquisition of the voicing contrast in Spanish: A phonological study of word-initial stop consonants. *Journal of Child Language* 7:433–58.

MacWhinney, Brian, and Catherine Snow. 1985. The child language data exchange system. *Journal of Child Language* 12 (2): 271–95.

Matheny, Adam, and Charlene Bruggemann. 1972. Articulation proficiency in twins and singletons from families of twins. *Journal of Speech and Hearing Research* 15:845–51.

McEvoy, Sandra, and Barbara Dodd. 1992. The communication abilities of 2- to 4-year- old twins. *European Journal of Disorders of Communication* 27:73–87.

Paradis, Johanne. 2001. Do bilingual two-year-olds have separate phonological systems? *The International Journal of Bilingualism* 5:19–38.

Vogel, Irene. 1975. One system or two: An analysis of a two-year-old Romanian–English bilingual's phonology. *Papers and Reports on Child Language Development* 9:43–62.

Volterra, Virginia, and Traute Taeschner. 1978. The acquisition and development of language by bilingual children. *Journal of Child Language* 5:311–26.

16

Language Learning Strategies in Adult L3 Acquisition: Relationship between L3 Development, Strategy Use, L2 Levels, and Gender

HUI-JU LIN
Georgetown University

PART OF THE LATIN PROJECT,[1] the current study investigated the relationship between strategies reported by ninety L1 Mandarin speakers of three different L2 English levels (low, mid, and high) and of both sexes and L3 development when learning to assign semantic functions to noun phrases at the sentence level. One-way ANOVA analyses showed that female participants and higher L2 participants used strategies more frequently than their counterparts. Correlation analyses revealed positive relationships between compensation strategies reported by all the L2 learners and the grammaticality judgment pretest as well as the sentence written production pretest. Positive correlations were identified between the grammaticality judgment pretest and compensation and metacognitive strategies reported by male learners, whereas a negative correlation was found between the grammaticality judgment delayed test and social strategies reported by female learners. Correlation analyses also yielded statistical significance showing that the more frequently strategies were used by low L2 learners, the higher L3 scores they attained. Negative correlations were found for the higher L2 learners. Nevertheless, the overall results support previous studies showing that female and higher L2 learners use strategies more frequently and that strategies play a role in L3 learning (Nation and McLaughlin 1986; Nayak et al. 1990; Sanz et al. 2009; Wharton 2000) by including a measure of strategies with a different group of learners. The results also indicate that factors such as L2 proficiency, sex, and type of language tests, may influence the relationship between learning strategies and L3 development.

Introduction

Over the last few decades researchers and teachers have attempted to identify the characteristics of good language learners in order to understand what distinguishes them from others and to use the knowledge to enhance language learning and teaching in second or foreign language classrooms. One way researchers have tried has been to examine the performance of multilinguals or bilinguals with monolinguals learning another language because multilinguals or bilinguals are considered to be better and more experienced learners. For instance, research has shown that people with several language skills have different processing strategies than those with single language skills (see below). Although research in strategies has been one of the prominent fields showing that more successful learners use a variety of strategies and use them more frequently, little research has been done on the types of strategies employed by bilinguals or multilinguals when learning another language. As the number of bilinguals grows in the world, the current study attempts to contribute to this line of study by including a measurement of strategies to examine the relationship between strategies and L3 development and to investigate how certain variables, particularly L2 proficiency levels and both sexes, influence strategies used in L3 development. It is hoped that the findings of the current study can provide a more detailed picture of strategy use by bilinguals in L3 development.

Review of the Literature

Researchers have noted the importance of strategies (e.g., Dörnyei 2006) or published books on theoretical and pedagogical issues (e.g., Cohen and Macaro 2007). Many empirical studies have also been conducted to understand strategies used by L2 learners and variables that influence strategy use (see Wharton 2000 for a short review) or to examine the effects of strategy instruction (e.g., Rivera-Mills and Plonsky 2007).

Despite the extensive SLA research in strategies and the fact that researchers often consider bilinguals and multilinguals to be better and more experienced language learners, little research has investigated the strategies employed by bilinguals or multilinguals when they learn another language (Nation and McLaughlin 1986; Nayak et al. 1990; Sanz et al. 2009). Moreover, only one study (Wharton 2000) included a measure of learning strategies to investigate the relationship between learning strategies used by bilinguals when learning another language.

Nation and McLaughlin (1986) compared the performance of fourteen multilinguals with fourteen bilinguals and fourteen monolinguals to understand the strategies employed by multilinguals, bilinguals, and monolinguals when learning an artificial language. Nation and McLaughlin first exposed the participants to an implicit condition, in which the participants were told to pay attention to the stimuli, and then to an explicit condition, in which they were told to search for rules. Additionally, the participants were exposed to only random or structured stimuli. After the treatment, the participants completed a grammaticality judgment test and an introspective questionnaire. ANOVA results showed that the multilinguals outperformed the other two language groups only on the implicit condition and that all the participants performed better when being exposed to structured stimuli.

Based on the data collected from the introspective questionnaire, Nation and McLaughlin posited that multilinguals learned better than bilinguals and monolinguals in the implicit condition because multilinguals used strategies that helped them allocate processing resources more efficiently. They also explained that limited exposure to the input might explain why no differences were found between the bilinguals and monolinguals. However, no other measurements of strategies were included.

In a comparative study of forty-eight participants with different language skills, Nayak et al. (1990) collected verbalization data during the learning phase to elicit strategies employed by multilinguals and monolinguals. The verbalization data showed that visual cues were used significantly more than other strategies in an implicit condition, in which the participants were told to memorize each sentence presented, and verbal cues were used significantly less in an explicit condition, in which they were told to discover the rules. They also found that multilinguals used more mnemonic strategies than linguistic ones in the implicit condition although both groups used linguistic strategies. Moreover, the difference was significant for the multilinguals in that they used a greater variety of strategies in the explicit condition than in the implicit condition. No statistically significant differences were found for the monolinguals between conditions. Nayak and colleagues concluded that the flexibility of switching strategies may be one factor that leads to the superior performance of the multilinguals.

Sanz et al. (2009) also suggested a positive relationship between strategies and L3 development while investigating the effect of thinking aloud on L3 development in different conditions in which participants either received or did not receive a grammar lesson prior to a treatment. ANOVA analyses on the accuracy data showed that thinking aloud might enhance L3 learning, but the appearance of reactivity depended on the types of tests performed. Sanz and colleagues' results also showed that verbalizing under more demanding conditions seemed to help learners extract more information from the input. When looking at the performance of participants who scored higher, they found that reviewing and recalling of rules were the most commonly used strategies. Yet no other measures of strategies were included in their design.

Nation and McLaughlin (1986), Nayak et al. (1990), and Sanz et al. (2009) have demonstrated that strategies facilitate learning and that the effects of strategies on L3 development may vary depending on external conditions (implicit vs. explicit condition) and other factors, but few of them included strategy measures to observe learners' strategy use. More important, caution is urged in collecting data on strategies by using only introspective questionnaires or online verbalization data because it is difficult for learners to report their strategies when they do not need to make effects to exercise them, as pointed out by researchers (e.g., Nation and McLaughlin 1986).

To my knowledge, only one study (Wharton 2000) included a strategy questionnaire to examine the relationship between strategies used by adult bilinguals or multilinguals and L3 development. Wharton examined the relationship among strategies, motivation, sex, self-reported L3 proficiency, and the target languages studied (French or Japanese) by recruiting 678 bilingual university students in Singapore. He used the *Strategy Inventory for Language Learning* (SILL), a self-reported questionnaire to measure their use of strategies. ANOVA analyses showed that motivation, self-rated proficiency, and sex influenced the number and frequency of strategies used. He also identified a positive relationship between L3 proficiency and strategies: participants with higher proficiency levels used strategies more frequently. Moreover, he found that men used strategies more frequently than women did. Although Wharton's study helps us understand the strategies used by bilinguals learning an L3 in a multicultural context. However, a potential problem is associated with his participants' self-rated proficiency. Proficiency rating compared to one's classmates was the only measure. No other measures were used to support the learners' proficiency self-rating when they were from different classes (eleven introductory and two intermediate French classes and twenty-two introductory and four intermediate Japanese classes. In addition, the results are limited to the context of Singapore. More studies are needed to see if his findings are also held in studies conducted in other settings, as he pointed out (236).

To conclude, the current study's objectives are to investigate the relationship between strategies and L3 development and to examine the relationship between strategies used by learners of certain backgrounds (proficiency and sex) and their L3 development. The researcher also attempts to examine the findings of Wharton by using standardized L2 and L3 tests to eliminate the potential problem associated with self-rated proficiency levels.

Method

Ninety L1 Mandarin speakers of different L2 English proficiency levels learning in an EFL context participated in the study to learn a third language, Latin, in a laboratory environment. Among them, thirty-one were male and fifty-nine were female. The participants were undergraduates of various majors and ranged in age from seventeen to twenty-two (M = 18.74). Because of the time and location constraint, the participants completed only the grammar and reading sections of the test,[2] and they were divided into three L2 groups (low, mid, and high) based on the raw test scores.

Target Structure

L3 development was assessed by their acquisition of Latin, which has free word order and uses case to determine the agent and patient in a sentence: that is, "who does what to whom." The other two languages involved were the L1, Mandarin, and the L2, English. According to the Competition Model (e.g., Bates and MacWhinney 1982), speakers of different languages rely on different cues to correctly interpret a sentence. While English speakers rely on word order, Mandarin speakers depend on animacy (e.g., Su 2001). Mandarin, a topic-comment language, also allows the omission of a subject, which is understood from the context, and accepts more flexible word order. Because of the different processing strategies associated with the three languages (Mandarin, English, and Latin), the chances of positive cross-linguistic influence from one language to another are minimized.

Measurement of Strategies

Following Oxford (1990), strategies are operationalized as "specific actions, behaviors, steps, or techniques that learners use to facilitate their learning in a second or foreign language" (8). The ESL/EFL version of *Strategy Inventory for Language Learning* (SILL) developed by Oxford (1990) was translated into Chinese by Yang (1992) and used to measure strategies employed by learners. The SILL comprises six categories: memory, cognitive, compensation, metacognitive, affective, and social strategies. Notably, because the current study focused on foreign language learning in general, the word "English" that appears in the original version of SILL was changed into "a foreign language/foreign languages" in the Chinese version.

Treatment

During the treatment, participants interacted with three types of practice activities twice, with two sets of each type of activity. They chose one of two translations or pictures that matched the Latin sentence heard or read, they read a Latin sentence and chose the picture that matched the sentence presented, and they listened to a Latin sentence and decided whether the sentence heard matched the picture presented.

L3 Tests

A written interpretation test, an aural interpretation test, a grammaticality judgment test, and a written sentence production test were given to measure L3 development. For the interpretation tests, which use different delivery modes, participants read or heard a Latin sentence and then had to choose the picture or translation of two options that matched the Latin sentence. For the grammaticality judgment test, the participants decided whether the sentence was grammatically acceptable. A third option, "I don't know," was also given in each test item for the three tests. Unlike the other three tests, the participants had to form a Latin sentence to describe a picture by choosing the correct endings to match the two animate nouns and one transitive verb provided and ordering the elements in the written sentence production test.

Each of the first three tests (the written interpretation test, the aural interpretation test, and the grammaticality judgment test) consisted of twenty test items, including eight distractors. One point was awarded for each correct answer. The maximum possible score was twelve. The written production test had fifteen test items, including five items as distractors. One point was given for each correct ending attached to the nouns or verbs in a sentence, and the maximum score of a sentence was three points. The maximum score of the written sentence production test was thirty.[3]

Experimental Design

A time series design was used in the experiment (pretest–posttest–delayed posttest), and four sessions were held. The first session lasted for approximately one hour in which participants completed a background questionnaire, three Working memory (WM) tasks,[4] and an English test to determine their L2 English level.

In the second session, the participants took vocabulary lessons, vocabulary quizzes, and language tests. They first received a Latin vocabulary lesson and took a test to determine their knowledge of the vocabulary. Participants had to score 60 percent or higher in order to take the language tests, which were the pretests. If they failed to do so, they had to repeat the vocabulary lesson until they passed it. A vocabulary quiz was given before each language test, and only the vocabulary used in the language test was tested to ensure that participants' errors in the language tests were not due to their unfamiliarity with the vocabulary. At this time participants had to correctly answer each vocabulary item in order to take the language tests. If they failed to do so, they had to review the vocabulary items and retake the vocabulary quiz until they passed it.

The third session took place approximately one week later and lasted around two hours. Before beginning this session, participants of each L2 level were randomly assigned to two feedback groups.[5] During the treatment, the participants practiced with the target language, and feedback was always provided after each response. Upon the completion of the treatment, participants completed an immediate posttest. The SILL was given at the end of the session.

The final session, in which delayed posttests were given, was held two weeks later. Before the language tests, vocabulary tests were again given. After completing the four language tests, a debriefing questionnaire was given. Lastly, two WM tests were given.

Analyses and Results

The descriptive statistics of the L3 test scores by all the participants are presented in table 16.1. The descriptive statistics of strategies reported by all the participants are as follows: memory strategies (M = 3.0284, STD = .49286), cognitive strategies (M = 2.8763, STD = .58709), compensation strategies (M = 3.2889, STD = .63097), metacognitive strategies (M = 2.8123, STD = .63548), affective strategies (M = 2.5944, STD = .61405) and social strategies (M = 2.8241, STD = .69345).

To examine the strategies employed by participants of different backgrounds (sex differences and L2 proficiency levels), one-way ANOVA analyses were run by using participants of different backgrounds (i.e., sex differences and L2 proficiency levels) as independent variables and strategy categories as dependent variables. When significance was identified, post hoc tests were used to identify where the differences occurred. The results are presented later.

Correlation analyses were also administered by using the Statistical Package for the Social Sciences (SPSS) program and the alpha value was set at .05 to examine the relationship between strategies and L3 development when participants are learning to assign semantic functions to noun phrases at the sentence level in an L3. Correlation results reached statistical significance between compensation strategies reported used by all the participants and the grammaticality judgment pretest, $r(90) = .253$, $p < .05$, as well as the written sentence production pretest, $r(90) = .210$, $p < .05$. Correlation analyses were also run between strategies reported used by L2 learners of each variable (L2 proficiency levels and sex differences) and L3. The results are presented in the next section.

Table 16.1

Average Scores of the L3 Language Tests by All the Participants

Language Tests	Pretest		Posttest		Delayed	
	M	STD	M	STD	M	STD
Written Interpretation	5.69	1.519	8.63	2.607	7.79	2.190
Aural Interpretation	4.34	1.749	6.74	2.160	6.11	2.216
Grammaticality Judgment	5.26	2.162	5.86	2.236	5.80	1.950
Written Production	9.74	3.844	11.98	4.589	11.84	4.620

Table 16.2

Average Frequency of Strategy Use Reported by L2 Levels and Both Sexes

Strategies	L2 Proficiency Levels			Sexes	
	Low L2	Mid L2	High L2	Male	Female
Memory Strategies	2.8667	2.9852	3.2333	2.8853	3.1036
	(.58022)	(.37223)	(.44478)	(.55220)	(.44534)
Cognitive Strategies	2.5004	2.9498	3.1786	2.7676	2.9333
	(.50137)	(.60409)	(.44181)	(.55475)	(.09964)
Compensation Strategies	2.9833	3.3778	3.5056	3.1935	3.3390
	(.58942)	(.48331)	(.69822)	(.69402)	(.59529)
Metacognitive Strategies	2.4741	2.8593	3.1037	2.5806	2.9341
	(.52679)	(.62031)	(.60713)	(.65904)	(.59268)
Affective Strategies	2.4833	2.5944	2.7056	2.4462	2.6723
	(.61018)	(.60756)	(.62466)	(.59689)	(.61352)
Social Strategies	2.5722	2.8444	3.0556	2.7043	2.8870
	(.72672)	(.75675)	(.50350)	(.68138)	(.69718)

Note. Standard deviations are within parentheses.

Learning strategies by sex and L3 development

Table 16.2 summarizes the average frequency of strategy use by sex and L2 proficiency. One-way ANOVA analyses with sex differences as an independent variable and strategies as dependent variables revealed that female learners used memory strategies, $F(1,88) = 4.126, p < .05$, and metacognitive strategies, $F(1,88) = 6.688, p < .05$, more frequently than male learners. Positive correlations were identified for the males between the grammaticality judgment pretest and compensation strategies, $r(31) = .534, p < .01$, as well as metacognitive strategies, $r(31) = .377, p < .05$, while one negative correlation was found for the females between social strategies and the grammaticality judgment delayed posttest, $r(59) = -.257, p < .05$.

Learning strategies by L2 proficiency level and L3 development

One-way ANOVA analyses examining the relationship between L2 proficiency and reported frequency of strategy use reached significance: memory strategy, $F(2,87) = 4.682, p < .05$, cognitive strategies, $F(2,87) = 13.203, p < .01$, compensation strategies, $F(2,87) = 6.242, p < .01$, metacognitive strategies, $F(2,87) = 8.796, p < .01$, social strategies, $F(2,87) = 3.902, p < .05$. Post hoc Sheffé tests revealed that both high and mid L2 levels used cognitive, compensation, and metacognitive strategies more frequently than the low L2 level and that high L2 group used memory and social strategies more frequently than the low L2 group.

The correlation analyses between the strategies reported by different L2 levels and L3 tests showed different patterns. While one negative correlation was found for the mid L2 group between social strategies and the grammaticality judgment delayed posttest, $r(30) = -.367, p = .05$, five positive and one negative correlations were identified for the low L2 group: (a) between compensation strategies and the gram-maticality judgment pretest, $r(30) = .417, p < .05$, as well as the written interpreta-tion delayed posttest, $r(30) = .487, p < .01$, (b) between cognitive strategies and the written interpretation pretest, $r(30) = .372, p < .05$, as well as its delayed posttest, $r(30) = .416, p < .05$, and (c) between social strategies and the grammaticality judg-ment pretest, $r(30) = -.391, p < .05$, as well as the written interpretation delayed posttest, $r(30) = .560, p < .01$.

Surprisingly, only negative correlations were identified for high L2 learners: (a) between memory strategies and the written interpretation delayed posttest, $r(30) = -.463, p < .05$, (b) between compensation strategies and the grammaticality judg-ment immediate posttest, $r(30) = -.411, p < .05$, (c) between metacognitive strate-gies and the written interpretation delayed posttest, $r(30) = -.395, p < .05$, as well as the aural interpretation delayed posttest, $r(30) = -.446, p < .05$, (d) between af-fective strategies and the written interpretation immediate posttest, $r(30) = -.425$, $p < .05$, as well as its delayed posttest, $r(30) = -.438, p < .05$, and the aural inter-pretation delayed posttest, $r(30) = -.455, p < .05$, and (e) between social strategies and the grammaticality judgment immediate posttest, $r(30) = -.410, p < .05$, the written sentence production immediate posttest, $r(30) = -.413, p < .05$, and the writ-ten interpretation delayed posttest, $r(30) = -.383, p < .05$.

Discussion

The results are consistent with SLA studies in strategies showing that females or learn-ers of higher L2 proficiency levels use strategies more frequently than their counter-parts (e.g., Green and Oxford 1995). More important, the current study provides new evidence to L3 studies (Nation and McLaughlin 1986; Nayak et al. 1990; Sanz et al. 2009) finding that strategies play a role in L3 learning by including a measure of strat-egy use. Moreover, the study supports the findings of Wharton (2000) to initial L3 development by recruiting Mandarin speakers learning English in an EFL context and studying a different target language in a different setting.

In looking at the relationship between L3 development and strategies used by both sexes, the current study showed evidence of sex differences in the use of learn-ing strategies in L3: compensation and metacognitive strategies helped male learn-ers in L3 learning and using social strategies more frequently was associated with worse L3 performance for females. The sex differences in strategy use may be ex-plained by learning styles (e.g., Cohen 2003; Oxford 1993) According to Cohen (2003), "Language learning styles are general approaches to language learning, while strategies are specific behaviors that learners select in their language learning." (279) He posits that learners tend to use strategies that are consistent with their learning styles when dealing with a task. Oxford (1993) also has similar arguments with some examples provided. For example, social strategies include questions, such as "I ask foreign language speakers to correct me when I talk." Those who are more concerned with answering correctly or asking others for help are usually females. Compensa-tion strategies include questions, such as "When I cannot think of a word during a conversation in a foreign language, I use gestures." Those who enjoy using gestures to convey meaning are tactile or kinesthetic learners and they are typically male.

A finding from the current study that using social strategies more frequently did not help females or learners of different L2 proficiency levels to learn an L3 suggests that factors other than learning styles may also play a role in L3 development. One explanation may be conditions or tasks (e.g., Cohen 2003; Nayak et al. 1990). For instance, Cohen (2003) argues that many factors such as contextual variables (e.g., in or out of class) and motivation to learn the language (e.g., for sociocultural reasons) may influence learning results. Nayak et al. (1990) also found that external conditions may influence the learning outcome. Thus, it is probable that the participants were learning the L3 in a laboratory setting, so using social strategies more frequently did not help female learners or learners of each L2 levels to learn an L3.

Separate correlation analyses examining strategies reported used by each level and L3 development revealed that using the strategies more frequently had negative effects on L3 development for learners of higher L2 levels. These results seem contradictory to previous studies showing that learning strategies facilitate second or foreign language learning. It is noted that the current study used correlations to separately examine the relationship between strategies reported by each L2 level and L3 development whereas the previous studies (e.g., Wharton 2000) used ANOVA analyses to investigate the relationship between strategies and self-rated proficiency levels. Regardless, it is suspected that because learners of higher L2 use strategies more frequently, limited exposure to the input may not be enough for them to learn an L3 better. More studies are needed to further examine the findings of the current study.

Finally, many correlations were found between the grammaticality judgment test and the compensation strategies, which include techniques such as guessing intelligently to make up for limited knowledge. An explanation may be that learning another language seems to help learners develop their sensitivity to language, which was measured by the grammaticality judgment test. Previous studies that used grammaticality judgment tests have also shown that learners with several language skills have heightened metalinguistic skills (e.g., Klein 1995; Thomas 1988) and other advantages to help them outperform monolinguals when learning another language. On the other hand, many correlations were also identified between the written interpretation test and several types of strategies. These results indicate that learners use a combination of strategies, not only one type in a task, as suggested by other researchers (e.g., Cohen 2003; Green and Oxford, 1995).

Conclusions, Limitation, and Future Research

The current study suggests that strategy use and L3 development is a complex phenomenon, related to a number of factors involved (sex, proficiency, learning style, and type of L3 language test). The current study has provided some evidence to show that strategies play a role in L3 development and that learners of different L2 proficiency levels and both sexes use strategies differently to learn an L3 when assigning semantic functions to noun phrases at the sentence level. Note, however, that strategy use in the current study is general use reported by learners, and they may not be the actual strategy or strategies used in the L3 learning task. Combining both questionnaires and other measures of strategies, such as online verbalization data, may give us a more detailed picture of strategies people use in language learning.

Next, the current study focused on the strategies reported by learners of both sexes and different L2 proficiency levels in learning an L3 in a laboratory environment and only examined one aspect of language learning, morphosyntax. SLA studies in strategies have suggested that other factors (e.g., motivation, condition, and type of acquisition) may influence strategy use. Researchers may consider examining the relationship in different conditions with different groups of learners or languages, so more consistent information becomes available and is verified within and across groups of learners, as also suggested by Wharton (2000).

As the population of bilinguals grows in the world, it is hoped that more studies are conducted to examine the strategies used by L3 learners and to investigate the effect of these strategies on L3 development. Such results may be beneficial to research in strategies as well as to language teachers.

NOTES

1. The current study is part of the dissertation of Lin (2009) and is also part of The Latin Project©, developed to investigate the relationship between bilingualism, cognition, and the acquisition of new linguistic knowledge. All materials, except for the nonword recall test, the sentence span test, and the computational digit span WM test, were originally developed by Cristina Sanz, Harriet Bowden, and Catherine Stafford with support from Georgetown University Graduate School grants to Sanz and assistance from Bill Garr of Georgetown's University Information Systems and Center for New Designs in Learning and Scholarship. Notably, the materials have been adapted for Mandarin speakers, and they are paper-based materials.
2. The English test is an older test of the General English Proficiency Test developed by the Language Training and Testing Center in Taiwan.
3. Half of the test items in each of the four tests were trained items, which participants had seen during the treatment. The other half were untrained items, which they had not seen during the treatment. The trained and untrained items were used to distinguish between chunked knowledge, in which memory could play a role, and generalized knowledge resulting from rule formation.
4. Different WM tests were administered and collected for another purpose. The test results are not analyzed here.
5. The grouping is for another purpose of the study. To indicate the source of an error, the more explicit feedback group received "right" or "wrong" as feedback along with a brief grammatical explanation. The less explicit feedback group received only "right" or "wrong" as feedback. A control group, which had similar L2 proficiency as the low L2 group, was also included in the design, and they received no feedback.

REFERENCES

Bates, Elizabeth, and Brian MacWhinney. 1982. Functionalist approaches to grammar. In *Language acquisition: The state of the art,* ed. Eric Wanner and Lila Gleitman, 173–218. New York: Cambridge University Press.

Cohen, Andrew. 2003. The learner's side of foreign language learning: Where do styles, strategies, and tasks meet? *IRAL* 41:79–291.

Cohen, Andrew, and Ernesto Macaro, eds. 2007. *Language learner strategies: 30 years of research and practice.* Oxford: Oxford University Press.

Dörnyei, Zoltán. 2006. Individual differences in second language acquisition. *AILA Review* 19: 42–68.

Green, John M., and Rebecca Oxford. 1995. A closer look at learning strategies, L2 proficiency, and gender. *TESOL Quarterly* 29:261–97.

Klein, Elaine C. 1995. Second versus third language acquisition: Is there a difference? *Language Learning* 45:419–65.

Lin, Hui-Ju. 2009. Bilingualism, feedbook, cognivity capacity and learning strategies in L3 development. PhD diss. Georgetown University.

Nation, Robert, and Barry McLaughlin. 1986. Novices and experts: An information processing approach to the good language learner problem. *Applied Psycholinguistics* 7:41–56.

Nayak, Nandini, Nina Hansen, Nancy Krueger, and Barry McLaughlin. 1990. Language learning strategies in monolingual and multilingual adults. *Language Learning* 40:221–44.

Oxford, Rebecca L. 1990. *Language learning strategies: What every teacher should know.* New York: Newbury House.

———. 1993. Instructional implications of gender differences in second/foreign language learning styles and strategies. *Applied Language Learning* 4:65–94.

Rivera-Mills, Susana V., and Luke Plonsky. 2007. Empowering students with language learning strategies: A critical review of current issues. *Foreign Language Annals* 40:535–48.

Sanz, Cristina, Hui-Ju Lin, Beatriz Lado, Harriet Wood Bowden, and Catherine A. Stafford. 2009. Concurrent verbalizations, pedagogical conditions, and reactivity: Two CALL studies. *Language Learning* 59:33–71.

Su, I-Ru. 2001. Transfer of sentence processing strategies: A comparison of L2 learners of Chinese and English. *Applied Psycholinguistics* 22:83–112.

Thomas, Jacqueline. 1988. The role played by metalinguistic awareness in second and third language learning. *Journal of Multilingual and Multicultural Development* 9:235–46.

Wharton, Glenn. 2000. Language learning strategy use of bilingual foreign language learners in Singapore. *Language Learning* 50:203–43.

Yang, Nae-Dong. 1992. Second language learners' beliefs about language learning and their use of learning strategies: A study of college students of English in Taiwan. PhD diss., University of Texas at Austin.

17

Effects of Bilingualism on Inhibitory Control in Elderly Brazilian Bilinguals

INGRID FINGER, JOHANNA DAGORT BILLIG,
AND ANA PAULA SCHOLL
Federal University of Rio Grand do Sul, Brazil

BILINGUALISM HAS ALWAYS BEEN a matter of interest and great polemic, and in the past two decades, there has been an important advance in the investigation of the effects of a bilingual experience throughout lifespan. Psycholinguists and cognitive science researchers, in particular, have focused on the relationship between bilingualism and the development of executive functions in children as well as the effects of a bilingual experience as a protective factor against cognitive decline in older adults.

In comparison to monolingual children, bilingual children have performed better in various nonverbal tasks demanding high levels of control, such as ignoring misleading features in a number concept task (Bialystok and Codd 1997); resisting previously relevant information in modified versions of Dimensional Change Card Sort (Bialystok and Martin 2004); solving problems based on reality questions (Bialystok and Senman 2004); apprehending an alternative perspective in an ambiguous figures task (Bialystok and Shapero 2005); managing conflicting attentional demands (Carlson and Meltzoff 2008); and solving complex tasks requiring control over attention to competing cues (Martin-Rhee and Bialystok 2008).

In the case of older adults, bilingualism has been associated with smaller Simon effect costs (Bialystok et al. 2004); advantages in planning and task management (Craik and Bialystok 2006); faster resolving of various types of response conflict (Bialystok, Craik, and Ruocco 2006); better performance in executive control tasks (Bialystok, Craik, and Luk 2008); and cognitive reserve associated with delayed onset of dementia symptoms (Bialystok, Craik, and Freedman 2007; Kempler and Goral 2008).

One possible explanation for bilinguals' advantage in inhibitory control is based on the evidence that suggests that both languages are activated even when bilinguals are using only one of them (Colomé 2001; Costa 2005; Dijkstra, Grainger, and Van Heuven 1999; Jared and Kroll 2001). This evidence leads to the question of how bilinguals monitor attention to two competing languages. To tackle this issue Green (1998) proposed a model called Inhibitory Control, according to which the unwanted language is suppressed by the same executive functions used to control attention and inhibition in general. According to Bialystok et al. (2004), the model being correct, a bilingual experience would result in great exercising of inhibitory control that could generalize to other cognitive domains.

Some important evidence for Green's model has been found through experimental and brain imaging research. Experimental data have shown bilingual advantages in nonverbal tasks requiring inhibitory control, which suggests the use of the same inhibitory mechanism to solve both linguistic and nonlinguistic conflict. In terms of brain imaging, a study from Bialystok, Martin, and Viswanathan (2005) using magneto-encephalography (MEG) has found that many areas associated with fast response in bilinguals were left hemisphere regions that bordered on language centers in the inferior frontal cortex. Thus, it is possible that the enhanced control processes in left frontal lobe are also available for other inhibitory tasks.

It has also been suggested in the literature that the cortical centers responsible for memory and attention processes are plastic and therefore can be affected by training (Gazzaniga, Ivry, and Mangun 2009). In line with these ideas, Bialystok, Craik, and Luk (2008) argue that bilingual individuals perform more efficiently in selective attention and inhibitory control tasks due to their increased ability to disregard distracting misleading information that result from their extensive practice of inhibitory function. Therefore, cognitive processing guided by selective attention and inhibitory control would mature faster in bilingual children. In the case of older adults, the result of well-practiced attentional control that accompanies many years of daily use of two or more languages, attending to one and inhibiting the other, would serve as a protective factor against cognitive decline.

Several studies have reported bilingual advantages in inhibitory control tasks in older adults. Even though the advantages seem to be generally consistent, they are limited by a number of factors, such as the kinds of stimuli presented in the tasks (Fernandes et al. 2007), the number of trials in the Simon Task (Bialystok et al. 2004), the degree of bilingualism (Zied et al. 2004), as well as the level of automaticity of the response elicited by the task (Bialystok, Craik, Ryan 2006). What all these studies have in common is the assumption that a bilingual experience may result in an inhibitory-control benefit for bilinguals. Some have also suggested that bilingualism enhances executive processes other than inhibitory control, that is, that a bilingual (or multilingual) experience may act as a cognitive reserve, thus attenuating the deteriorating effects of aging in executive functioning (Bialystok and DePape 2009; Bialystok, Craik, and Freedman 2007; Kavé et al. 2008).

Consistent with previous research, therefore, the basic underlying assumption of this investigation is that just as regular exercise helps retard the deterioration of the neuromuscular system that results from aging, the experience of using two or more languages on a daily basis slows down age-related cognitive decline in elderly individuals.

The present study thus examined the effects of bilingualism on inhibitory control within an unstudied bilingual—Portuguese/Hunsrückisch[1]—language group of older adults (sixty to seventy-one years old). Two versions of the Simon task were administered: the first version was biased for demands on inhibitory control (Simon arrows task), and the second was biased for demands on working memory (Simon squares task). A version of the Stroop task was also used to verify the participants' performance in an inhibitory control task involving linguistic stimuli.

On the basis of previous findings, we expected to find:

(a) Smaller inhibitory control costs in the Simon arrows task for bilinguals, reflected in higher accuracy levels, lower reaction time (RT) scores, and a lower Simon Effect (following Bialystok et al. 2004; Bialystok, Craik, and Luk 2008).

(b) Similar working memory costs in the Simon squares task for monolinguals and bilinguals since a bilingual advantage is expected to be found only in inhibitory control (following Bialystok, Craik, and Luk 2008).

(c) Similar costs of inhibitory control for monolinguals and bilinguals in the Stroop task due to the linguistic nature of the distracting stimuli (following Bialystok, Craik, and Luk 2008).

It should be stressed that the present study is relevant not only because it extends the research to an unstudied bilingual group (Portuguese/Hunsrückisch) but also because it compares the group's performance to a different monolingual group (Portuguese) as well, since most of the research has assessed bilingual performance in comparison to English-speaking monolinguals. Moreover, previous studies have investigated the performance of bilinguals and monolinguals with higher socioeconomic and educational backgrounds than the ones who were assessed in this research. Another important issue relates to the literacy level of the population tested, which differs considerably from the participants of previous studies. Although there were no specific predictions regarding differences in comparison to the groups that are normally tested, we argue for the importance of replicating previous research findings within distinct populations. We also draw on the ideas put forth by Morton and Harper (2007), who argue that the attested differences found in the literature may be the result of ethnical and socioeconomical characteristics of the populations studied.

Method

In this section we provide information regarding the participants of the study as well as the tasks and procedures used for data collection.

Participants

The sample comprised forty-two participants from the same village, divided into two language groups: twenty-one Portuguese monolinguals (ranging in age from 60 to 70 years, average 64.3) and twenty-one Portuguese/Hunsrückisch bilinguals (ranging in age from 60 to 71 years, average 63.8). A total of ten pairs of monolingual/bilingual participants were matched on age and the other eleven pairs differed by at most a year. There were equal numbers of men and women in each group. Most of the participants reported to have always worked as small farmers, shared similar backgrounds, and had had similar formal educational experiences (forty out of forty-two had attended school for one to four years). Bilinguals also had a similar language background experience—that is, all of them reported to have learned Hunsrückisch as their L1 at home and Portuguese at the age of seven or eight, when they started attending school. With respect to economic or social characteristics that were assessed in the questionnaire, no relevant differences between the language groups were found.

In addition, data from the language background questionnaire indicated that all the bilingual participants spoke Hunsrückisch and Portuguese on a daily basis since childhood. Participants who used to speak Hunsrückisch as children but did not use it on a daily basis after that were excluded from the sample to ensure that all bilingual participants tested had had an extensive bilingual experience. The monolingual participants did not speak or understand any other language apart from Portuguese.

One important characteristic of the population investigated here is that, even though they are literate, they have very little daily contact with samples of written language. The only newspaper that circulates in the village comes out once a week, and in their free time participants normally listen to the radio (shows in Portuguese and Hunsrückisch), watch TV, or meet friends and family. That means very little reading takes place in their daily routines.

Finally, the participants were interviewed and tested in their own houses and provided written informed consent for their involvement in the experiment. The data collection was conducted in Portuguese and all participants were tested by the same two experimenters using the same equipment and the same instructional protocols.

Tasks and Procedures

In what follows, information regarding the tasks and data-collection procedures that were adopted in the study will be provided. The information gathered in the language background and personal information questionnaire, as well as the scores in the Geriatric Depression Scale and the Mini Mental State Examination, were used in the selection of participants. The three experimental tasks that were used will also be explained.

Language background and personal information questionnaire. A questionnaire was filled out by the experimenter while interviewing the participants. There were questions related to the way languages were learned, the frequency they were used, the occasions and the people they were used with. At the end of the interview, participants were also requested to talk about their routine in Hunsrückisch and in Portuguese. Following the concept of domain of use (Fishman 1972), they were asked to talk about their routine in both languages in order to guarantee their language proficiency assessment in a topic they would be familiar with. The questionnaire also involved questions related to educational background, socioeconomic conditions, and general health conditions. No relevant differences were found between the two language groups.

Geriatric Depression Scale (GDS—Yesavage, Brink, and Rose 1983). The Geriatric Depression Scale is a thirty-item questionnaire in which participants are asked to respond by answering yes or no in reference to how they felt over the past week. The GDS was used to exclude participants who showed symptoms of depression.

Mini Mental State Examination (MMSE). The MMSE is a brief, quantitative measure of cognitive status, proposed originally by Folstein, Folstein, and McHugh (1975) and adapted to the Brazilian context by Bertolucci et al. (1994). It contains questions that assess six cognitive areas: short-term memory (retention), attention, short-term memory (recall), language, calculation, and orientation. The MMSE was adopted for two reasons: first, it is widely used to identify dementia symptoms; second, we followed a study conducted by Kavé et al. (2008), in which a significant effect of number of languages spoken was found in the MMSE.

Simon arrows task. This task was based on the stimulus–response conflict of the Simon task (Simon and Rudell 1967). The experiment was presented on a laptop with a fourteen-inch monitor. The sequence of events and collection of data were controlled by a program running E-prime. Each trial began with a fixation cross (+) in the center of the screen that remained visible for 800 ms and was followed by a 250-ms blank interval. At the end of this interval, an arrow pointing to the left or right appeared on the screen for 1,000 ms. There were two conditions. The first was a control condition to establish response speed when no additional processing is required. An arrow pointing either left or right appeared in the center of the screen, and participants pressed the left ("1") or right ("0") response key indicating the direction of the arrow as quickly as possible. There were twenty-four trials in this condition. The second was a conflict condition, in which the arrows were presented on the left or right sides of the display, creating congruent trials when the direction and position corresponded and incongruent trials when they conflicted. The instruction was to press the response key indicating the direction, irrespective of the position. There were forty-eight trials in this condition. There were eight practice trials in the beginning of the experiment and participants had to get them all correct to proceed to the experimental trials. If they made a mistake, they were given extra practice trials until they got eight trials correct.

Simon squares task. In this task all the stimuli appeared in the center of the screen in order to avoid conflict. The trial began with a fixation cross (+) that was presented for 800 ms, followed by a sound file "ding." The stimulus then appeared for 1,000 ms in the center of the screen. The stimulus presented was one of these four colors: blue, yellow, red, orange. Participants were instructed to press "1" when they saw a blue square, the "0" when they saw the red square, the "1" when they saw a yellow square, and the "0" when they saw an orange square. There were forty-eight trials in this condition. There were eight practice trials in the beginning of the experiment, and participants had to get them all correct to proceed to the experimental trials. If they made a mistake, they were given extra practice trials until they got eight trials correct.

Stroop task. This task was a version of the standard Stroop color-naming paradigm (Stroop 1935). The stimuli were the words "rosa" (pink) and "verde" (green) printed in capital letters in 100-point Arial font, presented in the center of the screen. The stimulus appeared immediately after a 250 ms sound file "ding" and remained on the screen for 1,000 ms. Participants responded by pressing "1" when a word in green font appeared and "0" when a word in pink font appeared. The word itself was the distracter. There were twenty-four trials in this condition. There were eight practice trials in the beginning of the experiment, and participants had to get them all correct to proceed to the experimental trials. If they made a mistake, they were given extra practice trials until they got eight trials correct.

Results

The aim of the present study was to explore the effects of a bilingual experience on inhibitory control (nonlinguistic and linguistic stimuli) and on working memory tasks. All participants (monolingual and bilingual older adults) were comparable on educational and social background, as shown in table 17.1.

Simon arrows task. To examine the effects of language group on the Simon arrows task, accuracy rates and reaction times (RTs) were analyzed. Overall, bilingual participants were slightly more accurate than their monolingual counterparts in all conditions. Analyses conducted on accuracy rates indicated a significant effect for language group under the incongruent condition of the Simon arrows task. Monolingual participants had an accuracy rate of 54.5 percent (SD = 29.2), whereas bilinguals obtained 77.9 percent (SD = 17.1) (p = .043). In the comparison of RTs between language groups, it was found that although bilinguals showed overall smaller RTs than monolinguals in the control condition (513.1 ms ± 98.3 vs. 553.5 ± 125.1), in the congruent trials (637 ± 85.6 vs. 655.1 ± 116.8) and in the incongruent trials (698.4 ± 86.8 vs. 721.6 ± 97.3), the advantages found in RTs were not statistically significant.

In addition, a comparison revealed a smaller Simon effect for bilinguals (61.3 ms) than for monolinguals (66.5 ms), but overall effect of language group was not statistically significant. The mean accuracy rates and RTs for control, congruent, and incongruent trials in the Simon arrows task as a function of language group are shown in table 17.2.

Simon squares task. The results for the task biased for demands on working memory are shown in table 17.3. Paired t-tests performed on the data demonstrate that a main effect of language was not found for the Simon squares task. The performance accuracy in the task was 87.9 percent for the monolinguals and 87.2 percent for the bilinguals and the RTs were practically the same.

Stroop task. Analyses revealed no main effect of language group in the Stroop task. The mean Stroop effect for monolinguals was 22.5 ms (SD = 56.3), whereas the Stroop effect for bilinguals was 16.4 ms (SD = 54.0). Mean reaction times of the congru-

Table 17.1

Mean Background Measures (and Standard Deviations) by Language Group

Measure	Monolinguals (n = 21)	Bilinguals (n = 21)*
Age (in years)	64.3 (3.1)	63.8 (3.2)
Schooling (in years)	3.5 (1.5)	4.2 (2.0)
MMSE	25.6 (3.3)	26.2 (3.0)

Note: MMSE = Mini Mental State Examination.
*p > .05

▓ Table 17.2

Mean Accuracy and Reaction Time (RT; in Milliseconds) by Language Group in the Simon Arrows Task

Language Group								Side
	Control	Accuracy (%)	Congruent	Accuracy (%)	Incongruent	Accuracy (%)	Simon Effect	
Monolingual	553.5 (125.1)	86.2	655.1 (116.8)	80.8 (12.9)	721.6 (97.3)	54.5 (29.2)	66.5 (48.7)	
Bilingual	513.1 (98.3)	94.1	637.0 (85.6)	86.6 (15.8)	698.4 (86.8)	77.9 (17.1)	61.3 (58.2)	

Note: Standard deviations are in parentheses.

▓ Table 17.3

Mean Accuracy and Reaction Time (RT; in Milliseconds) by Language Group in the Simon Squares Task

Language Group	Center-4	Accuracy (%)
Monolingual	632.7 (90.3)	87.9
Bilingual	633.1 (87.2)	87.2

Note: Standard deviations are in parentheses.

ent and incongruent trial of the Stroop task and the Stroop effect for both groups are reported in table 17.4.

Discussion

The main purpose of this study was to explore the effects of bilingualism on inhibitory control in a group of older adults. In particular, we tested whether bilingual advantages in controlled processing that are reported in the literature would also be found in a group of fluent bilinguals who had never been tested before, with low levels of formal education and very little daily contact with written language. The monolinguals and bilinguals tested were comparable on measures of cognitive status, years of formal education, and linguistic and socioeconomic background.

A few possible conclusions can be drawn from the analysis. First, in the Simon arrows task, incongruent items required longer RTs for both language groups. In the conflict condition (incongruent trials), bilingual participants were significantly more accurate, as predicted, and slightly faster (but not reaching significance). In addition,

▓ Table 17.4

Mean Accuracy and Reaction Time (RT; in Milliseconds) by Language Group in the Stroop Color Task

Language Group				Center			
	Congruent	Accuracy (%)	Incongruent	Accuracy (%)	Stroop Effect		
Monolingual	517.0 (93.2)	91.6 (13.6)	539.6 (103.6)	94.1 (0.6)	22.5 (56.3)		
Bilingual	525.2 (94.1)	91.6 (0.7)	541.7 (95.2)	86.6 (16.7)	16.4 (54.0)		

Note: Standard deviations are in parentheses.

bilinguals showed a Simon effect, but its magnitude remained smaller (though not significantly) than that for monolinguals, which suggests that incongruent trials were less disrupting for them. That is, to perform the task, participants were asked to press the key associated with the stimulus direction regardless of its spatial position in the screen in front of them. The smaller Simon effect scores obtained by bilinguals may be taken to suggest less inhibition cost and more efficient inhibitory processes. Finally, even though the overall results in the incongruent condition point to the hypothesized direction, they need to be viewed with caution, since only accuracy differences were found to be significant in the analysis.

It is relevant to note, however, that bilinguals were also slightly faster—though not significantly—than monolinguals in the congruent trials and in the control condition (when arrows appeared in the middle of the screen), which suggests a bilingual advantage even when inhibitory control was not particularly required. Actually, the difference in terms of performance between groups was similar to the difference in RT in the tenth block of study 3 in Bialystok et al. (2004). The difference in terms of performance was so small then that the researchers considered that monolinguals were as fast as bilinguals.

One of the possible reasons for the present finding might be related to the practice trials. Most of our participants had to repeat the practice set more than three times. The high number of practice sessions might have offered monolinguals enough practice to perform equivalently to bilinguals—as suggested by Bialystok et al. (2004), who observed that the performance of monolinguals and bilinguals in ten consecutive blocks of twenty-four trials revealed that even though bilinguals were much faster than monolinguals in the first blocks, monolinguals eventually managed to catch up and demonstrate similar scores after a few trials. Therefore, we assume that the number of practice trials might have affected accuracy rates and reaction times, thus skewing results.

Second, according to our initial predictions, participants from both language groups demonstrated similar performance in the Simon squares task, which was biased to increase working memory demands. As it turns out, mean accuracy and reaction time for both language groups were practically the same. These results seem to corroborate the evidence reported in Bialystok, Craik, and Luk (2008), in which monolinguals and bilinguals demonstrated largely similar performance on measures of working memory. Although it is assumed in the literature that working memory tasks might also involve executive control functions, it is difficult to isolate these constructs, since there are "indications that working memory may be a family of related constructs rather than a unitary entity; various tests of working memory do not necessarily correlate with each other" (870). Within this view, "it is perfectly possible that different working memory tasks may be differentially affected by bilingualism" (870), an assumption that could help explain the evidence found in this investigation.

Third, in the Stroop task, incongruent items also required longer RTs than congruent items for both groups. The Stroop effect was slightly higher (but not statistically) for the monolinguals, and accuracy scores did not differ significantly between groups either. In this task, even though a bilingual advantage in the incongruent condition would initially be predicted, beneficial effects of bilingualism in inhibitory control were expected to be canceled due to the interference of the linguistic stimuli (misleading linguistic information). Thus, the hypothesis predicted similar performance for monolinguals and bilinguals. Surprisingly, the bilinguals tested were slightly slower and less accurate than the monolinguals, although the results were not statistically significant.

One possible explanation for the above results relates to the participants' level of literacy, which might have played a role in their overall performance, since the task required participants to control the interference of misleading linguistic information (written word) when asked to respond to the color of the font. It is important to note that the same font size (100-point Arial) used in a previous study (Bialystok, Craik, and Luk 2008) was adopted here. However, it may have been too large, considering the particular group tested in this investigation—mostly farm workers, who claimed to have very little daily contact with reading materials. Thus, it is reasonable to assume that participants may not have realized the conflict involved in the task simply because they did not focus on reading the word itself, but rather focused on the color of the font, which was exactly what was asked of them. Actually, only three participants commented on the misleading effect caused by the linguistic information (word), and most of them reported to have found the Stroop the easiest task. Consequently, the fact that participants had lower educational levels than participants from previous studies (Bialystok et al. 2004, among others) may have thus contributed to a reduction of the conflict caused by irrelevant linguistic stimuli.

To conclude, although the findings reported here must be taken with caution, due to the small number of participants, we observed a trend that seems compatible with the suggestion that a bilingual experience increases skills associated with inhibitory control. Needless to say, more evidence from different language groups is required to confirm this assumption. In addition, degrees of formal education and literacy levels might have played a role in the development of executive functions in the case of our participants. Therefore, we emphasize the need for more studies exploring the interaction of bilingualism with other variables and the importance of testing different populations to verify the extent to which the bilingual advantage reported in the literature is indeed due to language experience or is the result of other factors, such as ethnicity, socioeconomic status (Morton and Harper 2007), education, and literacy levels.

NOTE

1. There are two official languages in Brazil, Portuguese and LIBRAS (Língua Brasileira de Sinais/Brazilian Sign Language). However, more than 200 languages (approximately 170 Indian languages and 30 immigration languages) are spoken throughout the country (Oliveira 2000); among them is Hunsrückisch, one of the languages spoken by the German immigrant population.

REFERENCES

Bertolucci, P. H., et al. 1994. The Mini-Mental State Examination in a general population: Impact of educational status. *Arquivos de Neuropsiquiatria* 52:1–7.

Bialystok, Ellen, and Judith Codd. 1997. Cardinal limits: Evidence from language awareness and bilingualism for developing concepts of number. *Cognitive Development* 12:85–106.

Bialystok, Ellen, Fergus I. M. Craik, and Morris Freedman. 2007. Bilingualism as a protection against the onset of symptoms of dementia. *Neuropsychologia* 45:459–64.

Bialystok, Ellen, Fergus I. M. Craik, Raymond Klein, and Mythili Viswanathan. 2004. Bilingualism, aging, and cognitive control: Evidence from the Simon task. *Psychology and Aging* 19:290–303.

Bialystok, Ellen, Fergus I. M. Craik, and Gigi Luk. 2008. Cognitive control and lexical access in younger and older bilinguals. *Journal of Experimental Psychology: Learning, Memory, and Cognition* 34:859–73.

Bialystok, Ellen, Fergus I. M. Craik, and Anthony C. Ruocco. 2006. Dual-modality monitoring in a classification task: The effects of bilingualism and aging. *The Quarterly Journal of Experimental Psychology* 59:1968–83.

Bialystok, Ellen, Fergus I. M. Craik, and Jennifer Ryan. 2006. Executive control in a modified anti-saccade task: Effects of aging and bilingualism. *Journal of Experimental Psychology: Learning, Memory, and Cognition* 32:1341–54.

Bialystok, Ellen, and Anne-Marie DePape. 2009. Musical Expertise, bilingualism, and executive functioning. *Journal of Experimental Psychology: Human Perception and Performance* 35:565–74.

Bialystok, Ellen, and Michelle M. Martin. 2004. Attention and inhibition in bilingual children: Evidence from the dimensional change card sort task. *Developmental Science* 7:325–39.

Bialystok, Ellen, Michelle Martin, and Mythili Viswanathan. 2005. Bilingualism across the lifespan: The rise and fall of inhibitory control. *International Journal of Bilingualism* 9:103–19.

Bialystock, Ellen, and Lili Senman. 2004. Executive processes in appearance–reality tasks: The role of inhibition of attention and symbolic representation. *Child Development* 75:562–79.

Bialystok, Ellen, and Dana Shapero. 2005. Ambiguous benefits: The effect of bilingualism on reversing ambiguous figures. *Developmental Science* 8:595–604.

Carlson, Stephanie M., and Andrew N. Meltzoff. 2008. Bilingual experience and executive functioning in young children. *Developmental Science* 11:282–98.

Colomé, Angels. 2001. Lexical activation in bilinguals' speech production: Language-specific or language-independent? *Journal of Memory and Language* 45:721–36.

Costa, Albert. 2005. Lexical access in bilingual production. In *Handbook of bilingualism: Psycholinguistic approaches*, ed. Judith F. Kroll, and Annette M. B. de Groot, 308–25. New York: Oxford University Press.

Craik, Fergus I. M., and Ellen Bialystok. 2006. Planning and task management in older adults: Cooking breakfast. *Memory and Cognition* 34:1236–49.

Dijkstra, Ton, Jonathan Grainger, and Walter J. B. van Heuven. 1999. Recognition of cognates and interlingual homographs: The neglected role of phonology. *Journal of Memory and Language*. 41:496–518.

Fernandes, Myra, Fergus. I. M. Craik, Ellen Bialystok, and Sharyn Kreuger. 2007. Effects of bilingualism, aging, and semantic relatedness on memory under divided attention. *Canadian Journal of Experimental Psychology* 61:128–41.

Fishman, Joshua. 1972. Varieties of ethnicity and varieties of language consciousness. In *Language and socio-cultural change: Essays by J. Fishman*, ed. A. S. Dil, 179–91. Stanford: Stanford University Press.

Folstein, Marshal F., Susan E. Folstein, and Paul R. Mchugh. 1975. Mini-mental state: A practical method for grading the cognitive state of patients for the clinician. *Psychiatric Research* 12:189–98.

Gazzaniga, M. S., R. Ivry, and G. Mangun. 2009. *Cognitive neuroscience: The biology of the mind*. 3rd ed. New York: Norton & Company.

Green, David W. 1998. Mental control of the bilingual lexico-semantic system. *Bilingualism: Language and Cognition* 1:67–81.

Jared, Debra, and Judith Kroll. 2001. Do bilinguals activate phonological representations in one or both of their languages when naming words? *Journal of Memory and Language* 44:2–31.

Kavê, Gigit, Nitza Eyal, Aviva Shorek, and Jiska Cohen-Mansfield. 2008. Multilingualism and cognitive state in the oldest old. *Psychology and Aging* 23:70–78.

Kempler, Daniel, and Mira Goral. 2008. Language and dementia: Neuropsychological aspects. *Annual Review of Applied Linguistics* 28:73–90.

Martin-Rhee, Michele, and Ellen Bialystok. 2008. The development of two types of inhibitory control in monolingual and bilingual children. *Bilingualism: Language and Cognition* 11:81–93.

Morton, J. Bruce, and Sarah N. Harper. 2007. What did Simon say? Revisiting the bilingual advantage. *Developmental Science* 10:719–26.

Oliveira, Gilvan Müller. 2000. Brasileiro fala português: Monolinguismo e preconceito lingüístico. In *O direito à fala: a questão do preconceito lingüístico,* ed. F. L. Silva and Heronides M. Mouras. Florianópolis, Brazil: Insular.

Simon, J. Richard, and Allan P. Rudell. 1967. Auditory S-R compatibility: The effect of an irrelevant cue on information processing. *Journal of Applied Psychology* 51:300–304.

Stroop, J. Ridley. 1935. Studies of inference in serial verbal reactions. *Journal of Experimental Psychology* 18:643–62.

Yesavage, Jerome A., T. L. Brink, and T. L. Rose. 1983. Development and validation of a geriatric depression screening scale: A preliminary report. *Journal of Psychiatric Research* 17:37–42.

Zied, Mohamed K., A. Phillipe, Pinon Karine, Valerie Havet-Thomassin, Aubin Ghislane, Roy Arnaud, and Lee Gall Didier. 2004. Bilingualism and adult differences in inhibitory mechanisms: Evidence from a bilingual Stroop task. *Brain and Cognition* 45:254–56.